THE
12-WEEK
EXECUTIVE
Health
PLAN

DR DAVID ASHTON

KOGAN
PAGE

Kogan Page Limited
120 Pentonville Road
London N1 9JN

British Library Cataloguing in Publication Data

A CIP record for this book is available from the British Library.

ISBN 0 7494 0223 7

Typeset by Photoprint, Torquay, Devon
Printed and bound in Great Britain by Clays Ltd, St Ives plc

Contents

To my father, Richard

ABOUT THE AUTHOR

Dr David Ashton is the Clinical Director of BMI Healthcare and the London Heart Clinic. After graduating in Medical Sciences from the University of St Andrews, David Ashton underwent clinical training at the Victoria University of Manchester. He subsequently took up various post-graduate appointments in general medicine and was formerly a member of the Department of Cardiology at Manchester Royal Infirmary. During this period he developed a strong interest in preventive medicine, particularly in relation to exercise, coronary artery disease, diet and cancer.

He is the author of several books including *The Corporate Healthcare Revolution — Strategies for Preventive Medicine at Work* (Kogan Page, 1989), as well as numerous papers and articles on a wide range of topics in prevention and health promotion. At present he is collaborating with the Royal Brompton National Heart & Lung Institute on a major study into the causes of heart disease in women.

David Ashton has wide experience of cardiovascular assessment including exercise electrocardiography, measurement of aerobic capacity, and exercise prescription. He has been the medical adviser to several world-class athletes and recently wrote guidelines on exercise for the World Health Organisation.

Dr Ashton is a member of the International Society and Federation of Cardiology and the Royal Society of Medicine.

PREFACE

When it comes to health and fitness, have you ever wondered what the stars and media personalities have that the rest of us don't? What sustains this army of 'experts', each eager to promote their own unique formula for health, beauty and even longevity? After all, given the vast number of books, articles, TV programmes and videos already available, we could be forgiven for believing that the elixir of life was now available to all — at a price. Popular books on health and fitness sell so well precisely because they promise an enormous amount of benefit for not very much effort — the 'no pain, no strain, no sacrifice' formula. Of course, it is an illusion. Whatever the promises may be they are rarely realised and our resolve invariably weakens because the results are poor or non-existent. Most of us give up and wait for another year of accumulated guilt to generate a fresh posse of New Year's resolutions. To paraphrase Dr William Kannel of the Framingham Heart Study, 'For too many of us, will-power usually lasts about three weeks and is soluble in alcohol!'

But the reality is that many of these self-styled experts are just as stressed, overweight, unfit and prone to disease as the rest of us. So how can they continue to be so convincing to so many people? The answer is that they are not constrained by the need for scientific accuracy and are therefore free to say and claim anything they want — and they usually do. This is clearly an enormous advantage if all you are seeking is commercial success, because whatever the claims of your 'unique system', you cannot ever be shown to be wrong. You are perfectly at liberty to claim that thousands of people have benefited from your programme — and who is to say otherwise? In some ways this is, perhaps, not that important. After all, much of the advice is harmless enough even if it does sometimes verge on the bizarre. Fortunately, most of us have an inbuilt and self-regulating commonsense mechanism which allows us to stop short of some of the more loopy ideas, such as drinking our own urine — a practice strongly recommended by one or two friendly experts from the far side. Nevertheless, I continue to be amazed at the readiness with which so many of us are prepared to accept advice about an issue as important as our health, from those who are among the least qualified to give it.

So in what way is this book different and how can an addition to the already groaning bookshelves be justified? Let me explain. As a physician who is familiar with the scientific literature I have no need of magic formulas — the reality of recent advances in preventive medicine is exciting enough. *Thus, everything I have included is based solely upon studies published in the medical and scientific literature. Moreover, the information presented here applies just as much to women as to men.* My challenge has been to make this new knowledge understandable and, above all, adoptable by as wide an audience as possible.

If you apply the information in this book conscientiously and with real commitment over the next **twelve weeks**, I guarantee that you will:

• be able to make immediate scientifically informed choices about your health
• increase your chances of a longer life and substantially reduce your risks of developing premature disease
• improve the overall quality of your life both now and in the future.

These are not simply words. The goals are achievable and the results measurable provided you have the determination to succeed. This is a book very much about **health**, not disease. It is about **informed** choices, not inconsequential anecdotes. It is about what you **can do** for yourself, not the wishful, the fanciful or the unobtainable.

ACKNOWLEDGEMENTS

Writing a book while continuing to fulfil the rigorous demands of a busy professional life is never easy. Moreover, writing for a lay audience is, in many ways, more difficult and time consuming than for a strictly medical one. Inevitably most of the writing has been done at weekends and during holiday periods and it follows that the heaviest burden has fallen (yet again) on my wife, Kerry, and our two young sons. It is never possible to compensate for lost time, but I hope they will forgive my long absences.

Without question, the greatest debt I owe is to the vast army of epidemiologists, scientists, biologists and physicians who, through their painstaking research and moments of insight, have created the tremendous body of evidence upon which the advice and information in this book is based. Individual acknowledgement of all whose work has informed me, either directly or indirectly, is impossible. Suffice it to say that without them this book would not exist. I sincerely hope that my attempt at translating their findings into a form more accessible to the lay reader, is not entirely unworthy of them.

In the nature of things, most of those who are involved in the business of producing a book remain anonymous. However, there are those who have made a special contribution and it would be unforgivable for me not to mention several of them by name.

Firstly, I would like to thank Robert Mathers and John Jackson for somehow finding the time to read through the manuscript and for their perceptive and constructive criticism. Whatever deficiencies now remain are entirely my responsibility, not theirs.

Thanks are also due to Patricia Parker and Stephen Browne. As on previous occasions Pat sacrificed a great deal of her own time in typing the manuscript, a task she accomplished with her usual cheerfulness and patience. Stephen made helpful observations and suggestions at almost every stage. I am deeply grateful to them both.

Finally I must express my gratitude to Philip Mudd, Pauline Goodwin and Anne Owen of Kogan Page for their unflagging support and encouragement. This was a book with a long gestation period but, by a combination of sympathy, cajolery and threats, they finally achieved their objective. I sincerely hope they feel it was worth the effort.

HOW TO USE THIS BOOK

Good management practice is an absolute prerequisite for success in any business enterprise, whether it be a large multinational corporation or a small family concern. Effective management, in turn, does not come about by accident. It requires the consistent application of sound management principles and a considerable amount of commitment and energy. When management is indifferent, inefficient or poorly informed, the business invariably suffers and may even collapse completely.

The principles of good health management are actually no different. You need a certain amount of basic background information but you also need the commitment to apply the principles in practice. As in business poor management may have potentially serious consequences. It may sometimes lead to disease, to premature disability or even death. It almost invariably leads to a poorer quality of life.

Of course we all tend to take our health for granted. Only when it is called into question or when we have actually lost it do we begin to realize its true value. Because of this we tend to give it a rather low priority for most of the time. It's something to pay attention to when everything else is done if we have any time or energy left. Typical comments that I hear quite frequently are, 'I know I should pay more attention to my health, but there seem to be so many other things going on', or 'I will get around to it — I just need to get the next couple of months over then I'll have more time'. Of course, we never quite manage it.

The fact that one may be in possession of good health at the moment does not, of course, give any guarantee for the future. In fact it is extremely difficult to motivate someone to continue to work for something which they apparently already have. Actually, there is a motivator which is capable of bringing about rapid, and sometimes dramatic, changes in attitudes and lifestyle; so powerful that almost overnight it can be the catalyst for a complete re-ordering of priorities. It's called a heart attack. Almost all of my heart attack patients say the same thing; 'I wish I had paid more attention to my health all those years ago'. In fact, they are fortunate — because they survived. Many others will not have the benefit of a second chance.

The British tend to regard good health as something of a lottery. If the 'health dice' roll in your favour, then you are one of the lucky ones. If not, well it just can't be helped. It is a curious attitude, and a strange form of gambling. Perhaps it is this sense of inevitability which may help to explain why we have been prepared to tolerate some of the highest death rates from heart disease and cancer in the developed world.

Of course it isn't merely a question of luck, except perhaps that the harder you work at your health, the luckier you will get. The fact is that to a very large extent your own health and well-being is **your** responsibility and is determined primarily by choices which **you** can make for yourself. But, like management in business you have to be committed, you need a certain amount of basic information and you need to be prepared to make a definite investment in terms of your own time. My aim in writing this book is to help you make that investment sensibly, safely and with the maximum return. The book is divided into three parts which are summarized below.

PART I

This contains Chapters 1, 2 and 3.

Chapter 1 is intended to provide the backdrop for the remainder of the book, by reviewing the most important trends in the most common causes of illness and disability. It will also introduce you to a major theme throughout the book, ie the 'risk factor' concept. The *seven* most important lifestyle-related risks and the *seven* major disease groups with which they are associated, are discussed.

In Chapter 2, 'More about Risk Factors', you will be provided with some more detailed information about each one of these factors and, very importantly, their interrelationships.

In Chapter 3 you will be able to carry out a simple Health Risk Appraisal (HRA) by using your personal 'health numbers'. After completing this assessment, you will have a very good idea about which particular aspects of your health and lifestyle need attention. The seven individual risk factors are then addressed in Chapters 4 to 10, which comprise Part II of the book. You can work through any one or all of the chapters depending upon your particular needs as identified in the initial assessment. Your HRA should then be repeated after a twelve-week period to assess your progress, and at regular intervals thereafter.

PART II

Part II of the book contains Chapters 4 to 10 and is entirely devoted to **self-assessment** and **action**. Each chapter discusses a specific risk factor and each has a similar structure, ie:

- Basic background information.
- Self-assessment.

- Interpretation of results.
- Action Plan.

Thus if your initial risk appraisal identified obesity or high blood pressure as a problem, you can turn to the relevant chapter (10 or 5), where you will find information and guidance to help you modify these risk factors.

PART III

Part III is devoted entirely to diet and nutrition. Here you will find a great deal of up-to-date advice on the principles of healthy eating, particularly with respect to avoiding heart disease and cancer. You will also find some useful advice on how to read a food label.

Part I

THE BACKGROUND TO HEALTH RISK APPRAISAL

Chapter 1

THE 7 × 7 PROGRAMME — RISK FACTORS, HEALTH AND DISEASE

When we look at health trends in this country (and in most other Western, industrialized nations), the two major causes of premature death and disability are cardiovascular disease (principally heart disease and stroke), and the various forms of cancer (see Figure 1.1). But many other diseases, although less serious in themselves, are responsible for a great deal of ill-health and a poorer quality of life for many thousands of people. Obesity, joint and back problems and alcohol abuse, are examples of common, important and almost entirely preventable illnesses, affecting people of all ages.

In fact we can identify the seven most common diseases, and seven important risk factors with which they are known to be associated (see Table 1.1).

Of course, not every risk factor is associated with every disease and the relative strength of the contribution from each factor differs greatly. Smoking, for example, contributes to almost all of the seven diseases, whereas hypertension is primarily related to heart attack and stroke. Table 1.2 gives more information about which risk factors are associated with which diseases, as well as some idea of the strength of the association.

We shall be discussing the risk factor concept in much more detail in Chapter 2, and each factor individually in Part II of this book.

In this chapter, I want to concentrate on the seven diseases identified above, starting with diseases of the cardiovascular system, ie coronary heart disease and stroke. You may already be familiar with much of what is covered here, but I would recommend that you should read through it anyway. This background information is fundamental to a full appreciation of the individual risk factors and their modification covered in Part II (the most important part) of the book.

1. CORONARY HEART DISEASE (CHD)

Recent surveys suggest that the general public is aware that coronary heart disease is the main cause of death in this country, and they are generally

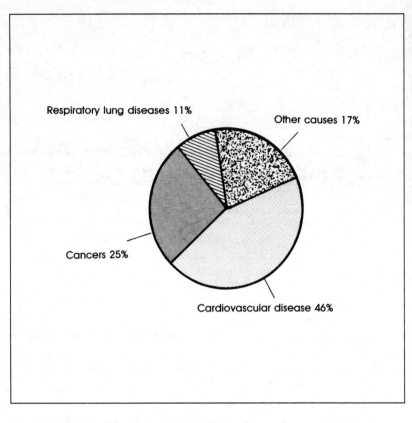

Source: *The Health of the Nation*, 1992, HMSO, London

Figure 1.1   Major causes of death (England and Wales 1991)

Table 1.1   7 risk factors × 7 diseases

Risk factor	Disease
Smoking	Heart attack
Hypertension (raised blood pressure)	Stroke
Physical inactivity	Cancer
Raised blood cholesterol (associated with high fat diet)	Respiratory (lung) disease Diabetes (Type II)
Obesity	Liver disease
Heavy alcohol consumption	
Stress	Musculo-skeletal disorders

Table 1.2   Contribution of risk factors to diseases

	Heart attack	Stroke	Cancer	Diabetes (Type II)	Liver disease	Respiratory (lung) disease	Musculo-skeletal disorders
Smoking	++	+	++			++	+
Hypertension	++	++					
Physical inactivity	++	+	+	+		+	++
Raised blood cholesterol (+ high fat diet)	++		+				
Obesity	+	+	+	++		+	++
Heavy alcohol consumption		++	+		++		
Stress	+	?	?				

? — Possible association
+ — Definite association
++ — Strong association

knowledgeable about its causes, although there is still much confusion about many of the factors involved. What is often not realized is that coronary heart disease is almost exclusively a twentieth century phenomena. Even in the 1920s and 1930s, the disease was regarded as uncommon. In 1920 the physician Sir William Osler wrote, 'Angina Pectoris (pain from the heart due to diseased coronary arteries), is a rare disease in hospitals, a case a year is about the average, even in the large metropolitan hospitals'. In 1928 there was a professional outcry when a question on coronary heart disease was included in an examination for doctors; it was felt that they were so unlikely to see such an obscure disease in practice, that a question in an exam on such a subject was totally unwarranted. Today, we rightly refer to this disease as a modern day epidemic, and it is the cause of a simply unimaginable amount of suffering and disability. Here are some facts about coronary heart disease:

* Coronary heart disease (CHD) is the leading cause of death in the United Kingdom.
* In the UK one in three men and one in four women will die from coronary heart disease.
* In 1991, around 170 000 people in the UK died from CHD — 92 000 men and 78 000 women.
* Unskilled men aged 20–64 are twice as likely to die from CHD as professionals.

- For every 100 people who have a heart attack, 57 will survive one year, and 25 will die immediately.
- The estimated annual cost to the NHS of heart disease, is around £700 million.
- CHD causes over 11 per cent of working days lost to illness, over 50 million in 1990, resulting in lost production worth £3.3 billion.

These figures give some idea of the total number of deaths but, of course, the problem of heart disease is very much bigger than this because a great many people who suffer heart attacks survive, but continue to suffer disability due to angina, breathlessness and fatigue.

Women and heart disease

Because coronary heart disease continues to be viewed by many as an essentially 'male disease', the size of the problem in women is often overlooked. This is partly because of the striking differences in death rates from heart disease between the sexes, with men aged 35 to 54 years having a rate some five to six times higher than women of the same age. Heart disease does not appear to become a major cause of disability or death in women until the age of 55 years onwards, probably because women are protected to some degree by their hormonal function. However, this protection appears to be mainly a postponement phenomenon, since as their hormone levels begin to decline after the menopause, women gradually experience the same rate of cardiovascular disease as men. It is also important to note that once a woman develops symptoms of heart disease, she is actually *more* likely to die from it than her male counterpart. In fact she is twice as likely to die from a first heart attack, and twice as likely to have a second. By any measure, therefore, heart disease in women is an important cause of illness, disability and death. Since the standard risk factors which have been shown to predict disease in men have a comparable influence in women, the opportunities for prevention must not be overlooked.

Is it getting worse?

Contrary to what is generally believed, the general trend is improving. Coronary heart disease rates in England and Wales have been declining slowly since reaching a peak in the early 1970s. Since that time, death rates in men in the 35 to 74 age group have declined by an average of 23 per cent in the UK. Whilst these trends may seem encouraging, it is important to recognize that these rather modest improvements compare poorly with the major reductions in death rates experienced by many other developed countries, such as Australia and the United States of America. For example, since 1968 the death rate from CHD in men aged 35 to 74 has fallen by 51 per cent in Australia, and by 55 per cent in the USA.

What about other countries?

International comparisons are both instructive and depressing. Available evidence shows that Scotland and Northern Ireland have the highest death rates from coronary artery disease in the world with England and Wales in sixth place (see Figure 1.2). Moreover, the UK position at the top of the International League Table is not changing. Men aged 35–74 in England and Wales are twice as likely to die from CHD as men in Italy, almost three times more likely than those in France, and eight times more likely than those in Japan.

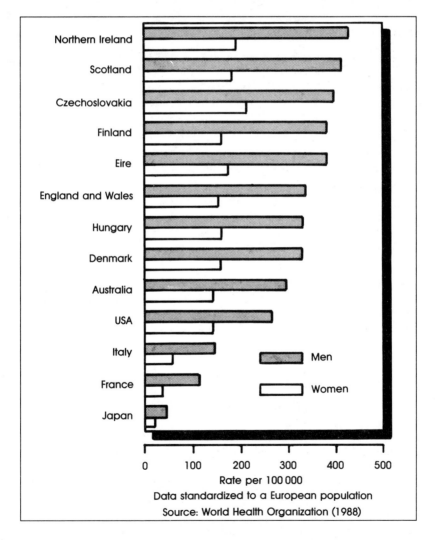

Figure 1.2   CHD death rates by country (all ages)

Who gets heart disease?

Most people believe that the typical heart attack victim is the highly stressed, high flying executive in his mid-50s, who finally pays the price for his dissolute existence. Contrary to public perception, however, coronary heart disease is more prevalent in manual than professional social groups. This has not always been the case. Back in the early 1950s, heart disease was much more common amongst professional and managerial groups and it is presumably a hangover from this period that still tends to assume an association between heart disease and 'executives'. Some people might see this as evidence that stress does not make a major contribution to heart disease, since if it were so important why is it that highly stressed executives have much lower rates of heart disease than those in manual groups or the unemployed? The answer, of course, is that executives do not have a monopoly on stress. The stress experienced by the chronically unemployed or the single parent must surely be equally telling.

Figure 1.3 shows the difference in mortality rates between various occupational groups in the 1950s compared with the 1980s. You will see that the relative positions have, in fact, reversed.

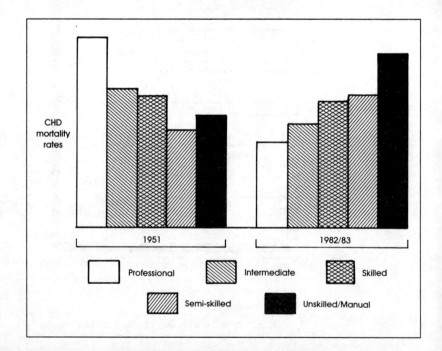

Figure 1.3   CHD mortality rates and occupational group

What exactly is a heart attack or stroke?

The heart is a muscular pump about the size of a fist and it weighs around ten ounces. In order to sustain life it has to beat about 72 times per minute, or roughly 40 million times per year. During the average lifetime it will beat an awesome three billion times. It supplies blood to every organ in the body, including itself. However, the extraordinary thing is that the heart muscle can only receive its blood supply (and hence oxygen) via two small arteries about an eighth of an inch in diameter. These arteries are called the coronary arteries (see Figure 1.4).

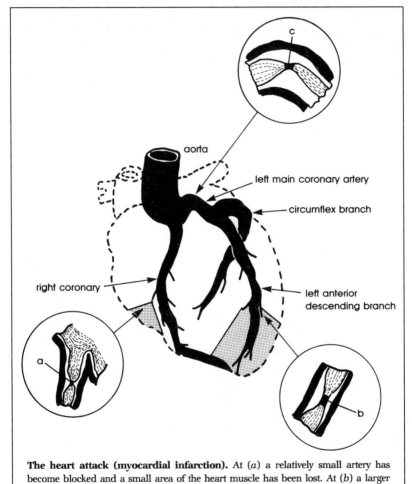

The heart attack (myocardial infarction). At (*a*) a relatively small artery has become blocked and a small area of the heart muscle has been lost. At (*b*) a larger vessel is involved and there is more extensive damage. A lesion at (*c*) threatens a large section of the heart muscle and is potentially lethal.

Figure 1.4 The arterial blood supply to the heart, showing the effects of a heart attack

Coronary Heart Disease (CHD) — the pathology

There are two fundamental processes involved in the development of coronary heart disease;

1. The development of fatty deposits or *plaque* in the lining of the artery.
2. The development of a blood clot (thrombosis) in the artery as a result of these fatty deposits.

Plaque (Atheroma) development

The essential problem in heart disease and stroke is that the blood vessels supplying the heart or the brain undergo a process of degeneration and become progressively blocked by fatty deposits, particularly cholesterol. These fatty deposits are sometimes referred to as 'plaque' or to use the proper medical term — *Atheroma*. In the newborn child, the inner lining of the coronary arteries is smooth, glistening and pearly white. The arteries themselves are flexible and supple and if our coronary arteries were to remain in this condition then we would never have heard about heart disease or stroke. The problem is that because of our Western lifestyle, our diet in particular, the healthy condition of our arteries gradually deteriorates. As the fatty deposits accumulate, the inside diameter of the vessel is reduced and it begins to lose its normal flexibility. This whole process is known as 'atherosclerosis', and as it continues the risk of a blood clot (thrombosis) on the surface of the plaque increases (see Figure 1.5).

Two other points about plaque formation are important:

1. The more plaque, the greater the risk of developing symptoms.
2. Individuals who have known risk factors such as cigarette smoking, high blood pressure or diabetes, have more plaque than those who do not have such factors.

Thrombosis

When the blockage in the artery has reached a critical level, a sudden and complete blockage — a thrombosis or blood clot — may occur (see Figure 1.5). The blood, which carries vital oxygen to the tissues, is no longer able to get through to supply the heart or the brain. Body tissues deprived of oxygen can only survive for a couple of minutes or so, and after that the tissue will die. In the case of the heart this will result in a heart attack, or in the brain a stroke.

The outlook for an individual suffering either of these events is largely dependent upon the site and the size of the artery involved (see Figure 1.4). The mechanisms involved in the production of a blood clot in the diseased

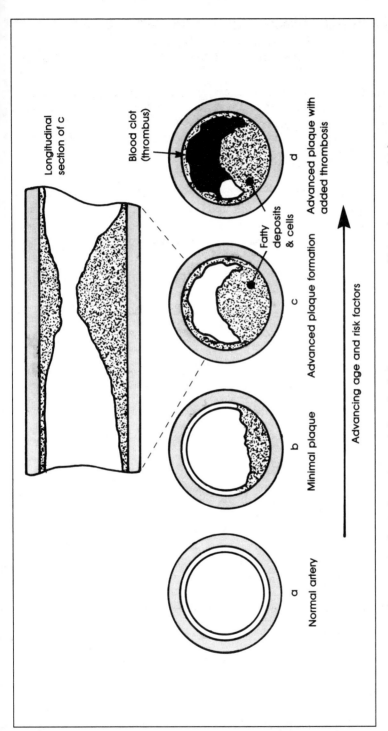

Figure 1.5 Plaque formation and thrombosis in a coronary artery (Artery in cross-section)

artery are complex and incompletely understood. However, individuals with disease in their coronary arteries often have other factors which tend to make the blood sticky, and which therefore increase the likelihood of a thrombosis.

Plaque formation and thrombosis are closely linked. In the first three or four decades of life it is the development of plaque and the risk factors associated with it which is the crucial factor. Once this has become established, the importance of factors likely to cause thrombosis increases (see Figure 1.6).

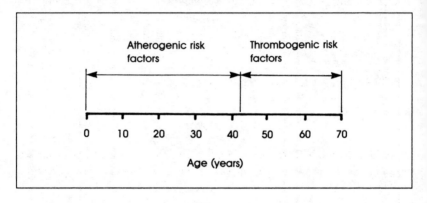

Figure 1.6   Atheroma and thrombosis in cardiovascular disease

In the overwhelming majority of cases, some degree of plaque deposition is necessary before thrombosis can occur. Occasionally the plaque itself may progress sufficiently to block the artery without thrombosis. It is important to understand that these are two separate but strongly related processes, which both contribute to the development of heart attacks and stroke. It also helps to explain why many patients who already have heart disease, are given drugs to reduce the stickiness of the blood and therefore reduce the likelihood of thrombosis in the future.

What are the symptoms of heart disease?

The first, and sometimes the only manifestation of heart disease, may be sudden death. More often, instead of progressing to a heart attack immediately, the formation of plaque within the arteries results in a condition called *angina pectoris*. Angina was first described by the English physician William Heberden, although he was unable to explain the cause. We now know that the formation of fatty deposits in the coronary arteries leads to 'coronary insufficiency', which means that the heart cannot receive enough blood (and therefore oxygen) to meet its requirements. This is particularly so during exercise when, as the heart rate increases, the demand for oxygen by the heart also increases. If the arteries are too narrow to permit an increased blood flow, the result is the pain which we call angina. Patients usually describe this as a crushing or 'gripping' sensation across the chest, or feeling as though a tight band had been placed across the chest wall. Other patients describe a feeling of constriction in the throat (angina means 'to strangle'). Sometimes there may be associated pain in the left arm (or both arms), and occasionally 'pins and needles' in the fingers.

Whatever the specific symptoms may be, a cardinal feature of angina is that it usually occurs on **exertion**, eg walking up a hill, or hurrying for a bus. When the patient rests, the pain usually recedes within a few minutes.

Modern drug therapy means that most patients with angina (and there are between 2–3 million of them in this country), can be controlled perfectly well. For others, in whom the disease is progressive and the pain unresponsive to medical treatment, surgical intervention may be recommended.

2. STROKE

A similar, though not identical pathological process which leads to damage to the coronary arteries, may also occur in the arteries supplying blood to the brain. If these become blocked, then a stroke will be the result. Stroke often results in death or serious disability, with some degree of residual paralysis affecting either the right or the left-hand side of the body. In England, there are about 65 000 stroke-related deaths each year, accounting for about one-quarter of those due to cardiovascular disease and 12 per cent of all deaths. About 100 000 people each year have a first stroke; some 25 000 are less than 65 years of age, and another 29 000 are between 65–74. Stroke is also a leading cause of disability, consuming about 5 per cent of NHS resources. Each year approximately two people per 1000 experience a first stroke and about two-thirds of these require some form of medical intervention.

Analysis, by age, of the number of cases of stroke indicates that it is predominantly a disease of the elderly. Indeed, roughly 50 per cent of the total number of first strokes occur in the over 75 years age group. But this does not mean that stroke is an unimportant cause of premature death and disability in younger people. In 1986, more than 4800 deaths from stroke occurred in individuals in the 55–64 year old age group.

So what actually causes cardiovascular diseases?

If the formation of plaque in the arterial wall is the fundamental cause of cardiovascular disease, then what exactly is the cause of plaque development?

The answer is that there is no one single cause, but rather a number of factors which have been identified as being strongly associated with an increased risk of developing the disease. The scientific evidence in support of the 'risk factor' concept has been gathered from many major studies, some of them lasting decades. In the case of heart disease, more than 250 such risk factors are said to exist, although only about 12 have been consistently associated with an increased risk (see Table 1.3). Of these, seven of the most important are readily modifiable, and they are exactly the same factors shown in Figure 1.2 and 1.3 at the beginning of this chapter. They will not be discussed any further here, since they are covered in detail in Part II. In addition there are two partially modifiable, and three non-modifiable factors.

Table 1.3   Risk factors for cardiovascular disease

MODIFIABLE	High blood cholesterol (hypercholesterolaemia)
	High blood pressure (hypertension)
	Cigarette smoking
	Physical inactivity
	Stress/Personality
	Obesity
	Heavy alcohol consumption
PARTIALLY MODIFIABLE	Diabetes
	High blood fibrinogen
NON-MODIFIABLE	Age
	Sex
	Family history (heredity)

Partially modifiable factors

1. **Diabetes:** Diabetics have an increased risk of developing various forms of arterial disease, including coronary heart disease. Nevertheless, much of the increased risk in diabetics is probably due to the presence of other risk factors — such as obesity — and it is therefore important that diabetics should control these additional risk factors as closely as possible. Diabetes starting early in life usually requires insulin, but the late onset variety is often associated with obesity and

can often be managed by dietary modification alone, or in combination with drugs.

2. **Increased blood fibrinogen**: Earlier in this chapter I described the development of atherosclerosis as involving two distinct, but closely related processes, ie plaque formation and subsequent thrombosis. The blood clotting mechanism contains two special proteins, one of which, fibrinogen, may increase the risk of a heart attack (as does a high blood cholesterol). Although recognized only fairly recently this contribution to risk of heart attack and stroke is now generally accepted. Indeed, the evidence to date would suggest an association between the blood fibrinogen level and risk of CHD or stroke that is about as strong as for cholesterol.

There is evidence that vigorous physical activity will help to reduce fibrinogen levels, thereby reducing the clotting tendency of the blood (see Chapter 7).

Non-modifiable factors

1. **Age** The older you are the greater the risk, and this applies to both sexes.
2. **Sex** There is a striking difference in death rates from heart disease between the sexes, with men aged 35 to 44 years having a rate five or six times higher than women of the same age. However, the difference diminishes gradually with increasing age, so that by the time men and women reach the age of 80 years and over, they have almost (but not quite) the same mortality rate. It seems likely that women are protected to some degree by their hormonal function, although the exact mechanism is still not completely understood. This hormonal protection diminishes progressively during and after the menopause.
3. **Family history** It is widely accepted that a 'bad' family history will tend to increase your own risk of developing heart disease. This is particularly true if it occurred in a first degree relative (mother, father, sister or brother) before the age of 60. However, it is extremely important to understand that merely having a family history does not mean to say that you **will** develop heart disease — merely that your risk of so doing is increased. This is actually a very complex question, and it is very unlikely that there is a specific genetic factor which is responsible for the mass public health problem of coronary heart disease. Moreover, it is sometimes difficult to know whether individuals with a family history of heart disease tend to develop the disease merely because they adopt the same bad health habits that their parents practised, or whether the disease would have occurred anyway. It is well known, for example, that you are much more likely to smoke if your parents smoked, and you will probably also tend to emulate their dietary habits.

Obviously you cannot alter your genetic inheritance, but you can and should pay close attention to risks such as hypertension, cigarette smoking and obesity, which are modifiable.

3. CANCER

The first thing to make clear about cancer is that it is quite wrong to think of it as a single disease; it is, rather, a whole collection — perhaps many hundreds — of different diseases. Whether the many different forms of cancer have a single origin is not yet known.

Cancer occurs when cells in our body which are normally under close control, begin to multiply and act in an abnormal and uncontrolled way. This forms a group of abnormal cells, and in time a very large number of these abnormal cells may form a tumour. It is precisely because our bodies are made up from many different types of cells, that there are so many different forms of cancer. Cancer of the breast, for example, is a completely different disease from bone cancer simply because the cells of breast tissue are entirely different from bone cells. The type of cell involved also helps to determine the degree of malignancy, ie how virulent the cancer is and how quickly it will spread. This, in turn, will greatly influence the prospects for making a full recovery. Lung cancer, for example, has an extremely poor outlook with very few patients (less than 10 per cent) being alive after five years. Skin cancer, however, has an extremely good prognosis with more than 90 per cent of patients still alive after a five year period.

How common is it?

Cancer is second only to heart disease as a killer in the developed world and a few dominant forms of the disease account for more than half of all cancer deaths. Lung cancer accounts for about 25 per cent; bowel cancer about 12 per cent; breast cancer 10 per cent and stomach cancer 7 per cent (see Figure 1.7).
Here are some other facts about cancer:

- In the UK, there are about 160 000 cancer deaths each year.
- Thirty per cent of all cancer deaths are caused by tobacco smoking.
- In the UK, almost one in four deaths are caused by cancer.
- There are about a quarter of a million new cancer cases every year.
- One in three people will develop cancer at some time in their lives.
- Lung cancer causes about 40 000 deaths a year in the UK.
- Breast cancer kills about 15 000 women every year in this country, with 25 000 new cases being diagnosed.
- Britain has the highest death rate from breast cancer in the world, and the disease is on the increase.
- Among an average 1000 young adults who smoke cigarettes regularly,

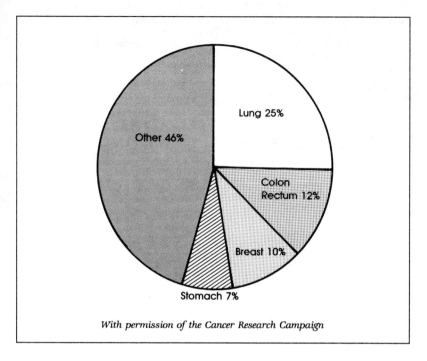

With permission of the Cancer Research Campaign

Figure 1.7   Cancer mortality in the UK (1986)

one will be murdered, six killed on the roads, but 250 will die prematurely because of tobacco.

What causes cancer?

Because cancer should not be thought of as one disease but many diseases, there is obviously a large number of potential causes. What causes one type of cancer does not necessarily cause another. For example smoking is undoubtedly the main contributory factor in lung cancer, but not of skin cancer.

We now have a very good idea of what causes certain types of cancer in human beings. In 1981, two of our most distinguished scientists, Doll and Peto, produced a major review, *The Causes of Cancer*, for the American Congressional Office of Technology Assessment. This report emphasized the importance of lifestyle factors in the origin of many forms of cancer. Smoking, obviously, is the best example. It is very strongly related to lung cancer, but also to a variety of other cancers. We also know that diet has a big part to play in cancer causation, particularly in relation to fat content and alcohol consumption. Table 1.4 indicates some of the more common forms of cancer, and the lifestyle related risk factors which are thought to be associated with them. You will see that once again, the seven factors identified at the beginning of this chapter are strongly represented.

Table 1.4 Cancer & lifestyle — associated risk factors

Cancer site		Associated risk factors
♂ + ♀	Lung	Tobacco smoking
	Mouth	Tobacco smoking, alcohol
	Oesophagus (Gullet)	Tobacco smoking, alcohol
	Stomach	Tobacco smoking, alcohol, diet
	Gall bladder	Obesity
	Pancreas	Tobacco smoking, alcohol
	Liver	Alcohol, diet
	Bowel (Rectum & Colon)	Diet, obesity, sedentary lifestyle
	Bladder	Tobacco smoking
	Breast	Diet, alcohol, oral contraceptive pill, Obesity, ?stress, sedentary lifestyle
	Skin (Esp. Melanoma)	Prolonged exposure to sunlight
♀	Cervix	Tobacco smoking, multiple sexual partners
	Uterus	Obesity
	Ovary	Diet
♂	Prostate	Obesity, diet, sedentary lifestyle

Of course there are many other factors involved. Some chemicals and certain types of infection are very important and undoubtedly environmental factors have an important role to play. Nevertheless, when we look at the whole range of potential causes, it is probable that tobacco, alcohol and diet account for about two-thirds of all cancer deaths (see Table 1.5).

Table 1.5 Causes of cancer

Cause	Estimated percentage of all cancer deaths (%)
Tobacco	30
Alcohol	3
Diet	35
Food additives	Less than 1
Occupation	4
Pollution	2
Industrial products	Less than 1
Medicines and medical procedures	1
Infection	10
Other and unknown	13

Source: *The Causes of Cancer* (OUP 1981) by Doll and Peto

How much does each factor contribute?

It is important to understand that the relative contribution of each risk factor to the cancers mentioned, varies considerably. In the case of lung cancer, the association with cigarette smoking has been so clearly demonstrated that we can reasonably regard cigarette smoking as the *cause* of lung cancer. The fact that not all smokers develop lung cancer is probably because some people are genetically more susceptible to developing the disease than others. In the case of some forms of skin cancer, particularly malignant melanoma, prolonged exposure to sunlight is probably the most important contributory factor. But in many other cases the contribution of specific lifestyle-related risk factors may be much less certain. The association between heavy alcohol intake and breast cancer, for example, is by no means conclusive and, of course, this is not the only factor involved. In the case of breast cancer we need also to take into account the possible contribution of the contraceptive pill and, again, a hereditary factor.

Despite these limitations in our understanding, there is now a great deal of information to communicate about cancer prevention and there is much that each and every one of us can do to minimize our risk of developing it.

Is cancer on the increase?

It is perfectly true to say that there are more recorded cases of cancer now than there were say 20 or 30 years ago. However, nowadays more people can expect to live into old age and so more of them will get cancer simply because cancer is primarily a disease of the middle-aged and elderly. Some types of cancer, for example cancer of the breast and skin, are on the increase.

For women, breast cancer is the commonest cause of cancer death, except in Scotland where deaths from lung cancer exceed those from breast cancer. In fact, lung cancer in women has increased by 21 per cent since 1980, although it has decreased by five per cent amongst men. This sharp upward trend in death rates from lung cancer in women is a reflection of the fact that women started smoking at a later stage than did men, and the consequences of this are only now becoming apparent.

Malignant melanoma is a comparatively rare but serious form of skin cancer, which develops in the pigment-producing cells of the skin (usually a pre-existing mole). During the last ten years there has been a 50 per cent increase in the number of people developing and dying from malignant melanoma in the UK. Although melanoma only accounts for about 1 per cent of all new cancer cases, the disease is of particular concern because it has an impact on young adults as well as older people. A number of risk factors are known to be associated with an increased risk of melanoma, including skin type, hair colour and pre-existing moles. However, the major trigger factor is prolonged exposure to sunlight. Depletion of the ozone layer due to atmospheric pollution may be contributing to an increased incidence of skin cancer, because of increased radiation.

Is cancer hereditary?

Very few forms of cancer can be shown to be purely hereditary and those that are are not common. There is almost certainly a genetic component in most types of cancer, but in all probability this is relatively small. To a very large extent, the relative importance of a family history of cancer depends upon the type of disease in question. A strong family history of breast or ovarian cancer undoubtedly increases the risk, as it does in the case of bowel cancer. Indeed, in cancer of the breast and ovary, the presence of a genetic predisposition may increase the risk by as much as 60–80 per cent.

The gene responsible for inherited (familial) breast and ovarian cancer is one of the most sought after in cancer gene research. Once the defective gene is finally identified, it will be possible, with a blood test, to distinguish with certainty those family members who are carriers and need high-risk management, from those who do not have the gene.

In many other forms of cancer the genetic contribution appears to be much less important. Remember that most diseases (cancer included) are the result of an interaction between a genetic, a lifestyle-related and an environmental factor, although the relative contribution of each may vary.

Is cancer caused by stress?

Despite assertions to the contrary which appear in the popular press, there is no convincing evidence that cancer can be initiated by stress, although there is some evidence that recurrence of cancer may be more likely to occur in those who are subject to chronically stressful situations. It remains a highly controversial area. The argument for a specific 'cancer personality' which may increase risk for some individuals, remains unconvincing.

What about diet?

Evidence would suggest that about 35 per cent (with a range of 10 to 70 per cent of cancer deaths) could be avoided if people changed their eating habits. Indeed, changing diet may be almost as important as stopping smoking. This important subject is discussed in much more detail in Chapter 11, but in general, diets high in fresh foods and vegetables, but low in salt, sugar and fats are beneficial.

Is cancer curable?

In recent years there have been truly remarkable advances in cancer therapy so that many forms of cancer are now completely curable. Moreover, the current revolution in genetics will add enormously to the list of available treatments. In the majority of cases the outlook for the cancer patient depends upon three main factors: the site of the tumour, the type of tumour and the stage at which the cancer was diagnosed. Generally speaking the earlier the diagnosis the better the prognosis, and the higher the chances of a full recovery.

4. RESPIRATORY (LUNG) DISEASE

By far the commonest forms of preventable lung disease in this country are chronic bronchitis and lung cancer, both of which are almost invariably associated with cigarette smoking.

In bronchitis, the constant irritation of the smoke causes the lungs to become inflamed, infected and inefficient. This irritation leads to the production of phlegm (sputum), increasing breathlessness, reduced exercise tolerance and eventually death from respiratory failure or heart disease. Sometimes the inflammation in the air sacs leads to the trapping of air in the lungs, a condition known as *emphysema*. Every year, more than 30 000 men and women in the UK die from the effects of chronic bronchitis, and many thousands of others are seriously disabled or have their quality of life impaired by their symptoms. The smoker's cough is the first sign that bronchitis is developing and that the lungs are being damaged. Tests of lung function in habitual smokers are almost invariably abnormal. There is a natural tendency for smokers to be primarily concerned about the risk of lung cancer, but a slow death from progressive lung failure is, in many ways, even more distressing. Itsi also worth bearing in mind that patients with chronic lung disease represent a much greater anaesthetic risk, and are also much more liable to developing post-operative chest infections and other complications.

Lung cancer kills more than 40 000 people in the UK each year, and over 90 per cent of cases occur in cigarette smokers. A regular smoker's risk of developing the disease is up to 40 times that of the non-smoker. Lung cancer in women is increasing, and in some parts of the UK it has now overtaken breast cancer as the leading cancer-related death in women. Unfortunately once the disease has developed, the outlook is extremely poor; only about 7–8 per cent of lung cancer patients are alive five years after diagnosis.

Other forms of lung disease, whilst not actually caused by cigarette smoking, are made very much worse as a result of exposure to tobacco smoke, asthma being perhaps the best example. Finally, although tobacco use is clearly the most important risk factor for lung disease, obesity can add to the breathing difficulties, reducing exercise tolerance still further. The capacity of the lungs to function normally deteriorates as obesity increases, and this will be even more pronounced in the presence of lung disease. Smoking and related diseases are discussed in more detail in Chapter 6.

5. DIABETES

In the normal person, insulin transports glucose from the bloodstream into the cells throughout the body; the cells are then able to turn this fuel into energy. When insulin is absent, or when the body becomes resistant to it, glucose levels in the blood begin to rise, and the condition known as *diabetes mellitus* develops.

There are two main forms of diabetes mellitus:

1. **Type I (also known as 'juvenile-onset', or 'insulin-dependent') diabetes**.
    This is the genetically determined form of the disease, in which the body is unable to manufacture insulin. As its name suggests, it is usually diagnosed early in life and requires life-long insulin injections. The disease is important because it is associated with an increased risk of heart, eye and kidney problems. The clinical course of coronary heart disease is likely to be more severe and the progression more rapid. Males have a mortality rate from heart attack which is four times that of non-diabetics. Females are even more susceptible, being six times more liable to a heart attack.

2. **Type II (also known as 'maturity-onset' or non-insulin dependent diabetes mellitus [NIDDM])**
    In this form of the disease which usually occurs after the age of 40, the main factor appears to be that the body has increased resistance to insulin. Although patients with this form of diabetes can usually be managed without insulin injections, it is a mistake to think of it as a 'mild' and relatively unimportant disease. Some patients with this type of diabetes will develop the same serious medical complications as those with Type I diabetes: coronary artery disease, kidney disease, stroke and eye problems.

    Obesity, a family history of diabetes and physical inactivity are all factors which may increase your chances of developing this condition. About 80 per cent of sufferers are overweight, and losing weight is sometimes sufficient to bring the disease under control.

6. LIVER DISEASE

The most important preventable cause of liver disease is excessive alcohol consumption, which is discussed in Chapter 8. Alcohol — in sufficient quantities — can damage almost every organ in the body, but the liver is particularly susceptible. There are four main forms of damage, and some individuals will progress inexorably through all of them.

1. The most common sign of liver distress is a **fatty liver.** Fat accumulates in the liver cells, leading to liver enlargement which often occurs within a few days of heavy alcohol intake. A fatty liver is often the first warning of more serious trouble ahead, but it can be cured by a combination of a sensible diet and alcoholic abstinence.
2. Inflammation of the liver, or **hepatitis,** is much more serious. There is damage to the liver cells and, as a consequence, the liver will function abnormally. In severe cases the patient may become jaundiced. About half of those with hepatitis will go on to develop cirrhosis of the liver.
3. **Cirrhosis** is a dangerous and frequently fatal condition, characterized by inflammation and scarring (fibrosis) of the liver tissue. It is irreversible, and frequently leads to progressive liver failure and death. Those who have been seriously alcohol dependent for more than ten years have about a 10 per cent chance of dying from cirrhosis.
4. A serious complication of cirrhosis is **liver cell cancer,** which develops in between 3–11 per cent of people with alcoholic cirrhosis. As with lung cancer, once the disease appears it is almost always fatal, and the treatment options limited.

7. MUSCULO-SKELETAL PROBLEMS

Lower back pain and other problems with joints and ligaments are extremely common in this country. In addition, loss of bone mineral, which is the hallmark of osteoporosis, is an important cause of pain and disability in post-menopausal women, resulting in fractures of the hip, wrist and vertebrae (spine). In fact, by the age of 70 about 40 per cent of women have experienced a fracture resulting in considerable discomfort for the individual, and a major economic burden for the Health Service.

The principal risk factors for musculo-skeletal problems are lack of regular physical exercise and obesity. There is good evidence that regular exercise can increase the strength of muscles, tendons, ligaments and bones, thus making injury much less likely. Those who are the least physically fit are more likely to suffer with back problems, and will take longer to recover. Conversely, regular exercise can help prevent back problems occurring in the first place.

Weight-bearing exercises can also help to prevent osteoporosis by increasing the mineral content and mass of the bones, even in individuals who have already been diagnosed as osteoporotic. The beneficial effects of exercise on bone density and the musculo-skeletal system in general are discussed in Chapter 7.

Finally, it is important to bear in mind that obesity almost invariably accelerates the progress of bone and joint damage, worsens symptoms, and delays recovery.

THE 7 × 7 PROGRAMME

In this first chapter I have identified the seven most important modifiable risk factors, and discussed the seven diseases with which they are known to be associated. This is the core of the 7 × 7 programme.

If you have read through this carefully, you will have made several important observations. Perhaps the most striking fact is that many of the risk factors contribute to several diseases; in the case of heart disease and cancer, for example, the risk factors are very similar. This is important because, as I shall be stressing later, eliminating one important risk factor will reduce your risk for several diseases. A quick check with Table 1.2, for example, shows that stopping smoking would reduce your risk of developing five out of the seven diseases listed.

It's also important to realize that many of the risk factors can be regarded as diseases in themselves. High blood pressure (hypertension) for example, is the major risk factor for stroke and heart attack, but in itself can cause damage to the heart, eyes and kidneys. Conversely, some diseases also act as risk factors for other diseases; diabetes can cause serious damage to the eyes and kidneys, but is also a major risk factor for heart attack. I shall be discussing the interactions and interrelationships between the various risk factors in more detail in the next chapter.

Chapter 2

MORE ABOUT RISK FACTORS

Before going any further, let's just recall the seven important **modifiable** risk factors which we discussed in Chapter 1. They are as follows:

1. High blood cholesterol level.
2. Cigarette smoking.
3. High blood pressure (hypertension).
4. Physical inactivity.
5. Obesity.
6. Stress/Personality.
7. Excessive alcohol consumption.

You will also recall that there were two **partially modifiable** factors, ie

- Diabetes (maturity onset).
- High blood fibrinogen.

The **non-modifiable** factors — age, family history and sex — need to be borne in mind because they have an important influence in determining the level of risk in any one individual. The risk factor concept is an important one and it is essential that you should understand its value, but also its limitations.

RISK FACTORS AND DISEASE — THE FRAMINGHAM HEART STUDY

Most people have never heard of Framingham — a small town (population 28 000) which lies about 18 miles west of Boston, south of the Massachusetts Turnpike.

In 1948 Framingham was chosen as the location for a major study into the origins of cardiovascular disease because of the worrying increase in heart disease in the USA. Some 5000 men and women volunteers, aged 30–59 years, underwent a thorough physical examination and regular reviews over a number of years, and their lifestyles were also recorded. Scientists were able to build up a picture of which factors were most likely to be associated with the development of a heart attack or stroke. Using sophisticated statistical methods, they were also able to calculate the independent contribution to risk made by each individual risk factor.

The Framingham Study continues to this day, revealing ever deeper insights into why cardiovascular disease occurs and, most importantly, how it may be prevented. Of course it is now only one of many hundreds of major studies into the origins of heart disease, but despite the fact that the data originate from a small community on the east coast of the USA, the name of Framingham has become synonymous with the risk factor concept.

Of course it is not only in relation to heart disease that the risk factor concept is important. Studies on many other diseases have also been able to identify specific determinants of risk, particularly for certain forms of cancer. For example, cigarette smoking is **the** major risk factor for lung cancer. Moreover, as we saw at the beginning of Chapter 1, several risk factors are common to a number of important diseases.

CAUSE AND ASSOCIATION

Whilst it is extremely important to be aware of what the risk factor concept means, it is also important for you to be aware of what it does *not* mean. There is much confusion in the use of the words 'cause' and 'association' which may lead to woolly thinking and inappropriate conclusions.

Let's consider first a simple example of a cause and effect relationship. If I apply heat (*cause*), to a metal bar, the bar will expand resulting in an increase in length (*effect*). There is an inevitable and almost immediate relationship between the two variables, and we are quite happy to accept that the heat (X), causes the metal bar to increase in length (Y). In statistical terms we measure the strength of the association or *correlation* between two variables, X and Y, by calculating something called the 'correlation coefficient'.

However, situations which are relevant to human health and disease are rarely as simple as this. Biological systems are infinitely more complex, and there are relatively few situations in which we can confidently say that a particular factor *causes* a specific disease. This may come as something of a surprise, but it is true nevertheless. This means that we have to be cautious in our interpretation of experimental data and avoid reaching conclusions which cannot be justified.

Let's take a concrete (and topical) example.

We know from many studies that there is a clear association (or correlation) between high blood cholesterol levels in a given population, and the risk of heart attack. As cholesterol levels rise, the death rates from heart disease rise, so there appears to be a clear positive correlation. However, we are not necessarily entitled to draw the conclusion that a high blood cholesterol **causes** heart disease.

Unlike the case of the metal bar, there are many other factors to be taken into account. For example, many (perhaps the majority) of individuals with high blood cholesterol levels never develop heart disease. It is also quite possible that other factors, including genetics, are at work. Few experts would deny that an elevated cholesterol level is an important risk factor for heart disease, but many of them would say that it falls short of a cause and effect relationship. All one can say is that a high cholesterol level (X), is associated (or correlated) with an increased risk of heart disease (Y), **not** that X *causes* Y.

In other situations the correlation may be so strong, and with a biologically plausible explanation, that we can safely regard the association as (for all practical purposes) one of cause and effect. The best example is the association between cigarette smoking and lung cancer. There is, without doubt, a strong and consistent positive correlation between the numbers of cigarettes smoked and the incidence of cancer, ie as cigarette consumption rises, cancer rates also rise. Conversely when cigarette consumption falls, the incidence of lung cancer also falls. In well over 90 per cent of lung cancer cases, the victim is a habitual cigarette smoker. What we are entitled to say is that there is very strong correlation between smoking and the risk of lung cancer, and that the strength of this association is such as to constitute a cause and effect relationship.

But not only do we need to be cautious about the degree or the strength of the association, we also need to ask whether the correlation is relevant or real. Often, two observations (variables) may be strongly correlated, without any plausible explanation. For example, in children there is a strong positive correlation betwen shoe size and reading ability, both of which increase with age. Nevertheless, the mere presence of a mathematical association would not lead us to suppose that shoe size and reading ability are actually linked in any way. To quote Stephen J Gould in his book, *The Mismeasure of Man*, 'One of the most elementary mistakes in logic is to state that if two or more entities are correlated or associated, they must therefore be causally linked in some way'. This principle applies in medicine just as well as anywhere else. The mere ability to demonstrate an association between two entities is not enough. There has, in addition, to be a biologically plausible explanation which makes the association relevant or 'real'.

The reason I am labouring this point here is because I suspect that many of the 250 so-called risk factors for heart disease, are nothing more than parallel observations which are not actually related at all. Since there is no plausible biological explanation for some of them, it may be better to call them 'risk markers' rather than risk factors. A risk marker for heart disease is nothing more than a factor which appears to have an association with an increased risk of developing disease, whereas for a risk factor there must be a reasonably well defined biological mechanism by which it exerts its influence. The popular press, of course, makes no such distinction which is why newspaper reports of yet another threat to life and limb appear at least once a week — an event which nowadays is likely to elicit a collective groan from most of us and complete indifference from the rest. When we read that the 'risk list' now includes snoring, not eating mackerel and not taking an afternoon siesta (all said to be risks for heart disease), we begin to wonder if this is all some part of a laughable cosmic plot.

A HEALTHY SCEPTICISM

Recognizing what is likely to be a true risk factor, as opposed to nothing more than a risk marker, is an important contributor to sanity. The press and the media are fond of any editorial which identifies a new form of risky behaviour, simply because it makes popular reading and sells newspapers. Nothing wrong with that, you might say, but the problem is that it often leads to confusion and sometimes real concern. There is usually no attempt whatsoever at critical evaluation of the evidence, because in general newspapers do not regard this as part of their function.

Not very long ago one of our major Sunday newspapers published a headline suggesting that the cholesterol story was all a great big mistake, and that recent scientific evidence had demonstrated that attempts to reduce blood cholesterol and reduce risk of heart disease were a waste of time. I was not able to obtain the scientific reference for this, because it was not provided in the article. On the following day, another national newspaper ran exactly the same story. When I telephoned them to find out the source of the data, I was told that they weren't actually very sure of where it all originated. In fact, they had simply taken the copy from the Sunday newspaper the day before, and re-published it in a different version. I asked whether they felt that was a responsible approach, and was told that they had to 'get something out', simply because the story was topical. They were not academics, and they could not accept responsibility for the scientific veracity of what they were publishing. It was getting the story out that was important. Incidentally, the study which formed the basis for the story was largely discredited following scientific peer review — a fact ignored by the newspapers in question.

Even if you are a non-scientist, I hope that being aware of all this will at least encourage you to think critically about the latest health fad featured on the covers of glossy magazines, or in the multitude of promotional videos produced by various fitness 'experts'. The next time you hear that head circumference is a risk factor for coronary artery disease, or you see a tabloid headline exclaiming 'Mango Eating Increases the Risk of Stroke in Middle-aged Men', you can regard it with a healthy degree of scepticism!

INTERRELATIONS BETWEEN RISK FACTORS

Apart from making its own individual contribution to risk, each of the factors listed at the beginning of this chapter has important interactions with the others. This is an important fact to bear in mind, since modification of one lifestyle-related risk factor may well have beneficial effects on several others. An example will help to illustrate what I mean.

Obesity is known to increase the risk of heart disease, stroke and some forms of cancer. However, obese individuals are also much more likely to have high blood pressure, diabetes and high blood cholesterol levels. They also tend to take much less regular physical exercise than their non-obese counterparts. Because of these associated factors, the actual level of risk in the obese person is considerably greater than that conferred by the presence of obesity alone. In fact, there is still some debate as to whether it is the obesity itself which confers greater risk, or the hypertension, physical inactivity etc with which it is known to be associated. Recent evidence suggests that it does in fact make a contribution to risk, independent of its association with other factors.

Obesity is also known to be associated with certain forms of cancer, particularly those cancers which are hormone dependent. Heavy alcohol consumption is also associated with an increased risk of cancer, but also tends to increase blood pressure and, consequently, the risk of a heart attack or stroke. Moreover, obesity and excess alcohol consumption are themselves related, because of the high calorie content of most alcoholic drinks.

I have tried to illustrate some of these interrelationships in an example of a risk factor 'network' shown in Figure 2.1.

Although having one risk factor may, because of its additional associations, increase your risk even more, the converse is also true. Reducing your weight will tend to reduce your blood pressure, cholesterol levels and improve blood sugar levels in diabetics. This is why relatively modest lifestyle changes in one area can bring about a substantial reduction in overall risk.

THE INDEPENDENCE OF RISK FACTORS

Whilst there are important interactions between some risk factors, we also need to appreciate their *independent* contribution to risk. If we carry out a study of risk factors in relation to heart disease, we may be able to demonstrate that patients who die from heart attack tend to have high blood pressure, smoke cigarettes, take little exercise etc, but what is the contribution made by each of these factors individually?

The way to find out whether and to what extent individual factors contribute to risk, is to use a sophisticated statistical technique known as *multiple regression*. This allows researchers to isolate a particular risk factor, and quantify its contribution to risk independent of all other factors. So when we say that lack of regular physical exercise is an 'independent' risk factor for heart disease, we mean that it makes an individual

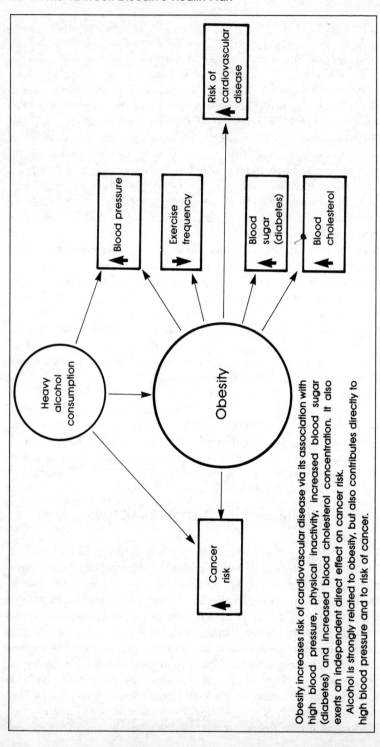

Obesity increases risk of cardiovascular disease via its association with high blood pressure, physical inactivity, increased blood sugar (diabetes) and increased blood cholesterol concentration. It also exerts an independent direct effect on cancer risk.

Alcohol is strongly related to obesity, but also contributes directly to high blood pressure and to risk of cancer.

Figure 2.1   Interactions between risk factors

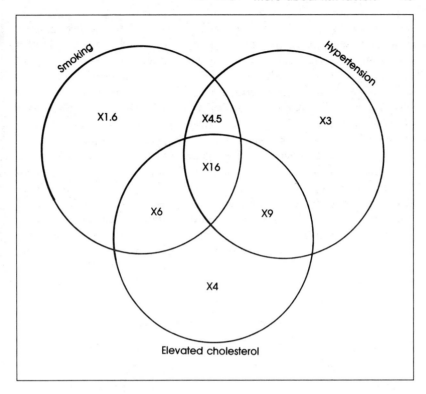

Source: Giuseppe Mancia, The Need to Manage Risk Factors of Coronary Heart Disease, *American Heart Journal* 115, no. 1, pt. 2 (January 1988): 240.

Figure 2.2 Multiplicative effects of risk factors

contribution to risk apart from any association with other factors such as obesity, high blood pressure etc.

MULTIPLICATIVE EFFECTS OF RISK FACTORS

In addition to being strongly interrelated, risk factors are also multiplicative (see Figure 2.2). For example, a cigarette smoker has about 1.6 times the risk of developing heart disease when compared to the non-smoker, and someone with hypertension has three times the risk. The combination of both increases the risk to 4.5 times that of the non-smoker with normal blood pressure. The addition of an elevated cholesterol level, in combination with smoking and hypertension, increases the risk of heart attack to 16 times that of the individual without these risk factors.

You must also bear in mind that relatively modest increases in **several** factors can be just as risky as a major increase in one. For example an individual who smokes only five cigarettes a day, with a slightly elevated cholesterol of 5.8 mmol/l and a mildly elevated diastolic blood pressure of 95 mm Hg, would probably be considered by most people to be at low risk. In fact, if you run these figures through the risk appraisal in the next chapter, this individual is at the same level of risk as someone with a blood cholesterol of 8 mmol/l, or someone who smokes 40 cigarettes per day!

The role of tobacco and alcohol in causing cancer is another excellent example of how two agents acting together can multiply the level of risk. The cancer causing effect of tobacco in the mouth, throat, gullet etc is not simply added to the effect of alcohol, but *multiplied* so that the effect of both drinking and smoking together, is many times greater than the effect of either one separately. Depending upon the number of cigarettes smoked, the particular combination of alcohol and cigarette smoking can increase the risk of cancer of the gullet (oesophagus) anywhere between 40 and 100 times.

RISK FACTORS AS DISEASES

Apart from their association with various forms of cancer, heart disease and stroke, many of the most important lifestyle-related risk factors may in themselves give rise to a whole range of ailments, some of which are serious.

Hypertension, for example, is a risk factor for stroke and heart disease but independent of these, it may cause damage to the kidneys and the eyes. Alcohol does appear to make a contribution to the development of certain forms of cancer and perhaps also to stroke, but equally important is its direct toxic effect upon almost every organ in the body. This can give rise to a whole spectrum of problems, ranging from cirrhosis of the liver and inflammation of the pancreas, to serious mental disorders and brain damage.

GAPS IN RISK FACTOR KNOWLEDGE

The risk factor concept provides a firm scientific basis for individual and population programmes designed to promote health and prevent disease. Evidence would suggest that major modifications in lifestyle-related risk factors throughout the UK population, would result in a very much healthier population and a considerable reduction in premature death and disability.

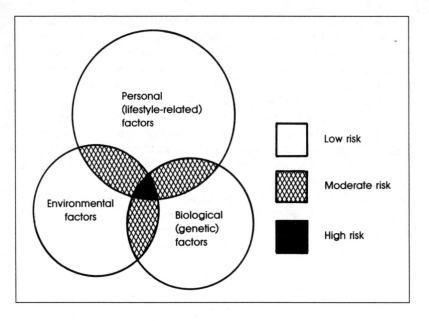

Figure 2.3   Contributors to risk

In the USA, for example, there has been a 55 per cent reduction in deaths since 1968. Some of this reduction can be directly attributed to improvements in medical care, and yet most of it — probably as much as 60 per cent — is attributed to better control of those aspects of health, diet and behaviour that tend to increase risk.

Even relatively modest changes in individual risk factors may have a substantial impact. Some recent studies have suggested that a 10 mmHg lowering of blood pressure in this country would produce a 30 per cent reduction in deaths. Another estimate suggests that a 10 per cent reduction in blood cholesterol levels through adult life would reduce heart disease by one-third. Individuals who exercise regularly may achieve a 45 per cent lower risk for heart disease, when compared with those who have sedentary lifestyle.

There is also enormous scope for preventing cancer. In *The Causes of Cancer* by Doll and Peto to which I referred in Chapter 1, the authors concluded that many cancers, perhaps the majority, could be avoided. Smoking contributes to at least 30 per cent of all cancer deaths and there is mounting evidence that diets relatively high in fat, but low in fibre, fresh vegetables and fruits, may significantly increase the risk of various cancers, including those of the bowel, breast, ovary and prostate. Obesity, as we have seen earlier, is also associated with an increased occurrence of cancers of the gall bladder, breast, bowel and prostate (see Table 1.4, page 32).

However, not everyone who has risk factors for a particular disease, will go on to develop that disease. Not all cigarette smokers will develop lung cancer, and not everyone who consumes alcohol to excess will develop liver cirrhosis. Although most of the individuals who develop heart disease have elevated blood cholesterol levels, many (perhaps 50 per cent) of people with a raised blood cholesterol will never develop heart problems. Clearly many other factors must be involved, many of which are, as yet, unidentified. Earlier in the book I explained that most diseases are the result of a genetic predisposition with a personal (lifestyle-related) factor. But there is also the possibility of an environmental factor exerting an influence. For example, some studies have shown a higher death rate from heart disease in those areas where the tap water is soft. This observation may be related to the relatively low levels of minerals such as calcium, magnesium and zinc, producing a deficiency state which may affect the heart muscle. Evidence for this is not conclusive, but it illustrates my point.

So, strictly speaking, there are probably three factors to take into account, ie genetic, personal and environmental. In all probability, the environmental factor is less critical than the other two — although still a contributor. Presumably when all three are present, the risk of disease is at its greatest (see Figure 2.3).

Key note

Lifestyle related risk factors increase susceptibility to many major diseases; are strongly interrelated; will have a multiplicative effect in terms of overall risk and may give rise to specific diseases in themselves.

In concluding this section, it seems clear that the risk factor concept provides us with firm scientific basis for personal action to reduce risk, although the story is far from complete. Two important points follow:

1. Lifestyle-related risk factors do not account for all cases of cardiovascular disease or cancer.
2. It follows that modifying these factors will not prevent all cases of these diseases.

Despite these caveats, you should be in no doubt that the scope for risk reduction via lifestyle modification is very considerable, and can make a major contribution to your current and future health prospects. That's what the rest of this book is about and it starts in the next chapter with your own Health Risk Appraisal (HRA).

Chapter 3

KNOW YOUR HEALTH NUMBERS!
YOUR HEALTH RISK APPRAISAL
(HRA)

A few years ago I was consulted by the managing director of a leading clearing bank who wanted some advice regarding his health status and, more particularly, how to improve it. I arranged for him to have a thorough physical examination which revealed that there were a number of risk factors present, for example overweight, lack of exercise, etc which needed urgent attention.

As I began to explain to him the implications of all this for his future health he interrupted and said 'I'm sorry if I appear to be a bit rude, but you don't need to give me a lot of justification for the recommendations you are making. I understand that they are important and I have every confidence in you, and trust what you tell me. But I like the fact that you are able to express these problems in the form of numbers because I work with numbers all day, and I understand them. So if you can explain to me what I need to do in terms of these numbers, in other words what the numbers are now and what you think they ought to be, then I will definitely do something about it. I just need the numbers!'

Well, I gave him the numbers, and (true to his word) he came back to see me about three months later and he had already achieved most of them. In fact he went on to make some pretty dramatic changes in his life and in his order of priorities. I still see him from time to time, purely on a social basis because he never seems to be ill these days. Interestingly, although it is in his outward appearance and his eating and exercise habits that the most obvious changes have taken place, from his own viewpoint the major benefit has been the enormous improvement in his psychological functioning. He feels that his work performance, particularly his intellectual performance, is much sharper and his problem solving skills considerably enhanced. There seems to be a definite 'edge' that was missing before.

I mention this example because it illustrates the fact that when individuals are given good quality information with realistic goals to achieve, they usually respond positively. Of course the level of that response varies enormously between individuals, but in my experience very few people remain totally indolent when they are made aware of their own specific health risks.

In this chapter you will be learning about your own **Health Numbers** and their significance via a personal Health Risk Appraisal (HRA) questionnaire.

WHAT IS A HEALTH RISK APPRAISAL (HRA)?

The concept of the Health Risk Appraisal (HRA) was introduced more than 20 years ago as a means of encouraging individuals to first identify, and then to modify, potentially significant risk factors. The essential component of most HRAs is a self-scored questionnaire which takes into account demographic and risk factor data, in order to highlight the most important areas of risk, and to translate these individual risk factors into an overall risk category (eg low, medium and high risk). The success of any HRA lies purely in its ability to communicate important information and to motivate individuals to modify negative habits and lifestyles.

WHICH HRA IS THE BEST?

If the purpose of an HRA is to communicate information to an individual in order to motivate them to take effective action, what is the best type of HRA in practice?

Obviously, the first requirement is that it must address those major risk factors which are known to be associated with disability, illness and death, eg blood pressure, blood cholesterol level, family history, exercise habits and so on. Whilst some HRAs now utilize very sophisticated mathematical modelling, there is no evidence that a complex 'Health Risk Statement' produced by a computer is any more effective in changing behaviour patterns than a simple self-scored questionnaire. The obvious advantage which computerized models have is that they provide a more complex scientific interpretation of the data and allow information from large number of HRAs to be processed very rapidly.

The one that you will be using is a 10 point inventory which takes into account all the major risk factors for cardiovascular disease. It therefore gives a risk assessment which is primarily directed towards heart attack and stroke. But please note that it includes all seven of the lifestyle-related factors which we discussed at the beginning of Chapter 1, so in fact it provides (albeit indirectly) a more general indication for a number of diseases, including cancer. This particular questionnaire also has the advantage that it is relatively simple to complete, and can be repeated at regular intervals without any difficulty. This will allow you to compare your progress over time. The other important advantage is that it does not require any advanced mathematical ability. Once you have gone through the process of scoring the questionnaire the first time, you will find it very much easier and quicker to complete on subsequent occasions.

COMPLETING THE QUESTIONNAIRE — THE RISK CATEGORY INDICATOR

The Health Risk Appraisal Questionnaire is shown on pages 52–54. There are ten items to be completed, each item attracting a certain number of points, depending upon your history, health habits etc.

Depending upon your overall score, you will see that there are five main risk groupings, ie low, relatively low, moderate, high and very high. This is reasonable as a rough guide, but does not reflect the fact that risk is on a continuum, ie there may be quite a difference between the lower end of a risk category and its upper end. For example, a score of 13 points will place you in the moderate risk category, but so would a score of 23 points. There is clearly a great deal of difference between the lower and the upper reference point for each of the five risk categories, and it is very important that you should be aware of this. For this reason, I have put the risk groupings on a linear scale, so that you can mark your risk level at exactly the right point. This way you will be able to see much more clearly whether you are at the lower or the upper end of a particular risk group.

I shall now run through the ten question areas in the HRA, so as to ensure that you enter the numbers/information accurately, and then I will give you some worked examples by way of illustration.

THE HRA QUESTIONNAIRE

Please note that for questions eight (Body Mass Index), nine (Stress) and ten (Alcohol) you will need to refer to other sections in the book. The page references are given in the following review of the questionnaire.

1. **Age & Sex:** Self-explanatory. The scoring reflects the fact that risk of heart disease increases with age, and tends (before the menopause) to be more common in men.
2. **Family history:** By blood relatives, I mean mother, father, brother or sister. The question relates to relatives suffering from heart disease or a stroke between 60–75 years old, or before the age of 60. The number of points awarded depends on how many there were in each group. For example, if my father died of a heart attack aged 70, and my sister died at 55 years, I would score 1 + 3 = 4 points.

7/10/94

HEALTH RISK APPRAISAL

	POINTS	SCORE
1. Age & Sex		
Female < 45	0	
Male < 40	1	
Female 45–55 or Male 40–49	②	
Female > 55	3	
Male 50–60	4	
Male > 60	5	
2. Family history of heart disease* (parents, brothers or sisters)		
No history	⓪	
1 Relative 60–75 years	1	
2 Relatives 60–75 years	2	
1 Relative < 60 years	3	
2 Relatives < 60 years	4	
3 Relatives < 60 years	5	
3. Tobacco smoking		
Never smoked	⓪	
Stopped smoking cigarettes more than 1 year ago	1	
Stopped smoking in past year *or* < 20 cigarettes per day	2	
Smoking 6 or more cigars per day *or* inhale a pipe regularly	2	
20–30 cigarettes per day	3	
31–39 cigarettes per day	4	
40+ cigarettes per day	6	
4. Diabetes		
No diabetes	⓪	
Diabetes controlled by diet *or* diabetes after age 55	2	
Diabetes at or after age 40 and now on insulin or tablets	4	
Diabetes before aged 40 and now on insulin	6	

* Heart Disease is defined as Angina or Heart Attack (fatal or non-fatal)

	POINTS	SCORE
5. Exercise Do you engage in regular conditioning exercise such as brisk-walking, jogging, running, cycling, badminton etc, at a level hard enough to make you breathless?		
3 or more times per week	0	
2 times per week	1	
1 period of exercise per week	3	
No exercise	(5)	
6. Total Cholesterol (TC) or TC/HDL ratio		
Cholesterol < 5.2mmol/L or TC/HDL Ratio 4.5 or less	0	
Cholesterol 5.2–6.4mmol/L (6.1) or TC/HDL Ratio 4.6–5.9 (5.5)	(2)	
Cholesterol 6.5–7.8 mmol/L or TC/HDL 6.0–7.9	4	
Cholesterol > 7.8mmol/L or TC/HDL 8 or more	6	
7. Blood pressure (mmHg)		
Systolic < 120	0	
120–129	1	
130–139 *guess*	(2)	
140–159	3	
160–179	4	
180 and above	6	
Diastolic < 80	0	
80–84	1	
85–89 *guess*	(2)	
90–104	3	
105–115	4	
115 and above	6	
8. Weight (BMI)	*just !*	
Body Mass Index (BMI)* within acceptable range for age	(0)	
A BMI < 30, but > upper limit of age-related BMI	2	
Body Mass Index > 30	4	

* Body Mass Index (BMI) $= \dfrac{\text{weight (kg)}}{(\text{height metres})^2}$

	POINTS	SCORE
9. Stress From questionnaires on pages 164–6		
0–24 points	0	
25–50 points 26 points	①	
51–70 points	3	
> 70 points	4	
10. Alcohol consumption (units/week)		
Male up to 21 units *or* Female up to 14 units	⓪ ?	
Male 22–50 units *or* Female 15–35 units	②	
Male > 50 units *or* Female > 35 units	4	
	TOTAL SCORE	

> Greater than
< Less than

Risk ranges by score

      0–7   Low
      8–12   Relatively low
      13–24 Moderate
      25–34 High
      35+   Very high

Now place a mark on the scale to indicate your level of risk

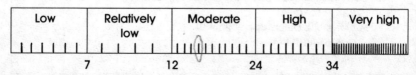

Please note that by a history of heart disease I mean a heart attack (whether fatal or non-fatal), heart surgery (for coronary artery disease), or a history of angina (by angina I refer to pain in the chest, usually on exertion, and usually treated by tablets). Heart surgery for anything other than coronary artery disease, eg valve replacement, does not count.

Obviously if there is no relevant family history, then you will not attract any points at all.

3. **Cigarette smoking**: This is straightforward. The question refers primarily to *cigarette* smoking, but note that you can also attract penalty points if you are a regular pipe or cigar smoker.

4. **Diabetes**: Again this should be self-explanatory.

5. **Exercise**: The question relates to how often you take regular conditioning (aerobic) exercise, for at least 20 minutes, at an intensity that will increase your pulse-rate and make you breathless. The activity should be regular, rhythmical and involve major muscle groups, eg *brisk*-walking, jogging, cycling, swimming and other sporting activities such as tennis, badminton, soccer etc. Walking only qualifies if it really is brisk; a casual walk to the local off-licence does **not** qualify! Your activity patterns may vary a little from week to week, but you should estimate your average number of weekly sessions.

Few people nowadays have a high level of occupational physical activity, but if your job genuinely does involve strenuous exercise, eg lifting, carrying or walking for a large part of your working day, then you should classify yourself as 'vigorously' active, and you will attract 0 penalty points.

6. **Cholesterol**: To answer this question you should ideally have your blood cholesterol measured, and some advice as to how you should go about this is given in Chapter 4, Part II. Cholesterol is measured in millimoles per litre (mmol/L) and so you simply need to give yourself the correct number of points, depending on the result.

If you are also able to obtain your HDL-cholesterol level, then this is better still. If you divide the Total Cholesterol result by the HDL, you have something called the TC/HDL ratio — a powerful indicator of risk. Again you simply allocate the number of points according to the ratio.

If you do have the TC/HDL ratio available, this should be used **instead** of the total cholesterol level; if not, the cholesterol alone will suffice.

7. **High blood pressure**: Chapter 5, in Part II, will give you more detailed information about how blood pressure is measured. The units of measurement are millimetres of mercury (mm/Hg), and the question relates to the two figures obtained, ie systolic pressure (the higher figure), and the diastolic pressure.

8. **Body Mass Index (BMI):** The formula for Body Mass Index (BMI) is given in the questionnaire. In order to save you calculating this, you need only to turn to page 192 where you will be able to find your BMI quite easily. When you have this number, you should see how this relates to the recommended ranges according to your age (page 194). If your BMI is 30 or greater, you will attract four points automatically. The point allocation for a lower figure depends upon whether it is within or above the age-related acceptable range. The importance of Body Mass Index is discussed in more detail in Chapter 10.

9. **Stress:** Stress is discussed in detail in Chapter 9, and one of the main items you will find there is a personal questionnaire designed to assess personality type, stress and coping skills. Turn to page 164, and work through the questionnaire completing all the items carefully. When you have completed this you will be able to work out which of the four categories you fall into, on the basis of which you will be given a specific stress score. This score will, in turn, attract a certain number of points in the Health Risk Appraisal questionnaire.

   So if, on the stress/personality questionnaire, you score more than 70 points, you should give yourself four points on the HRA form.

   If you score 51–70 points you should give yourself three points on the HRA.

   If you score 25–50 points on the Stress questionnaire, you should give yourself one point.

   If you score anywhere between 0–24 points on the Stress questionnaire, you will attract zero points on the HRA.

10. **Alcohol:** Chapter 8 in Part II, discusses alcohol and alcohol abuse in some detail. If you turn to Table 8.1 on page 142 you will be able to calculate the number of units (on average) which you consume over a period of one week. You then allocate the correct number of penalty points depending upon your **average** weekly consumption.

    Moderate amounts of alcohol (up to 21 units per week for males and 14 units for females) may actually carry some health benefits, particularly with respect to coronary heart disease. Above this level, however, the risks outweigh the benefits. Excessive alcohol consumption may contribute to the risk of stroke and heart disease because it is a potent hypertensive agent, ie it increases blood pressure. It also contributes to obesity and elevates blood fat levels, apart from its well documented potential to cause damage to the liver and other organs.

A NOTE ON FIBRINOGEN

You may recall from Chapter 1 that a high level of fibrinogen in the blood increases the risk of a heart attack and stroke. However, it is not included in the risk appraisal which you are about to complete, mainly because measurement of fibrinogen is seldom used as a routine investigation. Also, measures designed to modify or eliminate other risk factors will tend to have a beneficial effect on fibrinogen levels.

SOME WORKED EXAMPLES

I shall now work through three examples to show how the HRA can be used to assess the level of risk in any one individual case. More importantly, they will also serve to illustrate how relatively modest changes in these risk factors can bring about an appreciable reduction in risk. All three are taken from actual examples, although the names have been changed.

Example 1

John Barton is 55 years old and works as marketing director for a major multi-national corporation. He travels a great deal, and admits that he finds his job extremely stressful at times. On average he smokes 20–30 cigarettes per day, and drinks two to three whiskeys. At a height of 5 feet 10 inches (1.77 metres) he weighs 15 stones 4 pounds (97 kgs). Although Mr Barton does not have any heart problems himself, he revealed that his father died suddenly of a heart attack at the age of 59. After a recent health check he was told that his blood pressure was 165/102 mmHg and his blood cholesterol result came back at 7.1 mmol/L, with an HDL-cholesterol of 0.75 mmol/L. There was no history of diabetes. On the Stress/Personality questionnaire, he scored 58 points. Although he recognizes that regular exercise is important he says he 'cannot find time'.

Assessment and score

John Barton is 55 and male, so he attracts 4 points. He scores 3 points for his family history and a further 3 points for his cigarette smoking. He is not a diabetic and so scores 0 points. Currently he takes no regular exercise, and so gets another 5 points.

His Total Cholesterol (or cholesterol) result was 7.1 mmol/L, and the HDL 0.75 mmol/L, giving a high TC/HDL ratio of 9.5, for which he receives 6 points. His blood pressure is also somewhat elevated, for which he scores 7 points (4 for the systolic, and 3 for the diastolic).

Looking at the chart on page 192 we find his body mass index to be 31, and for this he attracts 4 points. His score on the stress/personality questionnaire gives him 3 points. He drinks on average four whiskeys per day (ie 4 units per day), or 28 units per week. This is above the recommended upper limit of 21 units per week, and so he receives 2 points.

Adding all the numbers up, John Barton has a risk score of 37 points, which puts him in the very high risk category.

After receiving appropriate advice about these important areas of risk, John Barton returned again after a period of twelve weeks for re-assessment. He had managed to reduce his alcohol and cigarette consumption, adopted a low fat diet and embarked on an exercise programme. The result was a reduced body mass index and TC/HDL ratio. Added to that, John feels very much better about himself both in terms of his appearance, and in the knowledge that he has greatly reduced his risk status. In just twelve weeks, John moved from the very high risk category, down to a moderate risk status. This major reduction in risk was accomplished by relatively modest changes in his lifestyle and behaviour.

Example 2

Jane Hurst is a 48 year old housewife who has had a problem with her weight for many years. At a height of five feet four inches (1.62 metres) she currently weighs 13 stones one pound (83 kgs). There is no family history of heart disease and she is not a diabetic. Mrs Hurst has never smoked.

In a renewed effort to lose weight, she recently started swimming once a week usually for a period of about 30 minutes. Her general practitioner found her blood pressure to be 168/90 and took the opportunity to check her blood cholesterol level which was found to be 5.3 mmol/L. She almost never touches alcohol and scored only 20 points on the stress/personality questionnaire.

Assessment and score

For her age and sex Mrs Hurst scored 2 points. In relation to family history, diabetes and smoking history, she scored a total of 0 points. Her blood cholesterol of 5.3 mmol/L (no HDL available), attracts a score of 2 points, and her blood pressure rating a further 6 points (4 for systolic and 2 for diastolic). Her body mass index of 32 means another 4 points but since she is exercising only once a week, she received an additional 3 points. Both stress and alcohol scores attracted 0 points.

If you work through this you will find that Mrs Hurst scores a total of 17 points, which places her in the moderate risk category.

After completing the HRA, Mrs Hurst increased her exercise sessions to three per week and pursued a low fat, high fibre diet more vigorously. She also restricted her salt intake in an effort to reduce her blood pressure. At a twelve-week reassessment, both her blood pressure and her blood cholesterol levels had dropped. Most importantly, she had lost a stone in weight, reducing her body mass index from 32 down to 29. She scored the same on the stress questionnaire and remains teetotal. As a result Mrs Hurst now scores a total of only 8 points, and moves easily into the relatively low-risk category — almost into the lowest risk group. Again this was achieved by relatively modest changes in her lifestyle and personal risk factors. Mrs Hurst found the improvement in her appearance and risk status enormously encouraging, and had the motivation to improve still further.

Example 3

Keith Matthews is 32 years old and works for the local housing department. He enjoys his job very much and does not find it unduly stressful. Much of his leisure time is spent pursuing various water sports, including scuba diving and water skiing, but he also runs several times each week. At a height of six feet one inch (1.86 metres) he weighs 12 stones (76 kgs). He was diagnosed as diabetic in childhood, but is remarkably well controlled on insulin. Otherwise he has enjoyed good health all his life, and has never smoked. He normally drinks about two to three pints of lager per week, but rarely any more.

There is some relevant family history in that his father died at the age of 51 from a heart attack. It was this fact that prompted him to take advantage of a recent offer for a free health check organized by his employers. As a result of this his blood pressure was found to be 120/70, but his blood cholesterol level was significantly elevated at 8.4 mmol/L, and with an HDL level of 1.2 mmol/L.

He scored only 21 points on the stress/personality questionnaire.

Assessment and score

For his age and sex Mr Matthews scored 1 point. For his family history he attracts 3 points, and for his history of diabetes 6 points. As a non-smoker who exercises regularly, he scores 0 points for questions 3 and 5. His TC/ HDL Ratio at 7, scored 4 points, but the remaining questions (7–10) amounted to 0. Keith Matthews attracted a total score of 14 points, which placed him at the lower end of the moderate risk category.

The important point to appreciate, however, is that most of his risk derives from what are non-modifiable risk factors, ie his family history of heart disease, and his diabetes. Because he scores so well on the remaining factors, he is still only at the lower end of moderate risk. The only real opportunity for improvement is in relation to his high cholesterol and TC/ HDL Ratio.

In fact, following his assessment he modified his diet to reduce the total amount of saturated fat, and had his cholesterol level checked again twelve weeks later. His total score had gone down to 12 points, which places him in the relatively low risk category. This example demonstrates that even if you are heavily loaded due to non-modifiable factors, there may still be an opportunity to improve.

NOW COMPLETE THE HRA QUESTIONNAIRE YOURSELF (PAGES 52–54), USING THE NOTES ABOVE AND THE RELEVANT SECTIONS IN PART II OF THIS BOOK

INTERPRETING THE RESULTS — WHAT DOES THE SCORE SIGNIFY?

The HRA which you have just completed provides you with a risk estimate for cardiovascular disease (heart attack and stroke) and (to a limited extent), for cancer and other diseases known to be associated with the seven modifiable risk factors discussed previously, and which are an integral part of the risk appraisal.

It is extremely important to recognize that being in a high risk category does not necessarily mean to say that you **will** develop heart or other problems. It merely means that your risk of so doing is greater than that of an individual who does not have your particular set of risk factors.

In the same way, being in a low risk category is in no way a health guarantee. All one can say is that the risk of your developing cardiovascular disease or some forms of cancer, is substantially less than in those individuals who have multiple risk factors. Moreover, the fact that you may be in a low risk category now does not provide you with a licence to do what you like in the future! This is an extremely important point. My own research suggests that about 40 per cent of individuals in high or very high risk categories will move into a lower risk category, provided they are given the necessary information and advice. Interestingly, however, I have also found that a significant number of individuals will move from low risk categories into moderate risk groups. The reason for this may be that they are under the impression that a low risk score initially, gives them *carte blanche* to do whatever they wish in the future. This is a false sense of security and illustrates an important point to remember, ie good lifestyle practices are for *life*, not just for the period up to and immediately following an HRA!

WHICH OF THE HEALTH NUMBERS ARE THE MOST IMPORTANT?

Most of the health numbers that you will have used in the questionnaire can be shown to have an independent predictive effect on the risk of developing heart disease, stroke and some forms of cancer. Some measurements are obviously less precise and therefore less meaningful than others. For example, the stress/personality questionnaire is extremely useful in getting some understanding of your level of stress, but it is not something which can be measured precisely. The same is true of exercise.

But some of the numbers which we have used can be measured very accurately. Three of these numbers, ie Blood Pressure, Total Cholesterol Concentration (TC) and Body Mass Index (BMI), are fairly precise measures which can give a great deal of information about your overall health. In many senses we can regard these three numbers as being among the most important because they provide an enormous amount of information about your current health status. This is worth explaining a bit further.

Blood pressure

Your blood pressure, and how to control it, is discussed in Chapter 5, Part II. We know that blood pressure is a risk factor for coronary heart disease, and stroke in particular. We also know that high blood pressure is related to obesity and also to alcohol consumption. Because excess alcohol consumption and obesity are also known to be associated with an increased risk of developing certain forms of cancer, liver disease and musculo-skeletal problems, it is clear that the level of your blood pressure does give some indirect indication of other potential risk areas.

Blood cholesterol

High blood cholesterol levels represent a major risk factor for coronary heart disease. This is discussed in more detail in Part II, Chapter 4 of this book. But since blood cholesterol is strongly related to the amount of saturated fat in your diet, and since saturated fat is thought to increase the risk of developing certain kinds of cancer, the level of your blood cholesterol may give an indirect indication of risk in this area also.

Body Mass Index (BMI)

Derived from your weight and height, this single number gives you a valuable insight into your general health. Obesity, of course, is strongly related to high blood pressure, high cholesterol levels, heart disease, some forms of cancer and excess alcohol consumption. It is also associated with Type II diabetes, and is much more common in those with a sedentary lifestyle. It may also worsen symptoms associated with lung disease and lower back problems.

So you can see by taking note of these three numbers, you will actually know a great deal about your current health status. You can record your baseline **'big three'** numbers in the space below.

Blood pressure (mmHg)	Blood cholesterol (mmol/L)	Body mass index

MONITORING YOUR PROGRESS

When you have completed your baseline HRA questionnaire as indicated above, you will have a good idea as to what your major risk areas are. Each of these risk factors is discussed in detail in Chapters 4–10 in Part II, and you should:

1. Identify the highest scoring (modifiable) risk factor from the seven covered in Part II. Alternatively, pick the one which you feel you will be most successful in changing to start with; early wins are great for morale.
2. Be realistic about what you are seeking to achieve. Set a **12-week** timescale, and stick to it, and go for fairly modest changes over that period. The examples given earlier on in this section illustrate that one can achieve a substantial reduction in risk, without dramatic alterations in lifestyle. If you're too ambitious you will fail early.
3. Repeat the HRA questionnaire at the end of the **12-week** period. This will give you some important feedback on your progress, and (assuming you have improved), encouragement to continue.

    Remember, even a few points reduction on the risk scale is beneficial.

I would then recommend that you repeat the HRA at 6, 9 and 12 months.

WHAT NOW?

Now comes the hard work! Part II is divided into seven specific chapters, each dealing with a modifiable lifestyle factor. If you have a problem with slightly elevated blood pressure, then you will turn to Chapter 5; if your blood cholesterol is elevated you will turn to Chapter 4; and if you want to start exercising you will turn to Chapter 7 etc. Each of the seven main sections consists of four basic headings, ie:

1. Basic background information.
2. Assessment/Self-assessment.
3. Interpretation of results.
4. Action Plan.

Because of the importance of proper nutrition, I would suggest that you should read Part III of the book carefully. You will find this invaluable in selecting nutritious, low fat foods.

So for the next twelve weeks, work hard, be committed and you will definitely see results. At the end of that time repeat your Health Risk Appraisal, and measure your progress. Go to it!

Part II

CHANGING YOUR HEALTH NUMBERS – REDUCING THE SCORE!

Chapter 4

HOW TO LOWER YOUR CHOLESTEROL LEVEL

Anyone can develop high blood cholesterol level, regardless of age, sex, race or ethnic background. Because there are no warning symptoms or signs, you may well be surprised at being told that your cholesterol is elevated. This is not a signal for you to become alarmed, but it is something to be taken seriously. Like other modifiable factors, it is a potential threat to your health that you can do something about.

WHAT IS CHOLESTEROL?

Although cholesterol is generally regarded as the villain of the piece, it is in fact a vital component of all the cells of the body, especially those of the brain, spinal cord and nerves. It is also an essential ingredient in the manufacture of bile salts and a number of hormones, including cortisone and the sex hormones. In short, you could not live without it.

Most people believe that cholesterol is some kind of fat but although it may have some of the physical properties of a fat, it is not actually a fat at all. In fact, chemically it resembles an alcohol and is a member of a group of substances referred to as *sterols*.

Despite its importance, we do not actually need cholesterol in our diet because the body manufactures its own — a process which can occur in every organ throughout the body except the adult brain. The majority of cholesterol synthesis, however, is carried out in the liver, which is capable of producing up to six times more cholesterol each day than is found in the average Western diet.

Blood fats (lipoproteins)

Cholesterol is transported around the body in packages called *lipoproteins*, the most important of which are Low-Density Lipoprotein (LDL) and High-Density Lipoprotein (HDL), each particle carrying a different proportion of cholesterol; about 50 per cent of LDL is cholesterol but only around 15

Table 4.1 Three measures of cholesterol and risk of CHD

Measurement	Abbreviation	Relationship to CHD
Total cholesterol concentration	TC	Increasing levels associated with increasing risk
Low-density lipoprotein cholesterol	LDL-C	Increasing levels associated with increasing risk. Constitutes about 70% of total blood cholesterol
High-density lipoprotein cholesterol	HDL-C	Increasing levels associated with progressively *lower* risk

per cent of HDL. About 70 per cent of the cholesterol in the blood is carried in the LDL form; usually called LDL-cholesterol, or LDL-C. The HDL form of cholesterol, HDL-C, carries around 20–25 per cent of the total cholesterol in your body. The remainder (about 10 per cent) is carried by other lipoproteins.

These two forms of cholesterol, ie LDL-C and HDL-C, have exactly opposite effects. LDL-C deposits cholesterol into the wall of the artery, leading to the formation of plaque and atheroma described in Chapter 1. This is why LDL-C is sometimes referred to as the 'bad cholesterol'.

In contrast, HDL-C helps to remove excess cholesterol from the wall of the artery, and is often called 'good cholesterol'. It follows that what determines your risk of coronary disease is not the level of blood cholesterol *per se*, but rather the form in which it is carried, ie LDL-C or HDL-C.

Laboratory tests

There are four main laboratory tests used to assess an individual's lipoprotein status, the three most important of which are shown in Table 4.1.

1. **Total Cholesterol (TC) concentration**: The most commonly used measure, and the one with which most people are familiar, is the blood cholesterol level. It is the sum of all the cholesterol present in LDL-C, HDL-C and other lipoproteins.

   A high blood cholesterol level is an important risk factor for heart disease, precisely because it reflects a high blood level of the harmful LDL-C. You can assume, therefore, that when I refer to a high blood cholesterol level (ie Total Cholesterol or TC), that this automatically infers an increased level of LDL-C, and vice versa.

2. **Low-Density Lipoprotein Cholesterol (LDL-C)**: Direct measurement of LDL-C is possible but complicated and expensive. This is why

advice is normally based upon measures of Total Cholesterol. than LDL-C.

3. **High-Density Lipoprotein Cholesterol (HDL-C)**: Unlike LDL-C, the level of HDL-C is more readily available and is an important indicator of risk for heart disease. Unlike LDL-C, high levels of HDL-C are associated with a low risk of heart attack.

4. **Blood Triglyceride level**: In some studies high levels of triglycerides are associated with an increased risk of cardiovascular disease, but because its role in the development of arterial disease is less clearly defined, we shall not be discussing it any further.

NB. Total Cholesterol (TC), LDL-C and HDL-C, are measured in units known as millimoles per litre (mmol/L). In the USA it is measured in milligrams per decilitre or mg/dl. To convert mmol/L into mg/dl you multiply by 38.7, hence 5.2 mmol/L = 200 mg/dl.

Key note

There are several types of lipoprotein packages or particles, each made up of varying amounts of protein, phospholipid, triglycerides and cholesterol. The two most important lipoproteins are LDL-C, and HDL-C, which have exactly opposite effects. High levels of LDL-C are associated with an increased risk of heart disease, whilst high levels of HDL-C reduce the risk. Total Cholesterol (TC) and HDL-C are measured routinely, but LDL-C is less widely available. However, because LDL carries about 70 per cent of the total cholesterol in the body, the TC level is a good indirect measure of LDL-C and of risk for coronary disease.

HOW DOES A HIGH LEVEL OF BLOOD CHOLESTEROL LEAD TO DISEASE?

We saw in Chapter 1 that cardiovascular disease is caused by a process known as *atherosclerosis*, the cardinal feature of which is the deposition of cholesterol and other fatty substances in the arteries that supply blood to the heart, brain and peripheral blood vessels (especially the lower limbs). This deposit, known as plaque or atheroma, may lead to thrombosis and thus precipitate a stroke or a heart attack (see page 25).

LDL-C particles encourage this process. Conversely, HDL-C removes cholesterol from the wall of the artery, and hence reduces the tendency to plaque formation.

It follows that the development and growth of plaque depends upon the amounts of LDL-C and HDL-C present in the blood. When cholesterol levels (and therefore LDL-C) are high, or when HDL-C is low, plaque formation tends to occur. Even if the LDL-C is raised, if the HDL-C is high enough, it may still be able to protect against plaque formation. This is why measurement of HDL-C is important, and why the TC/HDL-C ratio (see later) is such a powerful measure of risk.

Certain vitamins, notably E, C. and A may help to block the formation of LDL-C and therefore prevent the build-up of cholesterol in the arterial wall. Much more research is needed, but if this turns out to be true, dietary supplementation with these vitamins may become an important preventive strategy. This is discussed in more detail in Chapter 11.

HOW ARE LEVELS OF CHOLESTEROL RELATED TO RISK?

As we have seen, both HDL-C and LDL-C lipoproteins have totally different effects on risk. In general, the risk of developing heart disease increases as the level of cholesterol in the blood rises. Some experts believe that the relationship is linear, ie as the level of cholesterol rises, the level of risk increases proportionately. However, others have suggested that the relationship is curvilinear as indicated in Figure 4.1. The graph shows that there is a slight increase in risk for levels between 5.2 and 6.5 mmol/L, but a steep increase in CHD mortality rates with levels above 6.5 mmol/L.

Evidence suggests that about two-thirds of the adults in this country have blood cholesterol levels of 5.2 mmol/L or above, and one-quarter have levels greater than 6.5 mmol/L. Bear in mind, however, that in the British Regional Heart Study as many as 20 per cent of acute heart attacks (both fatal and non-fatal), occurred in those with blood cholesterol levels below 6.0 mmol/L. Clearly we should not ignore cholesterol concentrations in the 'borderline' range.

When we look at the graph showing HDL-C levels and mortality (see Figure 4.2), the reverse picture obtains. The higher the HDL-C the lower the incidence of heart disease, with a dramatic increase in risk with blood levels below around 1 mmol/L. It follows from this that the individual with the lowest risk has a blood cholesterol below 5.2 mmol/L and an HDL-C concentration above 2 mmol/L.

WHAT FACTORS INFLUENCE MY BLOOD CHOLESTEROL LEVEL?

- **Age and Sex:** During adult life, Total Cholesterol (TC) levels increase and continue to rise in both sexes. Up to the age of 55, levels are higher

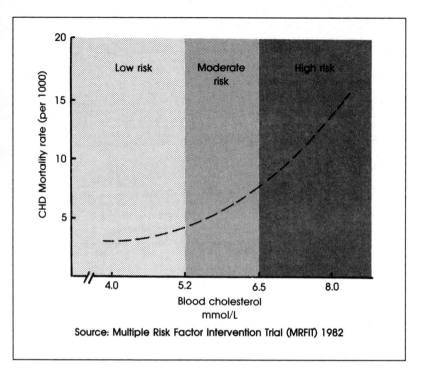

Figure 4.1   Blood cholesterol and CHD mortality

in men, but thereafter they tend to be higher in women (except in those
taking Hormone Replacement Therapy — HRT). The cause of the rise
in cholesterol levels with age is unknown. In addition to having lower
TC (and LDL-C) levels than men, women in their reproductive years
also tend to have higher levels of HDL-C. This favourable condition is
probably a hormonal effect (mainly oestrogens) and helps to explain
why pre-menopausal women have a much lower rate of coronary
disease than men. After the menopause, as the female hormone levels
decline, women gradually acquire the same risk of heart disease as
men. Recent evidence suggests that HRT helps to preserve the
favourable condition, and greatly reduces the risk of CHD in post-
menopausal women. It seems that oestrogens, not diamonds, are a
girl's best friend.

- **Diet:** Among the factors you can do something about, diet probably has
  the largest effect on your blood cholesterol level. Saturated fat is the
  main dietary component responsible for increasing blood cholesterol to
  dangerous levels. (For a more detailed discussion of dietary fats, see
  Chapter 11.) Strangely enough, cholesterol itself, as contained in foods
  such as egg yolk, liver, kidneys etc, has a relatively small effect on blood
  cholesterol levels. An article in the prestigious *New England Journal of*

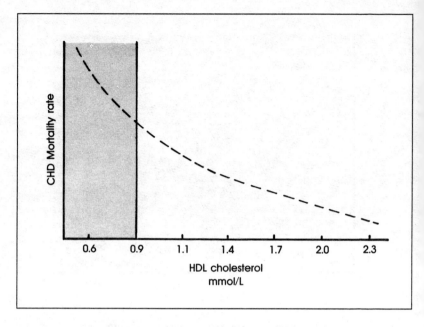

Figure 4.2   HDL-cholesterol and CHD mortality

Medicine entitled 'Normal Plasma Cholesterol In An 88-Year-Old-Man Who Eats 25 Eggs A Day' illustrates my point!

As you might expect, reducing the total amount of saturated fat in your diet can have a major impact in lowering your cholesterol to safer levels. However, diet will not have any beneficial impact on HDL-C.

- **Body Weight:** Being overweight may increase your blood cholesterol, and reducing weight will tend to lower it. Obesity is associated with low levels of HDL-C, but weight loss may provoke a rise in HDL-C concentration, and thus help to reduce CHD risk.

- **Physical Activity/Exercise:** Many people believe that regular exercise will help to burn up cholesterol, but actually it has very little cholesterol-reducing effect. Exercise does, however, tend to increase levels of HDL-C which may help to remove the harmful LDL-C particles. Presumably this is one of the mechanisms by which regular exercise is known to reduce the risk of CHD.

- **Genetic Factors:** For most of us, cholesterol levels are determined mainly by our saturated fat consumption. But a small number of people have an inherited tendency to high cholesterol levels; a condition known as *Familial Hyperlipidaemia*, or simply FH. There are 2 main forms of this:
  1. In the milder form, which occurs in about 1 in 500 of the population, the individual inherits one defective gene from one parent. Left untreated, individuals may suffer heart attacks in their

thirties or forties. They require aggressive cholesterol-lowering therapy with a combination of diet and drugs. Because it is a genetic disorder, it is important to measure the blood cholesterol levels of the patients' immediate family.

2. In the more serious form, which fortunately only affects one in a million people, the individual inherits a defective gene from both parents. The consequent rise in blood cholesterol is dramatic. These unfortunate individuals usually develop severe coronary heart disease in their early teens, often with fatal consequences.

- **Stress**: There is some evidence that chronic stress may tend to elevate blood cholesterol levels. There are, however, a number of possible explanations for this observation. For example, people who live pressurized, deadline-orientated lives, often have poor diets and are in the habit of eating junk food 'on the hoof'. Increased cholesterol levels in these individuals may be a function of a high fat diet rather than a specific response to stress.

- **Drugs**: Some prescribed drugs, eg oral contraceptives, diuretics and beta-blockers may have unfavourable effects on blood fats.

- **Coffee**: There is conflicting evidence about effect of coffee on blood cholesterol levels. Briefly, a number of surveys have shown ingestion of large quantities of coffee, particularly boiled coffee, is associated with a rise in blood cholesterol — in some by as much as 10–15 per cent. This is not observed when equivalent quantities of tea are drunk, nor with instant coffee, so is unlikely to be due to caffeine.

  More recent evidence also suggests that filtered coffee will raise blood cholesterol levels. However, this effects an increase in both LDL-C and HDL-C. In other words, the potentially negative increase in LDL-C is offset by an increase in the beneficial HDL-C. There is, therefore, no net increase in CHD risk.

  The message at the moment, then, is that if you drink coffee you should stick to the filtered type or the instant variety (which probably accounts for most of us).

Whilst all of these factors may tend to influence your cholesterol level, it is quite clear that you can actively do something about many of them. Dietary intervention (and consequent reduction of body weight) is usually sufficient.

ASSESSMENT/SELF-ASSESSMENT

There are three reliable ways of having your blood cholesterol measured:
1. Arranging the test with your family doctor is probably the most obvious. The more enthusiastic and knowledgeable GPs are usually quite happy to oblige — indeed many of them are introducing cholesterol screening as a general service offered by the practice.

Table 4.2   Interpretation of results

Blood level (mmol/L)	Desirable	Borderline	Abnormal
TC	< 5.2	5.2–6.4	6.5 and above
LDL-C	< 3.5	3.5–4.4	4.5 and above
HDL-C	> 1.0	0.9–1.0	< 0.9

> Greater than
< Less than

    Others, alas, are less cooperative and may not agree to have the test performed.

2.   Many private healthcare organizations will arrange the test for you, although a blood cholesterol test is usually a small part of a much more comprehensive screening package.

3.   Retail pharmacy outlets are beginning to offer cholesterol testing, usually using what are referred to as 'Dry Chemistry' analyzers (eg *Reflotron*). Instead of using chemical reagents in a test-tube, these instruments use chemically impregnated ('dry') paper strips. A finger-prick sample is all that is required and the result is usually available in less than three minutes. Provided that these instruments are properly calibrated and the operator has been well trained, the results are quite reliable.

Some chemist shops are also introducing cholesterol 'self-test' kits based on this principle, but they are generally unreliable and are best avoided.

    One practical point. Despite what you may have been told, you do **not** have to be in a fasting state for your blood cholesterol result to be accurate. (HDL-C measurement is not affected either — at least not significantly.) If your blood test is carried out in a pathology laboratory, other blood tests including HDL-C, Triglycerides and (possibly) LDL-C, may also be included.

    Note that for the risk appraisal the total cholesterol concentration (TC) or, if available, the TC/HDL ratio is used. Although you may also have results for LDL-C and triglycerides, these are not taken into account in the risk appraisal.

INTERPRETATION OF RESULTS

We shall consider results for TC (LDL-C) and HDL-C.

TOTAL CHOLESTEROL CONCENTRATION (TC)

We discussed earlier how increasing levels of cholesterol are associated with an increasing risk of heart disease. There are three ranges of cholesterol levels which we need to consider separately (see Table 4.2).

NB. *Because TC closely reflects LDL-C, I have focused primarily on the modification of TC levels for the remainder of this section. For readers who may be interested, the equivalent LDL-C levels (in mmol/L) appear in brackets.*

1. **Desirable:** Blood cholesterol (TC) less than 5.2 mmol/L (3.5).
2. **Borderline:** Blood cholesterol (TC) 5.2–6.4 mmol/L (3.5–4.4).
3. **Abnormal:** Blood cholesterol (TC) equal to or greater than 6.5 mmol/L (4.5).

HDL-C

At levels of HDL-C below 1 mmol/L, risk increases significantly. Average levels for males in this country are about 1.2 mmol/L, and for females around 1.6 mmol/L. Advice on how to increase your HDL-C is given shortly.

A NOTE ON THE TC/HDL-C RATIO

Since both TC and HDL-C are independently related to the risk of coronary heart disease, one way to combine their predictive value is to incorporate both measures into the TC/HDL-C ratio. This ratio also shows that it is perfectly possible to have a high blood cholesterol level with a below average risk of heart disease, because a large proportion of the cholesterol may be present in the protective HDL-C, not the harmful LDL-C, form. Even relatively small changes in HDL-C can make a major difference to CHD risk.

Various TC/HDL-C ratios and how they relate to risk are given in Table 4.3. The Health Risk Appraisal in Chapter 3 takes the TC/HDL ratio into account, if it is available. If not, the cholesterol concentration alone is used. Remember that death rates from heart disease in the UK are among the highest in the world, so having an 'average' risk ratio is not necessarily good news. Try to keep it at or below about 3.5 if possible.

Table 4.3 Total cholesterol/HDL ratios compared with the level of risk

Risk	Total Cholesterol HDL Cholesterol
½ average	3.5
average	5.0
2 × average	10.0
3 × average	20.0

ACTION

The action you need to take, if any, depends upon the range in which your cholesterol result falls. We shall consider TC (LDL-C) first, and then how to modify (increase) HDL-C.

TC (LDL-C)

1. **Blood cholesterol less than 5.2 mmol/L** (3.5)
   This is a very encouraging result indeed, and the level of your blood cholesterol does not pose any significant risk to your health. It follows that you do not need to follow any specific dietary measures, although you should obviously follow the basic principles of good nutrition which are discussed in more detail in Chapter 11.
2. **Blood cholesterol concentration 5.2–6.4 mmol/L** (3.5–4.4)
   This is a 'borderline' result. There is a slightly increased risk of developing cardiovascular disease at this level of blood cholesterol, but it is not necessary for you to follow a specific cholesterol-lowering diet. Nevertheless, the general recommendation is that you should make some effort to reduce the total amount of saturated fat in your diet. Even relatively small modifications in your diet can bring about a significant reduction in your total cholesterol level.

Key point — reducing dietary fat

The important points to bear in mind when reducing the amount of saturated fat in your diet are as follows:
— Choose lean meats, and trim the visible fat off before consumption (including chicken skin).
— Eat more fish and poultry.
— Try to reduce your consumption of chocolates, cakes, pastries and biscuits. Not only do they contain significant amounts of saturated fat, but they are also very high in calories.
— Try to use the frying pan less often. It is far better to grill, bake or boil instead. Microwave cooking is particularly helpful. If you do fry then try to use a polyunsaturated vegetable oil such as olive oil, sunflower oil, safflower oil or rapeseed oil.
— Try to limit your consumption of eggs, cheese, cream and other dairy products which tend to be high in saturated fat.
— Try and drink less whole milk and substitute either semi-skimmed or skimmed milk.
— Increase your consumption of fresh vegetables and fruit, and try to eat a purely vegetarian meal on one or two occasions a week.
— Use butter, margarine and other spreads sparingly.

Reducing the total amount of saturated fat in your diet is not difficult if you follow these guidelines. As well as tending to reduce your levels of cholesterol, it will also help you to lose weight.

3. **Blood cholesterol 6.5 mmol/L** (4.5) and above

    At this level, your risk of developing heart disease increases significantly. For this reason you need to follow a specific cholesterol lowering diet, an outline of which is given in Table 4.4 (overleaf).

MODIFYING YOUR HDL-C

Table 4.2 shows that the desirable level for HDL-C is greater than 1 mmol/L. Dietary measures will reduce your LDL-C levels and, therefore, your TC concentration but will have no significant effect on your HDL-C level. So how can you increase your HDL-C?

Key point — increasing HDL-C

- Levels of HDL-C tend to be lower in individuals who are obese, and who smoke cigarettes. So you can make a good start by giving up the cigarettes and getting your weight under control (see Chapters 6 and 10).
- HDL-C may also increase as a result of moderate and regular alcohol consumption. By 'moderate' I mean within the recommended safe-drinking guidelines of up to 21 units per week for men, and 14 units/week for women (see Chapter 8).
- Exercise. Perhaps the most consistent and impressive body of evidence is in relation to the effects of physical exercise. Sedentary people have much lower levels of HDL-C when compared with those who exercise regularly — an observation which helps to explain why exercise appears to confer a large measure of protection against heart disease. Many studies involving runners, cross-country skiers, middle-aged joggers, tennis players, brisk-walkers and even heart attack survivors, provide impressive evidence that regular physical exercise increases blood levels of HDL-C.

How soon can I expect my blood cholesterol levels to fall?

There is an enormous amount of individual variation in terms of a response to a cholesterol lowering diet. Some individuals appear to have quite dramatic reductions in a relatively short period of time, whilst for others the reduction may be relatively small and take quite a lot longer. Generally, your blood cholesterol level (both TC and LDL-C) should begin to fall two to three weeks after you begin your cholesterol lowering diet. Over time, you may reduce your blood cholesterol by 1 or 2 mmol/L, or even more.

Table 4.4 Your cholesterol-lowering diet

In general, try to choose foods less than 5g/100g of saturated fat (A). Foods in (B) are more than 15g/100g of saturated fat, and should be avoided. Foods between 5–15g should be taken in moderation.

	Choose (A)	Avoid eating/drinking (B)
Cereals	Wheatmeal flour/bread Oatmeal Sugar free muesli Wholegrain cereals Porridge, Oats Crispbreads Brown Rice, Wholemeal pasta, Sweetcorn	Fancy breads, eg croissants. Danish pastries, sponges, choux pastry, and all bought cakes Savoury cheese biscuits, cream crackers, biscuits Crisps and savoury snacks
Meat	Chicken and turkey (without skin) Veal Lean trimmed grilled steak Rabbit, hare, grouse, partridge, pheasant Venison Soya protein meat substitute	Ham, beef, pork, lamb, bacon, duck, goose, offal, liver, kidney, tripe, sweetbreads, heart, brain. Crackling and skin Sausage Salami Luncheon meat Pate, corned beef Scotch eggs, meat pies and pastries
Fish	All fresh, frozen, smoked, soused fish eg Cod, Plaice, Herring, Mackerel Tinnned fish in brine and tomato sauce eg Tuna and sardines Avoid oily fish and fried fish (in suitable oil) only if you are on a weight reducing diet	Battered fish Fish roe; Shellfish, taramasalata, caviar. Fish paste (unless made with permitted oils only). Potted fish. Fish fried in unsuitable oil (See Fats) or smothered in cheese
Fruit, vegetables and salad	All fresh, frozen, dried, bottled or tinned fruit, vegetables and salad, especially peas, beans, lentils, pulses and potatoes (baked or boiled), baked beans Olives	Chips and roast potatoes cooked in unsuitable oil or fat. (See Fats)
Nuts	Walnuts Almonds Pecan nuts Chestnuts Hazel (filbert) nuts	Coconut

Table 4.4 continued

Eggs and dairy produce	Skimmed milk Dried skimmed milk Soya milk Low fat yoghurt Cottage cheese Low fat curd cheese Egg white (meringue) (3 egg yolks per week only)	Whole milk, cream, imitation cream, full fat yoghurt. Ice cream. Evaporated or condensed milk. Excess eggs Hard cheese, cream cheese or processed cheese Quiche, soufflé
Drinks	Marmite, Bovril, tea, coffee, mineral water, fruit juice	Wholemilk drinks, bought soups, cream-based liqueurs Malted milk or hot chocolate drinks
Sweets, preserves, jams and spreads	Chutney and pickles Sugar-free artificial sweeteners, jam, marmalade, honey	Chocolates, chocolate spreads and sweets Toffee, fudge Butterscotch, lemon curd, mincemeat, coconut bars
Fats	All fats should be limited and used in moderation only. Choose margarines labelled 'high in polyunsaturates'. Ignore 'low in cholesterol'. Saturated fat should be less than 15g/100g. Suitable cooking oils are: sunflower oil, safflour oil, olive oil, rapeseed oil etc.	Saturated fats, ie butter, dripping, suet, lard, margarine, shortening, ghee, cocobutter, cooking oil, or vegetable oil of unspecified origin. Palm oil, coconut oil, cotton seed oil, peanut oil Peanut butter (especially hydrogenated)

The more you reduce your level, the more you will reduce your risk of heart disease. The higher your blood cholesterol level is to begin with, the greater reduction you can expect by following your new diet. Expected trends in your blood cholesterol levels are illustrated in Figure 4.3. This shows that, generally speaking, the most dramatic results are achieved in the first twelve weeks.

Checking your progress

If your blood cholesterol level is above 6.5 mmol/L (4.5), you should arrange to have your cholesterol measured again in three to six months to ensure that your dietary response is adequate.

If your level of cholesterol continues to be quite high, your doctor may need to consider what other methods of management are appropriate in your case. This will depend upon a whole range of factors, including any

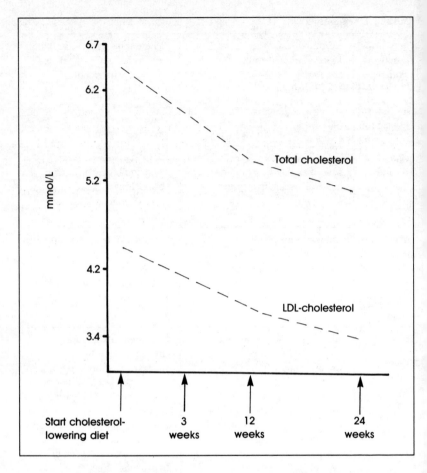

Figure 4.3 Expected changes in blood cholesterol level

relevant family history, your age and the presence of other coronary risk factors.

What should my blood cholesterol goal be?

Ideally your TC will be below 5.2 mmol/L (3.5), your HDL-C well above 1 mmol/L and your TC/HDL-C ratio below 3.5. However, for various reasons it may not be possible to achieve this, especially if your blood levels were quite high to begin with. These numbers are a guide — don't become a slave to them. Pay attention to other risk factors as well — your blood cholesterol is only one amongst several which need to be taken into account.

Cholesterol levels persistently above 6.5 mmol/L (4.5), may require further intervention, including drug therapy (see below).

(Remember that the aim of dietary intervention is to reduce the harmful

LDL-C. Measurement of TC is an indirect guide to this, but if you know your LDL-C so much the better — it is a much more specific marker of your response to a low fat diet.)

What about drugs?

Whilst dietary changes are the first and the most important action you can take to lower your blood cholesterol level, if it remains elevated your doctor may suggest other steps you can take. Normally, an individual should be placed on a cholesterol lowering diet for a period of six months before drug treatment is to be considered. Even if your doctor does recommend your taking some form of drug therapy, you should continue your cholesterol lowering diet since the combination may allow you to take less in the way of tablets to lower your levels. And, because diet is still the safest treatment, you should always try to lower your levels with diet alone before adding any medication. The combination of diet with drugs, is much more effective than the use of drugs alone.

How long do I need to follow this diet?

Your cholesterol lowering diet should be continued *for life.* The occasional piece of chocolate cake or sticky toffee pudding isn't going to do you any harm, but resuming your old eating patterns may. Surprisingly, after a while your new way of eating won't seem like a special diet at all, but will have become part of your normal routine — full of appetizing and nourishing foods. Remember, though, that there is a danger of finding too many excuses for special occasions!

How often should I have my blood cholesterol level checked in the future?

Again, this depends upon your baseline level.

If the initial cholesterol concentration was less than 5.2 mmol/L (3.5), then I would recommend that you have your cholesterol checked every three to five years.

If your cholesterol level is 5.2 mmol/L to 6.4 mmol/L (3.5–4.4), I would recommend that you observe the dietary advice given earlier, and have it checked annually.

If the initial TC level is at or above 6.5 mmol/L (4.5), then you will obviously have it checked at regular intervals (usually every twelve weeks) to ensure that the response to your diet is favourable. If it continues to be substantially above this level, then you may need additional therapy and your doctor will be best able to advise you as to how often future measurements should take place. If you manage to reduce your cholesterol to below 6.5 mmol/L (4.5) as a result of your dietary intervention, then I would recommend annual checks thereafter.

Does reducing blood cholesterol help to reduce my risk of developing heart disease?

Evidence would certainly suggest that by reducing your blood cholesterol level, you can significantly reduce your chances of developing heart disease in the future. The extent of that reduction in risk will tend to vary between individuals, but as a generalization it seems that a 1 per cent reduction in blood cholesterol concentration will be accompanied by a 2 to 3 per cent reduction in risk.

Key note

If you can reduce your blood cholesterol concentration by 25 per cent you will halve your risk of developing heart disease.

Treatment recommendations are summarized in Table 4.5.

Table 4.5   Treatment summary

A	TC < 5.2 (LDL-C 3.5) mmol/L **NO ACTION**
B	TC 5.2–6.4 (LDL-C 3.5–4.4) mmol/L Make modest reduction in dietary saturated fat (p76)
C	TC at 6.5 mmol/L (LDL-C > 4.5) or above Follow a specific cholesterol lowering diet (p78–9)
< Less than > Greater than	TC = Total cholesterol LDL-C = Low density lipoprotein cholesterol

Chapter 5

CONTROLLING YOUR BLOOD PRESSURE

High blood pressure, or hypertension to use the correct medical term, is a common and extremely important condition. At the present time it probably affects some 10 to 15 per cent of the adult population in Western countries, and since high blood pressure is associated with an increased risk of both heart attacks and strokes, it is clearly a public health problem of some significance.

Blood pressure is essential to life. This may seem a rather elementary point, but the fact is that many people are confused about what is meant by 'blood pressure', and are under the impression that blood pressure at *any* level is harmful. Some are also confused about the meaning of the word 'hypertension', believing it to be due to some form of mental tension or stress.

Blood pressure is nothing other than the pressure which the heart and arteries apply in order to move blood, and therefore oxygen, around the body. Because the heart and arteries function as a closed system, when the heart is actively contracting and forcing blood through the arteries, the pressure within the system rises. Pressure measured during this period is called *systolic* pressure. When the heart stops contracting, ie when it is resting between beats, the pressure falls to resting levels, and this pressure is termed *diastolic* blood pressure. These two figures are normally expressed in millimetres of mercury (mmHg) with one figure on top of the other eg 120/80 mmHg (120 being the systolic and 80 being the diastolic pressure).

The systolic blood pressure varies considerably, depending on the body's demand for oxygenated blood. During sleep, when all the various bodily systems are relatively inactive, the systolic pressure is low. But during hard physical exercise the muscles and tissues require enormous amounts of oxygen, and the heart supplies this by speeding up and pumping more blood through the system. This increase can be quite dramatic. At maximum exercise, for example, a trained athlete may increase his cardiac output (the amount of blood pumped by the heart), up to seven or eight times the resting level. Because the heart is beating much more rapidly (up to 200 beats per minutes), the systolic pressure in the system rises. A normal systolic pressure at rest would be around 120 mmHg, but during vigorous exercise this can increase to as much as 250 mmHg. Systolic pressure is very labile, and will vary considerably during a 24-hour period depending upon the level of activity. Stress, driving a car in heavy traffic, eating, alcohol, exercise etc, can all affect blood pressure levels.

Diastolic pressure, on the other hand, tends to be more stable with a much narrower range of variation during the day. Whilst the systolic pressure may increase by more than 100 per cent the diastolic pressure does not normally increase more than about 35 per cent. It represents, in effect, the constant background resting pressure (or 'tension') in the arterial system.

How is it measured?

The accurate measurement of blood pressure has only been possible since the beginning of this century, with the advent of an instrument called the sphygmomanometer. Given that blood pressure in the normal state can vary so widely, how is it possible for a doctor to make a reliable diagnosis of high blood pressure? The answer is that doctors always try to standardize their measurements by taking the blood pressure in a resting state, usually with the patient reclining on a couch. Even then, there may be considerable variation in the reading from one visit to the next. This is why your doctor will not be happy to make a diagnosis based on a single measurement.

Some people seem to have an aversion to having their blood pressure measured; the moment the cuff is placed on the arm, their heart rate and blood pressure increase dramatically — a phenomenon sometimes known as 'white coat hypertension', because of its association with the physician. In recent years modern computer technology has made it possible to measure, record and store blood pressure readings at regular intervals throughout the day. These ambulatory systems are not yet in general use, but some studies reveal that up to 30 per cent of patients diagnosed as hypertensive by their doctor, actually have normal blood pressures outside the surgery.

Why is high blood pressure important?

The reason, very simply, is that untreated hypertension is associated with a substantially reduced life expectancy due to its association with heart attack, heart failure and stroke.

Evidence from the Framingham Heart Study shows that people with hypertension are three times more likely to sustain a heart attack and four times more likely to have heart failure than those with normal blood pressure. Moreover, a heart attack in a hypertensive individual is more likely to be fatal and sudden cardiac death is also three to four times more common. The incidence of coronary heart disease rises by almost 20 per cent for each 10 mmHg increase in systolic pressure. At a systolic pressure of 160 mmHg, the risk is about double that if the pressure were 110 mmHg.

Hypertension is the most important risk factor for stroke, particularly when associated with cigarette smoking. In the British Regional Heart Study, cigarette smoking (without hypertension) increased the relative risk of stroke about two-fold and high systolic blood pressure (without smoking) increased the relative risk about four-fold. But the combination of smoking *and* hypertension increased the relative risk 12-fold. The relationship between blood pressure and stroke appeared to be predicted by the systolic blood pressure and knowledge of the diastolic blood pressure did not improve the ability to predict stroke events. In the same study, heavy alcohol consumption was associated with an almost four-fold increase in the risk of stroke compared to other men. Added to this, hypertension can also cause disease of the heart muscle, and damage to the kidneys and eyes leading to kidney failure and loss of vision.

Small wonder that insurance companies take careful note of an individual's blood pressure when determining life insurance premiums.

How does hypertension lead to disease?

The effects of high blood pressure can be divided into two main groups; those due to pressure changes within the heart and arteries, and those due to direct arterial damage.

The constant high pressure in the arterial system throws an enormous extra burden on the heart, which is able to compensate in the early stages by developing a thicker muscle wall (a process known as *hypertrophy*). Eventually, however, even a thickened heart muscle is not able to overcome the increased pressure in the arterial system, and it begins to fail. The patient begins to notice increasing breathlessness, initially on exertion, but later on also at rest. If this continues untreated, the heart failure will become very much worse as the heart muscle undergoes further decompensation.

Direct damage to the arteries leads to an acceleration of the atherosclerotic process, particularly in those who smoke or have high blood cholesterol. Exactly how or why this occurs is not clear. Apart from the heart and brain, this process can also damage the arteries supplying the eye and the kidneys, leading to deteriorating vision and kidney failure.

WHAT ARE THE SYMPTOMS OF HIGH BLOOD PRESSURE?

Contrary to popular opinion, most individuals with high blood pressure do not have symptoms. The prevalent idea that those individuals with high blood pressure have headaches is simply not true. Most people who have high blood pressure do not have headaches and most of us with headaches have normal blood pressures. Symptoms such as dizziness or lethargy, also commonly attributed to high blood pressure, are too non-specific to be of any real use in making the diagnosis.

What is normal blood pressure?

When we examine the statistics relating life expectancy to levels of blood pressure, it is clear that there is a linear relationship between long-term survival and levels of blood pressure, ie the higher your blood pressure, the less chance you have of living a normal lifespan. What is the ideal blood pressure? A simple answer is that the lower your blood pressure, the better. But this is neither scientific nor very helpful, so we have to try and be more precise. The World Health Organization defines 'normal' blood pressure as *below* 140/90 mmHg, and an 'abnormal' reading as 140/90 mmHg and above.

What causes high blood pressure?

In most cases of high blood pressure, the cause cannot be identified and we refer to this form of high blood pressure as 'primary' or 'essential' hypertension. In practice this accounts for the vast majority — about 95 per cent of patients with hypertension.

In the remaining 5 per cent, there is an underlying cause which can be identified and these cases are referred to as 'secondary', ie the high blood pressure is secondary to some underlying disease. The commonest cause is kidney disease, but in rare cases it may also be due to tumours and hormonal disturbances.

A number of lifestyle related factors have been identified as tending to increase blood pressure in some individuals. These factors are:

- Obesity.
- Heavy alcohol consumption.
- Smoking.
- Lack of regular exercise.
- Eating too much salt.
- High levels of stress.

I shall be discussing these in more detail later.

ASSESSMENT/SELF-ASSESSMENT

To get your blood pressure measured I would recommend that you visit your own general practitioner who will be able to do this for you. It takes only a few moments and is completely painless. Some retail chemist shops also offer a blood pressure testing service.

Your blood pressure should be taken in a resting state, while you are lying on a couch or sitting. Normally your doctor will take at least two readings, because the first reading is almost invariably higher than the second. Anxiety is a potent blood pressure stimulator, so trying to relax is very important. If your initial level of blood pressure is elevated, your doctor will probably ask you to return to his surgery again after a period of a week or so to carry out a further measurement. He may do this on several more occasions before deciding whether or not any form of treatment is required.

INTERPRETATION OF RESULTS

When you have obtained your blood pressure reading, you can enter this into the Health Risk Appraisal on pages 52–54. You will note that both systolic and diastolic values are taken into account.

It used to be thought that the diastolic blood pressure (the lower of the two values) was the most important predictor of heart disease, but recent evidence would suggest that the systolic blood pressure (the higher of the two values) may be even more important. In practice elevated systolic and diastolic blood pressure often go hand in hand. Remember, also, that although an initial high reading may fall on subsequent checking, a single casual reading should not be ignored. Even one high reading may be significant, and indicate a propensity to developing established hypertension in the future.

If your blood pressure is a bit on the high side, there is an enormous amount that you can do to reduce it to a more acceptable level. Perhaps as many as 80 per cent of individuals with borderline or mild hypertension can reduce their blood pressure to safer levels without resorting to the use of drugs.

ACTION PLAN

So what are the practical things that you can do to reduce your blood pressure to more acceptable levels?

- **Watch your weight — dropping pounds drops pressure:** The association between being overweight and high blood pressure has been demonstrated in scores of studies. It is not yet clear how excess weight raises blood pressure, but one theory suggests that fat cells stimulate the production of insulin, a hormone that is secreted by the pancreas and helps the body absorb sugar (and hence calories). Insulin has other effects, however, and may raise blood pressure by stimulating the nervous system and causing the body to retain salt and water. Whatever the mechanism, there is good evidence that reducing your weight will bring about a significant reduction in your blood pressure. Indeed, the loss of five to ten pounds can often make the difference between needing and not needing anti-hypertensive drug therapy. Since we know that obesity is also a risk factor for coronary heart disease and is associated with diabetes and high cholesterol, weight loss has health benefits beyond blood pressure reduction (see Chapter 10).

- **Limiting your alcohol intake**: Alcohol has a variety of effects on the cardiovascular system, and moderate alcohol consumption may have significant benefits. In heavy doses, however, it is a potent hypertensive (blood pressure raising) substance. In fact, heavy alcohol consumption is at present the commonest identifiable cause for high blood pressure in hypertensive patients. In the British Regional Heart Study, heavy drinking (more than 42 units per week) in men, was associated with an almost four-fold increase in the risk of stroke compared to other men. Individuals who consume four or more alcoholic drinks per day are twice as likely as teetotalers to develop hypertension, and some studies suggest that up to 11 per cent of cases of hypertension among men can be attributed to alcohol.

  Conversely, reducing your alcohol consumption will almost certainly help to reduce your blood pressure level, sometimes quite significantly. Cessation of even moderate drinking could be associated with an average systolic blood pressure fall of 18 mmHg. It follows that the potential for the prevention of stroke is considerable. However, it is not complete abstinence which is required, but merely a reduction of your alcohol intake to within the recommended number of units per week (ie, 21 for men and 14 for women).

- **Stop smoking**: The nicotine in cigarette smoke is not only highly addictive and carcinogenic, it provokes a transient increase in both heart rate and blood pressure. There are countless reasons why you should stop smoking, but one of the most important is that it will help to lower your blood pressure. Moreover, as we have seen previously, the combination of hypertension and cigarette smoking is particularly lethal.

- **Exercise regularly**: There is good evidence that regular exercise will, in itself, have a direct effect on lowering your blood pressure. A number of studies have shown that the resting systolic and diastolic blood pressures are significantly lower in physically fit persons, when compared with those who are in comparatively poor condition. Physical activity may lower blood pressure by 5–15 mmHg, and the antihypertensive effect of aerobic exercise may be achieved without the need for dietary alterations or even weight reduction. However, if your blood pressure is low or normal prior to training, regular exercise will probably have little effect on it.

  The type of exercise is important. Aerobic exercises such as swimming, jogging, brisk walking and cycling are fine, but strength-increasing isometric exercises such as weight training do not lower blood pressure. On the contrary, they may increase blood pressure to quite dangerous levels. If you have high blood pressure, avoid weight training and other strength exercises.

Although it is not known how aerobic exercise lowers blood pressure, it may have something to do with psychological relaxation and diminished nervous stimulation of the blood vessels. Part of the effect of exercise may also be accounted for by a reduction in body fat, which is another useful product of regular exercise. The effects of aerobic exercise on blood pressure are to some extent related to the degree of exertion — running or riding a bicycle produces greater blood pressure reductions than walking. Nevertheless, even gentle exercise can be effective; one study showed that 30-minute sessions of low-intensity stationary cycling produced reductions in blood pressure in men, which lasted longer than 12 hours.

Most patients with hypertension can exercise quite safely, assuming that they use a modicum of common sense. If you are overweight, then a non-weight bearing exercise such as swimming or the use of a stationary exercise bicycle for three or four, 30-minute sessions per week, has much to recommend it. If your blood pressure is very high and you are taking antihypertensive drugs, you will need closer supervision by your doctor. Some of these drugs will limit your heart rate response during exercise, and this will need to be taken into account if you are using your pulse rate as a measure of exercise intensity.

Finally, do not ignore symptoms such as chest pain, dizziness or undue breathlessness associated with your exercise session: stop exercising immediately and seek medical advice.

- **Reduce your salt consumption**: For decades, there has been evidence that diets low in salt might reduce blood pressure and, conversely, that excessive salt intake may contribute to high blood pressure in susceptible individuals.

Now recent research has demonstrated conclusively that salt restriction does lower blood pressure, particularly in hypertensives. Moderate dietary salt restriction can be expected to lower both systolic and diastolic blood pressure by about 5 mmHg on average, although in hypertensives the fall may be considerably greater. Indeed the higher the initial blood pressure and the older the patient, the greater the expected fall in blood pressure.

There is, of course, a considerable amount of individual variation in response to salt restriction, since some individuals appear to be much more 'salt sensitive' than others. We all know people who are heavy handed with the salt cellar, but have normal blood pressures. These people are able to adjust to an increased sodium load by increasing the excretion of sodium in the urine. Hypertensives, on the other hand, cannot tolerate a high sodium load. This is probably a genetically determined characteristic, and helps to explain why high blood pressure has a tendency to run in families. We eat an enormous amount of salt in this country — at least ten times more than we actually need. Healthy adults maintain a normal balance on as little as 3–20 mmol per day.

Every molecule of common table salt (sodium chloride) is made up of one atom of sodium and one atom of chloride, but it's the sodium which we need to be concerned about. This is expressed in millimoles (mmols), and each gramme of salt contains about 17 mmol of **sodium**.

It has been estimated that a reduction of daily sodium intake of 50 mmol (ie about 3g of salt) by a whole Western population, would reduce the incidence of stroke by 26 per cent and of heart attacks by 15 per cent. An additional reduction in the amount of salt added to processed foods would lower blood pressure sufficiently to prevent some 70,000 deaths a year in Britain, as well as much disability.

If you have high blood pressure, you are very likely to benefit from salt restriction. You should be able to achieve this quite easily. By simple dietary manipulation — that is, avoiding salty foods and not adding salt in cooking or at the table you can reduce your average daily salt intake by 30 per cent. Of course, only about one-third of the salt we eat is added in cooking or at the table. Another third occurs naturally in food, and the remainder is 'hidden' in processed foods. Tinned meats, tinned soups, salad dressings and bottled sauces are just a few examples of foods which are loaded with salt. This is why it's a good idea to get into the habit of checking the food label for the sodium content, and choose low-sodium alternatives.

Here are some guidelines (1 gram = 1000 milligrams):
— Sodium (salt) free: contains less than 0.005g (5 mg) per 100g.
— Very-low-sodium: contains less than 0.035g (35 mg) per 100g.
— Low-sodium: contains less than 0.14g (140 mg) per 100g.

Another way of avoiding the large amounts of salt in processed foods is to get into the habit of using fresh (unprocessed) foods. Try making your own salad dressings, soups and sauces — rich sources of sodium when obtained from a food store or supermarket. Instead of adding salt to dishes, be more creative and adventurous with your use of other spices and herbs; fresh lemon juice and flavoured vinegars go well with chicken and fish. However, too rigorous an attempt to control your salt intake is likely to mean that you will not stick to it. If you find giving up salt completely very difficult, there are quite a number of effective salt substitutes available at most chemist shops, and you may find that these are a suitable alternative. (Most substitutes use potassium chloride with a small amount of sodium chloride). Let's summarize the elements of dietary salt restriction:
— Cut out added salt at the table and in cooking.
— Read the food label, and choose low-salt products.

- — Use more fresh (unprocessed) produce.
- — Beware of sodium in other forms, eg sodium bicarbonate.
- — Use a wider variety of herbs and spices as a substitute for salt in your cooking.
- — Try using a salt substitute — usually potassium chloride. It still contains some sodium, but much less than ordinary table salt. You may think that you can't possibly get used to not having salt with your food, but you will surprise yourself. There is quite good research evidence that people do indeed adjust their tastes to a low sodium diet and they don't continue to miss salt. It may, however, take one or two months or so to make the adjustment.

- **Reducing stress:** Emotional stimuli, as I mentioned earlier, are potent stimulators of blood pressure. The mere process of walking into your doctor's surgery can be sufficient to provoke a rapid increase in blood pressure. More persistent stress, such as that associated with unemployment or a demanding job, can contribute to the development of chronic hypertension. The impact of these external pressures is often overlooked by doctors and patients, perhaps because they feel that occupational stresses are difficult to avoid. However, there is good evidence that stress-management techniques including yoga, biofeedback and transcendental meditation, can contribute much to blood pressure control. Reductions of at least 5–10 mmHg are quite possible, without adverse side effects — a very worthwhile strategy. Stress management is discussed in more detail in Chapter 9.

- **Dietary fibre:** Some recent studies have suggested that increasing the fibre in your diet — particularly from fruit — may help to reduce blood pressure. In a major study from Harvard Medical School, researchers found that in a four-year follow-up of 30 000 men, higher amounts of dietary fibre, potassium and magnesium were all associated with a lower risk of developing hypertension. This remained true even after adjusting for other factors such as age, weight and alcohol consumption. Fibre from fruit had the strongest relationship with lower blood pressure readings.

ARE THERE ANY OTHER FACTORS TO TAKE INTO ACCOUNT?

The major lifestyle factors likely to have an impact on your blood pressure have been reviewed above, but there are several others which you should be aware of.

- **Age:** In Western industrialized societies, there is a strong tendency for blood pressure to increase with age — up to 50 per cent of 65-year olds are hypertensive. One of the reasons for this is that as we get older and less active, we tend to put on weight and obesity is highly correlated with hypertension. However, in so-called primitive societies, high blood pressure does not appear to be an inevitable consequence of advancing age, so it seems reasonable to conclude that this is primarily a lifestyle-related phenomenon.

- **Family history of hypertension**: Hypertension undoubtedly runs in families. If your mother or father were hypertensive, then you are more likely to develop high blood pressure yourself. If both parents were hypertensive, then the chances are even higher. Some of this may well be due to behavioural factors — children tend to inherit the bad health habits of their parents, such as poor diet and obesity. But there is also an independent genetic contribution which may, for example, determine sensitivity to salt. Blood pressure levels in identical twins are more alike than those of non-identical twins, even though they are subject to similar family influences in relation to lifestyle.

  If there is a family history of hypertension, it does not mean that you will inevitably develop the problem yourself — only that you are more likely to. It follows that having your blood pressure checked regularly, and paying attention to the various factors set out above, is even more important for you.

- **Oral contraceptives**: In some women, the use of oral contraceptives may tend to increase blood pressure. The combination of the pill and cigarette smoking is particularly dangerous.

- **Potassium, calcium, magnesium and fish oils**: A variety of other dietary constituents may have a beneficial impact on blood pressure. Potassium supplementation has attracted considerable interest, and some studies suggest that hypertensive individuals can reduce blood pressure levels by as much as 5–10 mmHg as a result of additional dietary potassium. You can increase your potassium intake quite easily — orange and tomato juice, bananas and other fresh fruits, are rich in this mineral.

  Some research has also suggested that dietary supplements of calcium, magnesium and fish oils may have a modest blood pressure lowering effect in people with hypertension.

WHAT NEXT?

The important thing is to remember to have your blood pressure checked regularly. If, for any reason, your blood pressure does not respond adequately to the measures described above, your doctor may feel that intervention with antihypertensive drugs is necessary. There are many such drugs available, and your doctor will be able to advise you as to which one is the most suitable for you. However, even if you are prescribed medication this is not a signal to abandon the lifestyle-related strategies which we have discussed. They may allow a much smaller dose of drug to be used than would otherwise be the case. Since all drugs have potential unwanted side-effects, this is obviously of some importance.

Sometimes your doctor may decide to prescribe medication as a temporary measure, whilst encouraging you to make the lifestyle changes recommended above. As you make progress with your weight reduction, exercise etc it may then be possible to reduce the dose of medication or, in some cases, to stop it altogether.

What about stopping drugs?

If your doctor decides to treat your blood pressure with drugs because it has not responded sufficiently to other measures, will it be possible to stop the drugs in future? Until fairly recently the answer to that question would have been no — drug therapy for hypertension was for life. However, several recent studies have examined the possibility of stopping medication if the blood pressure is well controlled, particularly if the person is able to comply with various non-pharmacological measures such as reducing weight, salt restriction, regular exercise and so on. In one large study involving 2765 patients with mild hypertension, blood pressures remained in the normal range after two years of follow-up, in almost half the patients who had stopped taking their medication. It seems, therefore, that anti-hypertensive drugs can be safely discontinued for several months or even longer in some cases — but only after close consultation with your doctor and only if your blood pressure can be carefully monitored after withdrawal.

Will controlling my blood pressure reduce my risk of heart attack or stroke?

The short answer is *yes*. A number of major studies have shown that treating hypertension saves many lives by preventing strokes and heart failure. A sustained decrease in your blood pressure of as little as 5–6 mmHg may reduce your risk of coronary disease by as much as 25 per cent and for stroke by up to 40 per cent.

Taking control

Perhaps the most important lesson to be learned is that non-pharmacological methods of blood pressure control really **can** make a difference — particularly in mild hypertensives (ie about 80 per cent of those with high blood pressure). Exposing millions of people to drugs when relatively simple changes in lifestyle would be at least as effective, is an unnecessary waste of valuable resources. Even in more severe hypertensives, the evidence would suggest that lifestyle changes can make an important contribution by reducing the dose of antihypertensive drugs required. Let's just summarize the most important points for the last time:

Key note — reducing blood pressure

- Keep your weight under control.
- Limit your alcohol consumption.
- Stop smoking.
- Take regular, moderate aerobic exercise.
- Reduce your sodium intake.
- Learn to relax and control your stress levels.
- Eat more fibre, especially fruit fibre.
- Eat plenty of potassium rich foods.

Chapter 6

SMOKING: HOW TO STOP AND STAY STOPPED

Whatever anyone says, it's never easy to stop cigarette smoking. This is because nicotine produces both a physical and a psychological dependence. Although smokers develop a tolerance to nicotine, withdrawal symptoms do occur when nicotine is withheld. The psychological dependence which cigarettes engender is also very real — as any regular smoker will tell you.

I have already mentioned the importance of cigarette smoking in relation to lung diseases in Chapter 1, but I make no apology for repeating some of these points here.

- **Smoking is this country's most important avoidable cause of premature death and disease.** It accounts for at least 110 000 deaths each year (one every five minutes). Although smoking has declined in recent years, one in three of the adult population continues to smoke cigarettes (currently 30 per cent of women and 29 per cent of men).
- **Lung cancer kills more than 40 000 people each year in the UK.**
- **Between one-third and one-half of regular smokers will die from a tobacco-related illness.** In those aged 35 to 69 years, smoking reduces life expectancy by an average of 23 years. Contrary to popular belief, prolonged cigarette smoking causes even more deaths from other diseases than from lung cancer.
- **A regular cigarette smoker's chance of developing lung cancer is up to 40 times that of a non-smoker,** depending upon how many are smoked and for how long they have been smoking.
- **Smoking also increases your chances of developing many other forms of cancer,** especially cancers of the mouth, throat, gullet, pancreas and cervix.
- **Smoking is the major cause of many forms of chronic lung disease,** including bronchitis and emphysema.
- **Smoking is a major risk factor for coronary heart disease,** with a

regular smoker having two to three times the risk of a non-smoker. The risk is increased proportionally to the number of cigarettes smoked.

- **Lung cancer in women is on the increase.** In some parts of the UK it has now overtaken breast cancer as the leading cancer-related death in women.
- **In 1988/89, the Exchequer raised more than £6 billion from VAT and Excise duty charged on tobacco products.**
- **On average, for each cigarette smoked, a smoker shortens his/ her life by about five minutes.**
- **Out of every 1000 people who start smoking when they are teenagers and continue to smoke 20 cigarettes or more per day, one will be murdered, six will die in road accidents, and about 250 will be killed prematurely by smoking.**
- **Smokers are nearly six times more likely to have a stroke than non-smokers.**
- **In the UK, smoking-related illnesses kill 12 people every hour.**
- **At present just under 20 per cent of all deaths in developed countries are attributed to tobacco.** This percentage is still rising, suggesting that if these trends continue, just over 20 per cent of those now living in developed countries will eventually be killed by tobacco (ie about a quarter of a billion, out of a current total population of just under one and a quarter billion).
- **Stopping smoking produces tangible health benefits within hours, including a reduced risk of heart attack.**

WHAT'S IN TOBACCO SMOKE?

Tobacco smoke is produced by incomplete combustion of the tobacco leaf and composed of gases and vapours in which drops are dispersed. Chemical analysis of the smoke reveals more than 2000 different chemical compounds, more than 50 of which are known to be carcinogenic (cancer causing) agents. Mainstream smoke is the smoke inhaled directly by the smoker and then exhaled into the environment. Sidestream smoke, on the other hand, is the smoke emitted from the smouldering tip of the cigarette in between puffs. Harmful substances such as carbon monoxide, ammonia, tar, nitrozamines and polycyclic monocarbons tend to be more concentrated in sidestream smoke than mainstream smoke. The smoker, of course, inhales both mainstream and sidestream smoke while the non-smoker (passive smoker) inhales the more dangerous sidestream and the exhaled mainstream smoke of the smoker.

When tobacco smoke is inhaled into the lungs, the effect of cooling causes it to condense and this, in turn, produces the dark brown tar which collects in the lungs of smokers. After inhaling, 70–90 per cent of the chemical compounds in the cigarette smoke remain in the lungs. Moreover, the last few puffs on a cigarette have about twice the amount of tar as the first.

Apart from carcinogens, the two most harmful compounds are probably nicotine and carbon monoxide. Nicotine has a damaging effect on the heart and inhalation of cigarette smoke causes a transient increase in heart rate and blood pressure. Even in very small doses it is a stimulant, and in large doses it can be fatal. The carbon monoxide in tobacco smoke (and, incidentally, car exhaust fumes), displaces oxygen from the red blood cells, which is needed to supply the muscles, organs and other body tissues.

Exactly how cigarette smoking helps to promote the development of coronary disease is not known for certain, but there are some important clues. It is probable that the lining of the artery becomes damaged, and the formation of fatty plaque in the arterial wall is accelerated. A number of investigators have also reported an increased blood-clotting tendency in smokers, which increases the risk of thrombosis in the coronary and leg arteries. Smokers also have significantly lower levels of the highly protective HDL-cholesterol — another reason why they have a much higher risk of heart disease.

PASSIVE SMOKING — IS IT A PROBLEM?

The health implications of breathing other people's tobacco smoke (passive smoking) have become the subject of much scientific discussion and intensive research in recent years. On the basis of a growing body of scientific evidence, it is now clear that passive smoking can cause lung cancer in non-smokers as well as serious lung and breathing problems in children. Some recent evidence also suggests an association between breathing other people's tobacco smoke and heart disease. A Scottish study involving around 15 000 men and women, examined the effect on a non-smoker living with a spouse who smoked. After lengthy follow-up, the researchers found that the non-smoking partner had two and a half times the incidence of lung cancer and twice the incidence of heart disease of non-smokers who were themselves married to non-smokers.

Researchers at the Louisiana State University Medical Center, studied 1551 women who were lifelong non-smokers, 281 of whom had been diagnosed as having a type of lung cancer known as *adenocarcinoma*, and a further 139 with some other form of lung cancer. The remaining 1131 served as the normal control group. The study revealed that ever having lived with a smoking male raised a woman's risk of adenocarcinoma by at least 50 per cent and for lung cancer in general by 30 per cent. After a woman had been exposed to the smoke from 40 cigarettes or more for forty years, these risks increased to 70 per cent and 33 per cent respectively, compared with what the risk would have been if her husband were a non-smoker. Incidentally, pipes and cigars were implicated as well as cigarettes, although to a lesser degree.

The risks of active smoking are obviously much greater than those due to passive smoking, but the risks of passive smoking are much greater than those posed by any other indoor man made pollutant released into the general environment.

A major report from the US Environmental Protection Agency on the effects of tobacco smoking, was published earlier this year (1993). The study concluded that about 3000 US non-smokers die from lung cancer each year as a result of passive smoking. It is also said to cause between 150 000–300 000 cases of bronchitis or pneumonia in children under 18 months each year. On the basis of all this evidence, and notwithstanding the protestations of the tobacco industry, there can be no serious doubt that environmental tobacco smoke poses a significant hazard to health.

SMOKING IN PREGNANCY

There is compelling evidence that cigarette smoking in pregnancy can have a damaging effect upon the developing child. Babies of mothers who smoke weigh, on average, 200 grammes less than babies born to non-smoking mothers. Mothers who smoke, greatly increase the chances of their pregnancies ending in spontaneous abortion, stillbirth or neo-natal death. Maternal smoking in pregnancy has also been identified as a risk factor in cot death. On top of all this, as stated earlier, children of parents who smoke get more chest infections in the early years of life.

WHAT ABOUT CIGAR AND PIPE SMOKING?

The risk of developing lung cancer as a result of smoking pipes or cigars is significantly less than in cigarette smokers. However, pipe and cigar smokers have a high incidence of cancer of the mouth, tongue, lip, larynx and gullet, and this is probably due to the different way their smoke is inhaled. Pipe and cigar smokers tend to inhale less smoke into the lungs and hold more of the smoke in the mouth and upper respiratory tract.

Most studies show that there is only a very slightly increased risk of heart disease in cigar and pipe smokers, when compared with non-smokers. For this reason it is probably better to be a pipe or cigar smoker than a cigarette smoker, although it is obviously better not to smoke at all. The problem is that when cigarette smokers switch to a pipe or cigars, they still tend to inhale the smoke. In other words, they tend to smoke cigars or pipes in exactly the same way as they smoke cigarettes, and this is probably just as harmful.

WHAT ABOUT LOW TAR CIGARETTES?

Low tar cigarettes are probably less dangerous than high tar cigarettes, at least with respect to the risk of lung cancer. This is because the concentration of cancer causing agents in a low tar cigarette is significantly lower than in a high tar cigarette. Nevertheless, even smoking low tar brands carries a significantly increased risk of cancer when compared with a non-smoker.

Smoking a low tar cigarette probably does not reduce the risk of developing heart disease or other forms of chronic lung disease. Many smokers who switch to low tar brands inhale more deeply, take more puffs per cigarette and smoke more cigarettes than before.

The only safe cigarette is the one that hasn't been smoked.

ASSESSMENT/SELF-ASSESSMENT

Perhaps this is the easiest form of self-assessment in the whole book! It only involves answering one question, ie Do you smoke?

If the answer to this is *no*, then there isn't very much point in reading the rest of this section. If the answer is *yes*, then the next most important question is: do you want to give up smoking?

If the answer to this question is no, or you are not sure, then reading the rest of this section is probably not going to help you.

If the answer is *yes*, then having a better insight into the reasons why you smoke may help you to give up. Table 6.1 is a simple test which will help you to understand more about your smoking habit. It was adapted from the Smoker's Self-Testing Kit, USA Department of Health and Welfare.

INTERPRETATION OF RESULTS

Each of the six factors in the test, stimulation, handling, pleasurable, relaxation, etc, attracts a specific score. Scores of 11 and above on any factor are high; any score of seven and below is low.

SO WHAT DO THESE SCORES MEAN?

Let's take each item individually.

- **Stimulation:** If you score high or fairly high on this factor, it means that you feel stimulated by cigarette smoking — you may feel it helps to wake you up, keep you going when you are under pressure, organize your energies. If you are trying to give up smoking, it is important for you to try to substitute some other activity, for example, brisk walking or moderate exercise whenever you feel the urge to smoke.

- **Handling**: Handling things can be satisfying, but there are many ways to keep your hands busy without lighting up or playing with a cigarette. Why not play with a pen, a rubber or a pencil? Alternatively try doodling, or play with a coin, a piece of jewellery, or some other harmless object. After all, Mozart was said to have composed while rolling a billiard ball up and down the table!
- **Accentuation of pleasure/pleasurable relaxation**: It is not always easy to know whether you use the cigarette to accentuate positive feelings (statement C), or to minimize negative feelings (statement D). Evidence would suggest that about two-thirds of smokers score fairly high on accentuation of pleasure, and about half of these will also score as high or higher on reduction of negative feelings.

  Individual who apparently get real pleasure out of smoking will often find that a rational appraisal of the habit — and its potential risks — is enough to make them think seriously about giving up. Substituting other activities, for example social engagements and physical exercise, are often invaluable strategies in your plan to give up.
- **Reduction of negative feelings or psychological crutch**: Many smokers use a cigarette as a kind of psychological crutch in moments of stress or discomfort. It's almost a kind of reflex action. When the telephone goes and you know it is going to be a difficult conversation, you tend to reach for the cigarette immediately. If you are going in to a difficult meeting, you will light up a cigarette automatically just prior to the appointment — to steady your nerves (or so you think).

  The real question is whether or not the act of smoking the cigarette will help you to deal with the problem any more effectively. An honest answer to this question must be 'no'. After all, the circumstances which led to the problem in the first place have not changed merely by the act of lighting a cigarette.

  When it comes to stopping, this type of smoker typically finds it easier to stop when everything is going well, but will almost certainly revert to the weed when the going begins to get tough again. Substituting physical activities — eating or drinking (obviously in moderation) — may serve as a useful substitute for cigarettes, even in times of tension.
- **Psychological addiction or craving**: Of all factors this is probably the most difficult to overcome and anyone who scores high on this is not going to find giving up easy. For you the craving for the next cigarette begins to build up the moment you put the first one out, and so reducing the number of cigarettes over time is not likely to work very well. There is no easy way around this. You just have to pick the time, prepare for it and then kill the habit stone dead.
- **Habit**: If you scored high on this factor, the probability is that you are not actually getting all that much satisfaction from your cigarettes. Neither do you actually crave them very much. You will often light up your cigarette without actually realizing that you are doing it, and quite

Table 6.1   Why do you smoke?

Here are some statements made by people to describe what they get out of smoking cigarettes. How *often* do you feel this way when smoking them? Circle one number for each statement. *Important: Answer every question.*

	Always	Fre-quently	Occasion-ally	Seldom	Never
A. I smoke cigarettes in order to keep myself from slowing down.	5	4	3	2	1
B. Handling a cigarette is part of the enjoyment of smoking it.	5	4	3	2	1
C. Smoking cigarettes is pleasant and relaxing.	5	4	3	2	1
D. I light up a cigarette when I feel angry about something.	5	4	3	2	1
E. When I have run out of cigarettes I find it almost unbearable until I can get them.	5	4	3	2	1
F. I smoke cigarettes automatically without even being aware of it.	5	4	3	2	1
G. I smoke cigarettes to stimulate me, to perk myself up.	5	4	3	2	1
H. Part of the enjoyment of smoking a cigarette comes from the steps I take to light up.	5	4	3	2	1
I. I find cigarettes pleasurable.	5	4	3	2	1

Table 6.1 continued

		Always	Fre-quently	Occasion-ally	Seldom	Never
J.	When I feel uncomfortable or upset about something, I light up a cigarette.	5	4	3	2	1
K.	I am very much aware of the fact when I am not smoking a cigarette.	5	4	3	2	1
L.	I light up a cigarette without realizing I still have one burning in the ashtray.	5	4	3	2	1
M.	I smoke cigarettes to give me a 'lift'.	5	4	3	2	1
N.	When I smoke a cigarette, part of the enjoyment is watching the smoke as I exhale it.	5	4	3	2	1
O.	I want a cigarette most when I am comfortable and relaxed.	5	4	3	2	1
P.	When I feel 'blue' or want to take my mind off cares and worries, I smoke cigarettes.	5	4	3	2	1
Q.	I get a real gnawing hunger for a cigarette when I haven't smoked for a while.	5	4	3	2	1
R.	On occasions I've found a cigarette in my mouth and didn't remember putting it there.	5	4	3	2	1

Table 6.1 continued

How to score:

1. Enter the numbers you have circled to the test questions in the spaces below, putting the number you have circled to Question A over line A, to Question B over line B, etc.
2. Add the 3 scores on each line to get your totals. For example, the sum of your scores over lines A, G and M gives you your score on *Stimulation* — lines B, H, and N give the score on *Handling*, etc.

Totals

_____	+	_____	+	_____	=	_____
A		G		M		Stimulation
_____	+	_____	+	_____	=	_____
B		H		N		Handling
_____	+	_____	+	_____	=	_____
C		I		O		Pleasurable Relaxation
_____	+	_____	+	_____	=	_____
D		J		P		Crutch: Tension Reduction
_____	+	_____	+	_____	=	_____
E		K		Q		Craving: Psychological Addiction
_____	+	_____	+	_____	=	_____
F		L		R		Habit

Scores can vary from 3 to 15. Any score 11 and above is high; any score 7 and below is low.

often you will stub the cigarette out before you have smoked even half of it. For you stopping cigarette smoking should be relatively easy and the key to success is being aware of every cigarette that you smoke. So by asking yourself a simple question, 'why do I want this cigarette, do I really need it?' you can often prevent yourself from lighting up in the first place.

SUMMARY OF TEST RESULTS

If you do not score particularly high on any of these six factors, the chances are that your addiction to tobacco is not that great and, given a reasonable level of commitment, you should not find it too difficult to stop. If you score high on several categories (and you are very likely to if you have been smoking for a long time), you may need to adopt several different strategies to try to help you give up. We shall be discussing this in more detail in the next section — the Action Plan.

ACTION PLAN

Make no mistake, you really have to *want* to give up smoking if you are going to succeed. Whatever advice is given and however helpful any particular method might be, your success will always depend upon one thing, and one thing only — your personal commitment. Over 11 million people have now given up smoking — there is absolutely no reason why you should not become one of them.

SMOKERS' RATIONALIZATIONS

Smokers can be remarkably inventive when it comes to rationalizing their habit. As a smoker, you may have flirted with some of these yourself, but let's take a few of the more common ones and deal with them now.

1. **'If I stop smoking, I will gain weight'**: Evidence does not bear this out. A number of studies have shown that only about one-third of smokers who stop actually gain weight, and about the same number will actually lose weight.
2. **'Cigarettes help me to concentrate'**: On the contrary, the psychological effects of cigarette smoking are likely to have a negative impact on brain function rather than the reverse. This is because the carbon monoxide in cigarettes robs the brain of oxygen, decreasing concentration by as much as 12 per cent.
3. **'I have been smoking for most of my life; there is not much point in stopping now because the damage is done'**: This is one of the most common rationalizations. The fact is, however, that it is never too late. The moment that you stop smoking, the body begins to repair itself. This is true at any age, and whatever your smoking history happens to be.
4. **'I haven't stopped, but I have switched to low tar cigarettes and they are safe'**: It's certainly true that smoking a lower tar cigarette is better than smoking a high tar version. The problem is that many smokers inhale more deeply, take more puffs per cigarette, and smoke more of the low tar cigarettes as a result of the switch. The only safe cigarette (as I have said previously), is the one that hasn't been smoked.
5. **'I need a cigarette to help me relax'**: Nicotine is a powerful stimulant. It's probably the deep inhaling and exhaling that relaxes a smoker, not the cigarette itself.
6. **'Lots of my friends have smoked all their lives, and they don't seem to have suffered any ill effects'**: Many people smoke all their

lives and never develop lung cancer. But lung cancer is only one of the many diseases to which cigarette smoking has been linked, and it would be most unusual to find a long-term smoker without some evidence of damage. Smokers run a particular risk of chronic lung disease, a fact which is very easy to demonstrate using simple lung function tests.

Having dealt with some of these fallacies, let's move on to the more positive aspects of giving up. We are going to consider this in five separate stages which are as follows:

- **Step 1**   Think about why you want to stop smoking.
- **Step 2**   Picture yourself as a non-smoker — motivate yourself.
- **Step 3**   Prepare to stop.
- **Step 4**   Stop.
- **Step 5**   Stay stopped.

Let's go through these steps in more detail.

Step 1 — Why stop?

You have to think carefully about the reasons why you want to stop smoking. Write them down, and think about each one of them in turn. If you can, single out the most important reason of all. Then, whenever you are tempted, remind yourself of that single most important reason why you want to stop. For example:

- You will have more money to spend on other things — use the money to treat yourself to something you would normally regard as a luxury item.
- Your health will improve and your future health prospects will be much better.
- You will be free of the worry that you are preparing for an early grave.
- You will look better and smell better.
- You will not be exposing family or friends to the dangers of passive smoking.
- Your children are much less likely to start smoking.
- You will suffer fewer colds and other minor infections.

Step 2 — Motivate yourself

Motivation doesn't grow on trees, but you can think yourself into a motivated state. Essentially this involves contrasting your image of yourself in two different situations, ie as a lifelong smoker and then as a non-smoker. In the first image, try to imagine yourself being seriously ill, diseased and disabled as a result of your cigarette smoking. Try to imagine the huge sense of regret you will have at not giving up, and the circumstances that your family may be in because of your early disability or death. Think yourself into living a shorter life, and a retirement that is overshadowed by your deteriorating health.

Then imagine a completely different picture. Imagine being in good health, being vigorous well into your later years, having the time and the good health to enjoy your life to the full. Become a non-smoker in your mind, picture yourself refusing cigarettes, try to get right inside this picture and believe that you can become exactly what you are imagining.

Work on both these images. You have to make each of them as real as possible and when you feel tempted, bring each of the two images into your mind and experience them again. They really can work!

Step 3 — Prepare to stop

Planning your strategy carefully is extremely important. The more you know about your habit and the circumstances in which you smoke, the more successful you are likely to be in giving up.

Think about the situations in which you tend to smoke and when you tend to have your first cigarette of the day. Once you stop smoking, these times and places are obviously going to be the danger spots, so work out now how you are going to be able to cope with them. To be forewarned is to be forearmed.

Some may find it easier to reduce their cigarette consumption gradually rather than stop all at once. This may work for some, but make no mistake, this is no substitute for giving up completely. There is going to have to be a place and a time when you become a non-smoker. Keep on recalling the images you have created for yourself as a non-smoker and as a smoker.

Make sure you talk to your family and let them know that you intend to give up, and the date on which you intend to do it. This will help them to understand that you may be a little more irritable than usual, and it will also put additional pressure on you not to break the agreement.

Very importantly, plan other health strategies. Take more regular exercise, change your diet and moderate your alcohol consumption. Not only will the time taken up during exercise help to improve your overall standard of fitness, it will also reduce the time available for cigarette smoking. As you become fitter, the idea of smoking a cigarette will become even more absurd.

Another tactic which some may find useful is to make a contract between yourself and somebody else. The contract should state that from a particular date and time, you will never smoke again. You should sign it yourself, and have it witnessed by somebody else.

On the day before your stopping date, make sure that you get rid of all ashtrays and all remnants of the smoking ritual (ie pipe cleaners, lighters etc).

Finally, mentally run through the first few days of your programme. Try to rehearse some of the difficulties and make sure that the elements of the plan which you have set up for yourself are actually in place.

Step 4 — Stop

When the big day arrives, just focus on getting through that day without a cigarette. Try not to think about tomorrow or next week. Find ways of occupying your time and avoid circumstances in which you may be subject to temptation. Changing your routine is going to help and being with other non-smokers will also help.

Stick closely to your new exercise routine and whatever additional events you have planned to occupy your time. Keep recalling the images of yourself as being healthy and enjoying life to the full as a direct result of having stopped smoking. Occasionally remind yourself of the opposite image and of the single most important reason why you want to give up. Use these images whenever you feel tempted.

In the first few days you may find that you are subject to some of the side effects of tobacco withdrawal. These are discussed in more detail at the end of this section. Most of them are transitory problems and they should pass in a couple of weeks or so. If you do become unduly concerned, then you should discuss the matter with your own doctor.

Some people find that nicotine chewing gum (now available without a prescription), acupuncture or hypnosis may help. You may find such aids very helpful — some people certainly do. But remember, nothing will make it easy. It is still going to depend, essentially, upon your commitment and **willpower**.

Step 5 — Stay stopped

The probability is that the first few days will not be too difficult, but then the going really is going to get tough! Be determined, stick with it, and don't give up. Keep on recalling the mental images that you have constructed for yourself and use them again and again.

Make sure that you adhere closely to whatever routine you planned in support of your efforts to give up. Don't break this routine, because once that happens you are going to run into trouble. Continue to pay close attention to other aspects of your lifestyle, particularly diet and exercise.

Begin to take pride in your appearance, and in your increasing fitness. Tell others about it. Keep thinking about all the benefits which you are accruing as a result of your decisive action to stop.

Make sure that you saved all the money you would normally spend on cigarettes. You will be surprised and pleased at the rate at which it mounts up. Plan to treat yourself to something that you have wanted for some time (not a new cigarette lighter).

Do not ever succumb to the illusion that one cigarette won't matter. The moment you give in, you will be back where you started.

If you feel that you would like to have some more specific help, there are a number of organizations who may be able to assist. These are listed at the end of this section.

SOME WITHDRAWAL SYMPTOMS AND SIGNS

Some of the more common problems encountered by smokers who give up are as follows:

1. **Craving**: More than 90 per cent of smokers will experience craving during withdrawal. If you have been a heavy smoker, it will usually last for about three weeks, gradually easing off. The best way of overcoming this problem is to find some way to distract yourself each time you feel the craving. Go to the toilet, make some coffee, hang a picture, play the piano — anything to distract yourself. If there are certain parts of your routine which you invariably associate with smoking a cigarette, for example reading the paper, then don't read it. If you normally have a cigarette after the end of a meal have a mint and brush your teeth instead. If you are eating out, eat in the *No Smoking* part of the restaurant.

2. **Increased appetite**: Nicotine is an appetite suppressant, so many smokers find that when they give up smoking their appetite increases. It is also true that food in the gut is absorbed more efficiently in the non-smoker, which again may tend to increase weight. Sucking mints or nibbling other food items as a substitute for a cigarette may also add unwanted calories. Interestingly, however, studies indicate that only a minority of smokers actually put on weight when they stop.
    Try to limit the effects of this by nibbling carrots, celery or apples. If you do put on a little weight, don't worry unduly about this because you can quite easily shed it later. Increasing your exercise may also help.

3. **Irritability, anxiety and loss of concentration**: Most of these can be attributed to the upheaval of breaking a long-established habit as well as trying to adjust to the physical problems. There is no easy answer to this, and it may take two to three months to adjust. The support of those around you, both at work and at home, can be critical during this period.

4. **Worsening cough**: As your body tries to rid itself of all the filth caused by cigarette smoking, you may experience a temporary worsening of your smoker's cough. This will disappear after a few weeks or so.

5. **Feeling lightheaded or dizzy**: The carbon monoxide in your blood which is produced as a result of cigarette smoking, will obviously start to fall and the oxygen supply to your brain will increase. This is a short-lived phenomenon which should only last for about 7–10 days.

Other minor symptoms include nausea, constipation or diarrhoea and occasional headaches. Again, these will all disappear after a couple of weeks or so.

WHAT IF I REALLY DON'T WANT TO STOP?

If you are a smoker who really doesn't want to stop, there are still some things that you can do to limit the harm from cigarettes and tobacco. Obviously nothing is going to make smoking safe, and anything short of stopping completely is a compromise. However, it is a compromise that you may wish to accept. If this is the case:

- Choose a low tar cigarette.
- Don't smoke your cigarettes all the way down; you get most of the tar and nicotine from the last few drags. If you smoke half you will only get about 40 per cent of the total tar and nicotine. Try to get used to putting your cigarette out earlier.
- Take fewer drags on each cigarette.
- Try not to inhale as much smoke.
- Try to smoke fewer cigarettes each day. Perhaps you might like to consider not smoking at home, or only smoking during set times.

WHAT ABOUT NICOTINE SUBSTITUTES?

The evidence that nicotine replacement is helpful in quitting smoking is actually quite strong. The most commonly used method of nicotine substitution is in the form of nicotine chewing gum (eg *Nicorette*). Some people find this extremely helpful, and if you find it difficult to give up smoking any other way it may well be worth a try.

A more recent development is an anti-smoking 'patch' (*Nicorette*, *Nicotinell*, *Nicabate*). The device is worn on the body like a sticking plaster and is laced with nicotine, which is slowly but continuously absorbed into the bloodstream and is said to help wean smokers off tobacco without withdrawal symptoms. The patches deliver a steady flow of nicotine over 24 hours, at concentrations which are high enough to prevent or reduce the early morning craving for cigarettes. They should be used with caution in patients who have a history of angina or other manifestations of coronary artery disease.

The patches are not cheap but the cost is actually quite small when you set it against the costs of tobacco (and your ailing lungs). Beware of cheap substitutes which are coming onto the market; they may not release the nicotine gradually, or in sufficient doses to keep blood levels constant. Reported side-effects are palpitations, indigestion, nausea and insomnia, but many people do not experience any untoward effects at all. Again, if all else has failed, it may be worth a try. But you're still going to need willpower!

If you would like to try a nicotine substitute, you would be well advised to discuss it with your family doctor beforehand. Remember, however, that the general measures set out in this section are still applicable, and will increase your chances of success.

SUPPORT AND THERAPY

You may wish to obtain more information about how to stop cigarette smoking or take advantage of specific courses and programmes designed to help you. Some of the more useful contact points follow:

ASH (Action on Smoking and Health)
27–35 Mortimer Street
London W1N 7RJ.
Tel: 071–637 9843.
ASH provide 'Give Up' packs for smokers free of charge. They also supply information on how to start your own 'Stop Smoking' group.

Health Education Authority
78 New Oxford Street
London WC1A 1AH.
Tel: 071–383 3833

ASH (Scottish Committee)
6 Castle Street
Edinburgh EH2 3AT.
Tel: 031–225 4725.

Quit
Latimer House
40–48 Hansen Street
London W1P 7DE.
Ring Quickline on 071–487 3000.
Quit runs monthly, five evening, stop smoking courses in central London. Quickline can also refer you to other courses in your area.

These organizations can also give you useful advice about new products, services and programmes for smoking cessation.

I make no apology for devoting so much time and space to the subject of tobacco, because of its clear relationship to so many forms of preventable disease. You may have tried to quit or to cut down in the past (most smokers have — several times) and are now smoking again. But if you can learn to understand why you failed last time, you may be better prepared to achieve success the next time. After all, more than eleven million people in the UK are ex-smokers and there is no real reason why you should not be one of them.

Chapter 7

WHY EXERCISE?

When it comes to taking regular exercise, the British are a pretty indolent lot. A recent survey — of which more later — showed that we have a miserably low level of physically active adults in this country, with most of us failing to take even the minimum amount of exercise required to achieve a health benefit. Not that we're alone; similar surveys in Canada, Australia and the USA indicate that a sedentary lifestyle travels well, and the levels of activity (or inactivity) are broadly similar in all these countries.

In the early part of this century doctors and other supposedly intelligent people believed in the 'rate-of-living' theory, which basically stated that the heart was pre-programmed to beat a certain number of times, and then you were finished. Using them up during exercise was just a quick way to an early grave. Conversely, the lower your rate of energy expenditure, the longer you could expect to survive. If the results of the recent physical activity survey are anything to go by, this theory is still alive and well. Another source of concern was the 'athletes heart' which many doctors regarded as a hazardous side-effect of strenuous exercise, likely to reduce life-expectancy. Only in the latter half of this century has there been scientific evidence to show that hard physical exercise has many potential health benefits, and that 'athletes heart' is nothing more than a normal and reversible physiological adaptation.

Before the age of technology, many occupations demanded a great deal of physical activity and energy. A century ago, a third of the energy expended in USA farms and factories was supplied by muscle power as compared with only about 1 per cent today. Nowadays, many more people have to rely on exercising during leisure time as a means of maintaining fitness. Despite the tremendous growth in recreational exercise and sport, the fact remains that the overwhelming majority of people in this country still fail to take anything like enough physical exercise. Even in the USA, which has developed something of an exercise culture, it has been estimated that more than 60 per cent of its adults are still sedentary. As we shall see later, this has serious public health implications, a point well made by the USA Center for Disease Control; 'A sedentary lifestyle constitutes the greatest single risk to the collective hearts of America'.

THE ALLIED DUNBAR NATIONAL FITNESS SURVEY (ADNFS)

The Allied Dunbar National Fitness Survey (ADNFS) was published in 1992. It represents the most detailed and scientific assessment of the physical activity patterns and fitness levels of the English population ever carried out. Some 6000 randomly selected adults were surveyed, using a home interview followed by a physical appraisal.

The survey provides a rich source of information about current activity patterns — some of it disturbing. Some of the more important findings are as follows:

- In terms of physical activity, more than 70 per cent of men and 80 per cent of women fell below their age-appropriate activity level necessary to achieve a health benefit. Even among 16–24 year olds, 70 per cent of men and more than 90 per cent of women, fell below the recommended target activity levels.

- More than 80 per cent of males in the coronary-prone 45–54 age category reported inadequate levels of physical activity for their age. This is a finding of considerable concern, given the high incidence of heart disease in this group, and the well documented protective properties of exercise.

- Activity declines markedly with age — some 45 per cent of 65–74 year olds were almost completely sedentary. This is another worrying finding, since there is impressive evidence that elderly people respond well to graded exercise programmes, with consequent improvement in mobility and a reduced likelihood of hip fractures and other injuries.

- The percentage of women participating in more vigorous forms of exercise is much lower than men in every age group low (an average of 4 per cent compared with 14 per cent in men).

- About one-third of men and two-thirds of women would find it difficult to sustain walking at a reasonable pace (about 3 mph) up a 1 in 20 slope. It seems that even walking on level ground at 3 mph represents severe exertion for older women — more than 50 per cent of women aged 55–64 years are not fit enough to continue walking on the level at this speed.

- 30 per cent of men and 50 per cent of women aged 65–74 years did not have sufficient muscle strength or power to lift 50 per cent of their body weight — and as a consequence would have difficulty doing simple things such as rising from a chair without using their arms.

- Power to extend the legs was also low among women aged 55 years and above, with 50 per cent falling below the power needed to climb stairs without assistance.

If we assume that this is a truly representative sample, one has to conclude that this represents a scathing indictment of the average physical condition of millions of people in this country. Interestingly, however, the survey participants themselves took a decidedly more optimistic view of things, for despite overwhelming evidence to the contrary, 80 per cent of both men and women of all ages believed themselves to be fit and doing enough exercise to stay fit! This discrepancy between the perception and the reality may be just mass self-deception, but is more likely to reflect the fact that many people don't actually know what constitutes 'healthful' regular exercise.

THE SCIENTIFIC EVIDENCE FOR BENEFIT

Since the early 1950s, scientists and physicians all over the world have studied the relationship between exercise and disease, particularly heart disease. There have been some 53 major long-term studies, and literally thousands of articles published in the scientific literature. The overwhelming majority of these reports confirm the significant benefits of a physically active lifestyle compared with a sedentary one. Indeed, the estimated reduction in the risk of heart attack with the maintenance of an active, compared with an inactive, lifestyle is 35–55 per cent. There is therefore an enormous body of scientific literature supporting the case for exercise and its widespread and enthusiastic promotion in the general population. As James Rippe from the University of Massachusetts Medical School has said, 'For the first time, we have scientific evidence to support what has always seemed true: regular exercise helps prevent many diseases, lengthens lifespan, and improves quality of life'.

So what precisely are these benefits?

SOME OF THE BENEFITS OF EXERCISE

1. **Lower risk of premature death:** After taking into account multiple risk factors including cholesterol levels, blood pressure, weight, smoking etc, physically fit men have a 53 per cent lower risk of dying prematurely when compared with sedentary men. Physically fit women have an even greater level of benefit, being 98 per cent less likely to die prematurely when compared with their sedentary counterparts.

2. **Lower risk of coronary heart disease:** Men and women who are physically fit and exercise regularly are up to eight times less likely to die from heart disease than unfit persons. There is a large and consistent body of scientific evidence to suggest that a sedentary lifestyle is a major independent risk factor for coronary disease.

3. **Lower risk of cancer:** In recent years a number of studies suggesting that regular exercise may help to protect against various forms of cancer have appeared in the scientific literature. In general,

it appears that physically fit men die four times less often from cancer, and physically fit women die 16 times less often from cancer than unfit men and women. In particular, a physically fit woman may have a 50 per cent lower risk of developing breast cancer than a sedentary woman, and there may also be benefit in relation to cancer of the cervix and uterus. A number of studies have consistently demonstrated a risk of colon cancer which is 75–80 per cent higher for physically inactive men and women compared to their more active counterparts. For men, there is some preliminary evidence to suggest that regular exercise may help to protect against cancer of the prostate.

4. **Preservation of bone density:** Osteoporosis (weakening of the bone structure due to loss of minerals), is a particular problem in women after the menopause. Hormone Replacement Therapy (HRT) has been shown to protect women against bone loss, but there is also good evidence that regular, weight bearing exercise, can help to preserve bone density. Thus men, and particularly women, who remain physically active into old age are much less likely to suffer from osteoporosis.

5. **Reduced blood pressure:** Many studies show that resting blood pressures in physically fit persons are significantly lower than in those who are unfit. Regular exercise may be just as effective as drugs in reducing blood pressure (see page 88) and even relatively mild exercise has been shown to be beneficial in persons with hypertension.

6. **Reduced body weight:** Regular exercise helps to promote fat loss, whilst enhancing muscular strength and flexibility. By burning calories more efficiently, regular exercise helps to maintain optimal body weight and composition.

7. **Increased HDL-Cholesterol:** Contrary to what is generally believed, regular exercise will not actually reduce the total cholesterol concentration or LDL-cholesterol. The idea that you can 'burn off' the excess blood cholesterol just isn't true. Exercise does, however, raise the levels of the beneficial HDL-cholesterol, and reduces the TC/HDL-C ratio to a lower-risk profile (see page 75).

8. **Reduced clotting/coagulation:** An increased tendency for the blood to clot (coagulate) is an important factor in precipitating heart attacks. One measure of the clotting tendency is the level of a substance in the blood called fibrinogen; the higher the blood fibrinogen, the greater the risk of thrombosis. Exercise reduces blood fibrinogen levels, and therefore the risk of heart attack.

Another important factor is the effect of exercise on blood platelets, which prevent bleeding from cut or broken blood vessels by clumping together and initiating the formation of a blood clot (thrombosis). Unfortunately they sometimes mistake the fatty plaque inside a diseased coronary artery as a break in the wall which needs plugging, and by doing so precipitate a clot and a heart attack — hence the term 'coronary thrombosis'. Exercise has been shown to reduce platelet stickiness by up to 40 per cent, and by doing so reduces the risk of a heart attack.

9. **Reduced risk of diabetes:** Maturity-onset diabetes (NIDDM — see p.36) usually appears after the age of 40. Unlike those with juvenile onset diabetes, whose bodies do not manufacture any insulin at all, those with NIDDM do secrete some insulin, but not nearly enough. In addition, they have some measure of insulin resistance which makes them less responsive to whatever little of the hormone is available. (In simple terms, insulin moves blood sugar from the blood into the tissues and when it is either deficient or absent, blood sugar rises to higher than normal levels, and the individual becomes diabetic.)

   The most important risk factor for NIDDM is obesity: indeed the risk of developing this disease is directly proportional to body weight. Up to 80 per cent of people with NIDDM are overweight at the time of diagnosis, and losing weight is the first stage of treatment — indeed, in many cases, this is the *only* form of treatment required. Sometimes drugs are required to assist if weight loss is not sufficient, but insulin is rarely required.

   For many years, studies have suggested that regular physical exercise may help to prevent NIDDM. A Harvard study of more than 22 000 male physicians has been underway for the past decade. Those who did brisk exercise five or more times per week had a 42 per cent reduction in risk for NIDDM, compared with a 23 per cent reduction in those who had only one exercise session each week.

   Even younger, insulin-dependent diabetics, may benefit from regular exercise. Apart from improving cardiorespiratory fitness they will tend to see a reduction in their daily insulin requirements. However, exercise can also be hazardous if taken too close to an insulin injection and diabetics need to achieve close control over their blood sugar levels if they are to avoid problems.

10. **Improved cardiorespiratory fitness:** Obviously, if you exercise regularly then your general level of fitness will be much higher than a sedentary individual. Not only does this reduce your risk of developing many forms of disease, but it adds immeasurably to the quality of your life.

11. **Reduced stress and improved mood:** Prolonged exposure to stressful stimuli can bring about sustained release of the stress hormones. These hormones produce a heightened state of arousal characterized by increased heart rate and blood pressure, dilation of the pupils and an increase in blood fats and blood sugar. This rapid outpouring of stress hormones is an integral part of the normal 'Fight or Flight' response to an external threat — you either stay and try to

deal with it, or you leave as rapidly as possible! From a biological viewpoint, this is a survival mechanism, designed to be activated occasionally. But if the stress response is elicited too frequently, it can produce an almost continuous state of arousal. As a result, the body begins to show various signs of wear and tear, including an increased risk of heart attack and sudden cardiac death.

There is evidence that regular exercise can help to reduce the sudden hormonal surges which are a cardinal feature of the stress response.

Apart from helping to reduce potentially dangerous surges of stress hormones, regular physical exercise also improves mood. Although it was known for many years that people who are physically fit experience an enhanced sense of well-being, the sceptics tended to dismiss this as just another facet of a rather strange personality type found commonly in those who exercise. However, in 1974 the discovery of a group of proteins which became known as 'endorphins' provided a firm biological basis for the mood enhancing qualities of exercise. These substances have a chemical structure which is similar to morphine and, since they are produced by the body itself, speculation soon grew that this group of substances was the 'natural' pain-killer or analgesic of the body. It is likely that the endorphins work in concert with a variety of other complex chemical transmitters, acting as an anti-depressant which is as effective as psychotherapy. It is also a useful means of controlling anxiety and improves the symptoms of pre-menstrual tension.

Whatever the underlying mechanism, it is evident that regular exercise can make an important contribution to stress control and an enhanced sense of well-being.

12. **Improved sleeping pattern:** Insomnia is an extremely common problem, and most of us have experienced occasional sleeping problems during stressful life events such as job or domestic difficulties, a wedding, illness or an impending examination. For some, however, such difficulties can evolve into a chronic sleeping problem. Regular physical exercise can do much to help restore a normal sleeping pattern by promoting more continuous and restful sleep; it should be an integral part of any strategy for dealing with insomnia.

I think you will agree that by any measure, this is a pretty impressive list of real benefits that you can achieve by regular, moderate exercise.

ASSESSMENT/SELF-ASSESSMENT

Your self assessment here is made up of only two elements, ie a question and a simple test.

THE QUESTION

There is a consistent body of research to suggest that people need to be moderately or vigorously active at least three times a week in order to reduce their risk of heart disease and stroke. So far as we know, this also applies to the prevention of other diseases such as diabetes, obesity, and hypertension. So the question is actually quite simple: **do you exercise regularly?** More specifically, do you set aside time for regular moderate or vigorous exercise of 20–30 minutes duration, on three or more occasions per week?

I will be saying some more about what I mean by 'moderate' or 'vigorous' exercise later, but first let me make a few general points about the question. The type of exercise likely to produce benefit is going to be regular, rhythmical and involve major muscle groups. Typical examples are cycling, playing badminton or tennis, rowing, jogging or running and brisk walking. A list of exercises which 'qualify' and some that don't is given later in this section. The point is that the exercise has to be sufficiently vigorous to increase your pulse rate, as well as the rate and depth of your breathing. Moreover, the exercise must be sustained for 20–30 minutes. So when I am talking about swimming as being a good form of exercise, I *mean* swimming — not sitting at the side of the pool watching other people! Brisk walking would only qualify if it really *is* brisk, and not a casual walk to the postbox. You will also see that I have specifically asked whether or not you actually set aside time to take exercise. Some people may think that they get enough exercise at work, walking up and down the stairs all day. Whilst this is undoubtedly better than being entirely sedentary, it is unlikely to give you the same degree of benefit that a regular, set exercise period will (always assuming that you are not a lumberjack!). You may recall that the Allied Dunbar survey, to which I referred earlier in this chapter, showed that only 20 per cent of men and 10 per cent of women were engaged in occupations which would be classified as moderately or vigorously active.

If you are already taking a regular exercise, then I need only to encourage you to continue. There will still be much in this section that you will find of interest, and you may want to try the simple fitness test. If you are not exercising regularly, then having answered the above question in the negative I would suggest that you carry out a simple test to evaluate your current level of fitness. This will help to provide a baseline estimate, against which you can measure your future progress.

THE TEST

Before the test — a quick check

Before the simple fitness test, you should ask yourself the following questions:

- Have you ever been told that you have a heart problem and advised to limit your physical activity?
- Do you have chest pain or discomfort which is brought on by exercise, eg walking up a hill?
- Do you have episodes of dizziness or feeling faint?
- Are you a diabetic?
- Do you have any bone or joint problems that may limit, or be aggravated by, physical activity?
- Are you currently taking any medication for high blood pressure, angina or any other heart condition?
- Are you aware of any other health problem which may expose you to unnecessary risk during exercise?

If the answer to any of the above is *yes*, then you should seek advice from your family doctor before going any further.

Let me emphasize at once that embarking upon an exercise programme is perfectly safe for the vast majority of people. Very few individuals, even those with heart disease, have to avoid physical activity entirely. These few questions are simply meant to identify the very small minority of people for whom exercise may be inappropriate or who require close medical supervision.

A simple fitness test

To carry out your baseline fitness test, you need a stopwatch (or a watch with a second hand), some decent running shoes and some loose, comfortable clothing. These are basically two versions of the test, ie the distance covered in a time of 12 minutes or the time taken to cover 1.5 miles.

The 1.5 mile test: The aim is to measure the time it takes you to cover a 1.5 mile distance either walking or jogging (or both) — **SAFELY.** You obviously have to make a real effort, but you must **not** drive yourself to the point of exhaustion. Don't try the test with anyone else — it's likely to become competitive and turn into a race. If you find you need to walk the whole distance without jogging at all, that's absolutely fine.

The 12 minute test: If you feel that a 1.5 mile distance is a little too much to start with, then you can simply walk/run along the flat for a period of 12 minutes, and then measure the total distance covered. The safety comments about the 1.5 mile test apply equally to this test.

Key note

If you experience any symptoms during the test such as discomfort or pain in the chest, arms or jaw, or if you feel dizzy or in any way unwell, then you should stop the test immediately. If you are completely sedentary, undertake this evaluation with care.

These words of caution may seem a bit over the top, but I do assure you that some people (usually men) can be remarkably silly when it comes to performing this sort of simple assessment. They seem to regard it as an opportunity to prove to everyone else that the spark of youth and fitness still burns, even if it is covered in 30 lbs of adipose tissue and they haven't actually done any regular exercise for 20 years — a potentially dangerous illusion. This is a perfectly safe test, but if you haven't exercised for a long time, then do please *take it easy!*

INTERPRETATION OF RESULTS

In Tables 7.1 and 7.2 on pages 121 and 122 you will find five fitness categories based upon your 1.5 mile time or your 12 minute distance. The table takes into account that your aerobic capacity will also be a function of your age. You simply have to select which age group is appropriate for you, and on the basis of either your distance or your time, find your fitness category.

There is one additional item in the table which I should mention — your maximum oxygen uptake (VO_2 Max). In essence, this is a measure of your cardiorespiratory (aerobic) fitness, and is expressed as the number of millilitres of oxygen, per kilogram of body weight per minute (ml/Kg/min). The more efficient you are at delivering oxygen to the muscles and other body tissues, the higher will be your VO_2 max. Direct measurement of oxygen consumption requires expensive and sophisticated laboratory equipment and highly trained personnel. Few people will have ready access to such facilities. Fortunately it is possible to obtain a reasonable estimate indirectly because there is a correlation between your time over 1.5 miles (or distance over 12 minutes) and your VO_2 Max. So, for example, if you are 45 years old and completed your 1.5 mile test in 11 minutes and 15 seconds, your predicted VO_2 Max is 41–48 mls/Kg/min, which would place you firmly in the 'Excellent' fitness category.

As a rough guide, most sedentary individuals will have a maximum oxygen uptake of 35–40 mls/Kg/min. A more active individual who is perhaps exercising for three or four 30-minute sessions per week may have around 45–50 mls/Kg/min. In a good class club runner it will be 70 mls/Kg/min or more and in a world class marathon runner, 85 or above. You must bear in mind that these capacities are largely genetically determined. Put simply, you cannot become a great athlete — you are born one. Nevertheless, even if your VO_2 Max is only modest, it can usually be improved by 15–20 per cent.

The fitness assessment also takes age into account — an important point since, like it or not, your exercise capacity (VO_2 Max) diminishes with age. However, the good news is that if you maintain a good standard of fitness

Table 7.1 Predicted aerobic fitness classification: men

Category	Measure	Under 30	30–39	40–49	50+
			Age (years)		
Poor	12 min. distance (miles)	1.0–1.24	0.95–1.14	0.85–1.04	0.80–0.99
	1.5 mile time (min:sec)	14:31–16:30	15:31–17:30	16:31–18:30	17:01–19:00
	Predicted oxygen uptake (VO_2 max ml kg^{-1} min^{-1})	25.0–33.7	24.7–30.1	24.6–26.4	24.5–24.9
Fair	12 min. distance (miles)	1.25–1.49	1.15–1.39	1.05–1.29	1.0–1.24
	1.5 mile time (min:sec)	12:01–14:30	13:01–15:30	14:01–16:30	14:31–17:00
	Predicted oxygen uptake (VO_2 max ml kg^{-1} min^{-1})	33.8–42.5	30.2–39.1	26.5–35.4	25.0–33.7
Good	12 min. distance (miles)	1.50–1.74	1.40–1.64	1.30–1.54	1.25–1.49
	1.5 mile time (min:sec)	10:16–12:00	11:01–13:00	11:31–14:00	12:01–14:30
	Predicted oxygen uptake (VO_2 max ml kg^{-1} min^{-1})	42.6–51.5	39.2–47.9	35.5–44.4	33.8–42.5
Excellent	12 min. distance (miles)	1.75–2.00	1.65–1.90	1.55–1.80	1.50–1.75
	1.5 mile time (min:sec)	8:45–10:15	9:30–11:00	10:00–11:30	10:30–12:00
	Predicted oxygen uptake (VO_2 max ml kg^{-1} min^{-1})	51.6–60.2	48.0–57.0	44.5–53.6	42.6–51.6
Superior	12 min. distance (miles)	2.00+	1.90+	1.80+	1.75+
	1.5 mile time (min:sec)	<8:45	<9:30	<10:00	<10:30
	Predicted oxygen uptake (VO_2 max ml kg^{-1} min^{-1})	60.2+	57.0+	53.6+	51.6+

Source: *Why Exercise?* (1986) Ashton, D and Davies, B, Basil Blackwell Ltd, Oxford.

< Less than

Table 7.2 Predicted aerobic fitness classification: women

Category	Measure	Age (years)			
		Under 30	30–39	40–49	50+
Poor	12 min distance (miles)	0.95–1.14	0.85–1.04	0.75–0.94	0.65–0.84
	1.5 mile time (min:sec)	15:31–17:30	16:31–18:30	17:31–19:30	18:31–20:30
	Predicted oxygen uptake (VO_2 max ml kg^{-1} min^{-1})	23.6–30.1	23.5–29.4	23.4–28.9	23.3–27.0
Fair	12 min. distance (miles)	1.15–1.34	1.05–1.24	0.95–1.14	0.85–1.04
	1.5 mile time (min:sec)	13:01–15:30	14:01–16:30	15:01–17:30	16:31–18:30
	Predicted oxygen uptake (VO_2 max ml kg^{-1} min^{-1})	30.2–37.0	29.5–35.8	29.0–35.0	27.1–33.0
Good	12 min distance (miles)	1.35–1.64	1.25–1.54	1.15–1.44	1.05–1.34
	1.5 mile time (min:sec)	11:16–13:00	12:01–14:00	12:31–15:00	13:31–16:30
	Predicted oxygen uptake (VO_2 max ml kg^{-1} min^{-1})	37.1–47.9	35.9–45.0	35.1–40.9	33.1–37.0
Excellent	12 min. distance (miles)	1.65–1.85	1.55–1.75	1.45–1.65	1.35–1.55
	1.5 mile time (min:sec)	9:45–11:15	10:30–12:00	11:00–12:30	12:00–13:30
	Predicted oxygen uptake (VO_2 max ml kg^{-1} min^{-1})	48.0–55.2	45.1–51.6	41.0–48.0	37.1–44.6
Superior	12 min. distance (miles)	1.85+	1.75+	1.65+	1.55+
	1.5 mile time (min:sec)	<9:45	<10:30	<11:00	<12:00
	Predicted oxygen uptake (VO_2 max ml kg^{-1} min^{-1})	55.2+	51.6+	48.0+	44.6+

Source: *Why Exercise?* (1986) Ashton, D and Davies, B, Basil Blackwell Ltd, Oxford.

< Less than

in your 50s and 60s, you may well have a better physiological capacity than many people 30 or 40 years younger. The Allied Dunbar survey found that the average aerobic capacity of the most fit 10 per cent of men aged 64–75 was higher than the least fit 10 per cent of men aged 25–34 years. The same pattern applied to women.

ACTION PLAN — SO YOU WANT TO EXERCISE?

HOW SHOULD I START TO EXERCISE?

The short answer to this is 'with care'. If you have not exercised for a long time, then the most important thing is to start gently and increase the amount of exercise you take gradually. For example, if you intend to use jogging as your main form of regular exercise, then don't start jogging immediately. On the first few occasions, simply go out and walk for ten minutes or so. Carry on doing this until you are walking for about 15 to 30 minutes. When you are comfortable with this, jog for one minute and then walk for one minute. Over a period of time you then reduce the amount of time you spend walking, and gradually increase the amount of time you spend jogging. You will then be able to jog for 20 to 30 minutes non-stop.

But remember that this gradual approach applies to any sort of exercise you do. If you start too quickly and try to do too much, you risk getting injured and you may feel less inclined to exercise in the future. Some soreness in the muscles is almost inevitable if you have not been very physically active for a while, but this is nothing to worry about and it will disappear after a few days. In fact the best way to get rid of muscle soreness is to exercise again.

A word about proper clothing. It is important that you use the correct tools for the job otherwise you will be uncomfortable and increase the risk of injury. This is probably more applicable to jogging/running than anything else. Pounding on hard surfaces can be quite hard on the joints, so do make an investment in a good pair of running shoes. During a five mile run, each shoe will land on the ground some 5000 times, and for an average person weighing 170 lbs (77 Kg), this means a cumulative force of around 400 tons per shoe. Potentially, this places tremendous stresses upon the feet, ankles, knees, hips and spine and if you don't wear proper footwear you will literally run into trouble. Cushioning and stability are, without question, the key factors. The technology and the materials involved in designing and building running shoes nowadays is remarkable — take full advantage of it. The old pair of plimsolls which you found in the attic isn't going to do!

There are four essential elements to consider when talking about exercise:

Table 7.3 The effectiveness of various sports/activities in improving cardio-respiratory fitness

GROUP A Good/excellent effect		GROUP B Poor effect	
Swimming	Fencing	Yoga	Sailing
Jogging/running	Soccer	Cricket	Fishing
Brisk walking (2 miles+)	Hockey	Archery	Darts
Cycling	Rugby	Snooker/billiards	Weight-training
Squash	Basketball	Table-tennis	Gardening
Tennis/badminton	Rowing	Golf	Bowling
Orienteering	Aerobics	Shooting	Housework
Cross-country skiing	Handball		
Heavy gardening	Canoeing		
(eg digging)	Judo		
Disco dancing (hard)			
Ice-skating			

1. The type or form of exercise
2. The frequency and duration.
3. The intensity.

1. What type of exercise?

In terms of developing your cardiorespiratory fitness (fitness of the heart and lungs) dynamic exercise involving large muscle groups is required for maximum effect. Examples of this form of exercise are shown in Table 7.3, along with a list of 'non-qualifying' activities (Group B). The latter, whilst enjoyable, are unlikely to be of sufficient intensity to provide a training effect.

Choose something from Group A which you enjoy and are therefore likely to comply with — consistency is all important. You must try to exercise regularly (at least 3 times) throughout the week, and you're just not going to do this unless you actually enjoy your chosen form of activity. It's also quite a good idea to find a partner who is willing to work with you. This adds a social dimension to your exercise programme, making it more enjoyable whilst increasing compliance.

Apart from cardiovascular or aerobic fitness, other components of physical activity need to be considered. These include strength, flexibility and muscular endurance. No single exercise is 'pure' — all have several elements. However, it is improvements in cardiorespiratory fitness that are likely to bring the most important and immediate health benefits.

If you are overweight or obese, you would probably be better starting an exercise programme with non-weight bearing forms of activity such as swimming, a static exercise bicycle or a rowing machine. This will improve your fitness without risking damage to the joints and tendons. If you combine your exercise programme with appropriate dietary measures, it will also help you to lose weight. When your body weight has been reduced to more acceptable levels, you can safely add other activities such as jogging, brisk walking, tennis and running to your training schedule.

Let me make a few very brief comments about some of the more common forms of exercise.

Swimming

If I had to select one activity for everyone, it would be this one. It's a first class cardiorespiratory exercise, but also scores well for strength and flexibility (suppleness). Because the body weight is supported by the water, swimming is ideal for anyone with back or joint problems, or who is overweight. The obvious disadvantage is that you need to have ready access to a swimming pool. Even if this is geographically convenient, there may be other limitations. Pools are often crowded with children, especially during school holidays and at weekends. This may make steady, good quality swimming hazardous or impossible. However, most pools have adult sessions at specific times (often early morning), and if you choose your times carefully you should be able to establish a regular routine. It shouldn't cost much either — most pools have season tickets and special rates for lunch-time or early morning sessions. There are often special rates for the retired or unemployed.

One practical point. When you are using your heart rate to monitor your exercise intensity, it should be 10 to 12 beats *lower* than for normal, upright exercise. This is to do with the fact that in swimming, the heart is in the horizontal rather than the vertical position.

Cycling (outdoors)

A tremendous exercise for cardiovascular fitness and, to a lesser extent, strength. It will do little for your flexibility, so you should add some stretching/flexibility exercises to your programme. Professional racing cyclists are without peer in terms of their cardiovascular conditioning, and some may cover upwards of 25 000 miles in any one year. Fortunately one can achieve excellent results with much more modest mileages. There are few forms of exercise so enjoyable when the sun is shining and the leafy lanes beckon. The problem nowadays is that the roads are so congested with cars and heavy lorries, that cycling has become quite a dangerous form of recreation. It's also much more hazardous during the winter months when visibility is poor and the roads may be icy. Personally I stick to cycling in the summer months, and switch to swimming and running during winter.

One last word here — *always* wear a crash helmet! The technology has improved enormously during the last few years, and the helmets are so light and well-ventilated that there really cannot be any excuse for not wearing one.

Stationary cycling

If you're worried about the roads, a static exercise bike (an exercycle) is another option. It has the benefit of being very convenient and, used properly, is extremely effective.

As a non-weight bearing exercise it may have particular advantages for those with joint or weight problems. Unfortunately most people find it terminally boring — even with modern computer graphics which are meant to convince you that you're riding through the mountains of Colorado.

But if you enjoy it — great!

Jogging/running

Still very popular, regular jogging or running is an excellent form of cardiovascular exercise. What exactly constitutes jogging as opposed to running is difficult to say, although it's usually taken that jogging is slower and less vigorous than running. Few people would argue that if you can cover a mile in less than six minutes you are running. If you take 10 or 20 minutes, you're jogging. At what point the one merges into the other is anyone's guess.

You can run almost anywhere, and although you run the risk of injury to feet, ankles and knees, selection of proper footwear (discussed earlier) can reduce this to a minimum. Running shoes are not cheap, but the investment is well worthwhile. A word of caution; beware of heavy traffic, and if you run at night, wear some reflective clothing. When running on pavements look out for pot-holes and also for low-level branches from trees and shrubs — they can inflict serious damage to your eyes.

Walking

Walking is perhaps the most natural of all exercises, and has probably been undervalued in terms of its health-promoting properties. Recent research suggests that a *brisk* walk each day may offer health benefits comparable to those normally associated with more intense exercise. A large study known as the MRFIT (Multiple Risk Factor Intervention Trial) demonstrated that men who performed moderate activities such as walking for 30 minutes each day, had a 20 per cent lower overall death rate and 35 per cent fewer deaths from coronary artery disease, than did less active men. Regular, brisk walking reduces blood pressure and increases blood levels of the protective HDL-cholesterol. It may also help to protect against diabetes and premature bone demineralization (osteoporosis).

All in all, brisk walking is a very good exercise and one accessible to almost everyone — including the elderly and patients with heart disease.

Having decided which type of exercise suits you best, you then have to consider the frequency, duration and intensity required to produce health and cardiorespiratory benefits.

2. Frequency and duration

Many people put off embarking on an exercise programme because of concerns about the amount of time involved. In fact, lack of time is the most common excuse offered by people who need to rationalize their continuing inactivity.

The scientific evidence shows that 30 minutes of moderate/vigorous exercise on three or four occasions per week is the optimum, and this applies to all ages and both sexes.

(Two sessions of 30 minutes duration are probably adequate to *maintain* cardiovascular conditioning.)

Please note that **more** is not necessarily better. In terms of health benefits, exercising seven times a week offers no significant advantage over exercising three four times a week. Running 30 or 40 miles per week is no better than running a total of 12 miles per week. Naturally, if you are exercising more frequently your fitness and exercise performance will be at a higher level, but performance is not our principal goal — improved health is. The biggest advantage in health terms occurs as a result of moving from a sedentary lifestyle to a moderately active one. Further benefit may be derived from more frequent or intense exercise, but this is more performance-related than health related. Intensive training for seven days a week may be worthwhile if you are a competitive athlete, but for most of us the added 2 or 3 per cent improvement that daily training may provide, is simply not worth the effort.

We have covered the type, frequency and duration of your exercise, but what about intensity?

3. Intensity

One of the most frequently asked questions by individuals who are just beginning an exercise programme is 'How hard should I push myself?' In physiological terms we refer to this as exercise *intensity*. Intensity is nothing more than the rate of doing work. Running a mile in 7.5 minutes obviously requires a greater intensity of effort than walking the same distance. The best indicator of exercise effort or intensity, is your heart rate (pulse rate), expressed in beats per minute (beats/min).

Everyone has a maximum heart rate that is related to his or her age — the Age Predicted Maximum Heart Rate (APMHR). (Please note that this is a function of age, not fitness.) A simple way to calculate your APMHR is to subtract your age from 220, ie

APMHR = 220 − Age (in years)

So if you are 40 years old, your APMHR is 180 beats/minute. A slightly more accurate method is to use the following equation:

$$APMHR = 214 - (0.8 \times Age)$$

So for a 40 year old;

APMHR = 214 − (0.8 × 40) = 214 − 32 = 182 beats/min.

This simply means that if you were to exercise the average 40 year old at maximum intensity, the pulse would increase steadily until a 'ceiling' rate of around 180 beats/min was attained. Continuing physical exertion beyond this point would not result in any further increase in heart rate.

How does this help us in determining training intensity?

Scientific studies have shown that the intensity of effort required for effective aerobic training is in the range of 65–85 per cent of the APMHR. For a 40 year old this would be a heart rate of about 120–156 beats/min.

This is a concept of the utmost importance. Exercising at too high an intensity will quickly lead to exhaustion, and it may be dangerous for older individuals who have been sedentary for a number of years. Conversely, too low an exercise intensity will not lead to any significant improvement in cardiorespiratory fitness. So there is clearly an optimal heart rate which will produce the required training effect — the Training Heart Rate (THR). You can find the upper and lower limits of your THR *range* from Table 7.4 which gives a minimum and maximum heart rate based on 65–85 per cent of the APMHR, together with the relevant 10-second count (see the later section 'How to take your pulse').

Thus, if you are 50 years old you can see that your APMHR is 174 beats/min, and this gives you a THR range of 113–148 beats/min (based on 65–85 per cent of APMHR). The 10-second count during exercise is 19–25 beats/min, depending upon the individual.

If you are 33 years old your APMHR is around 186 beats/min, with a THR range during exercise of 121–158 beat/min — between 20–26 beats per 10-second count.

As an approximation, exercise at 65–75 per cent of APMHR can be classified as 'modest' and should be the range to aim for if you are sedentary. Aerobic activity at 75–85 per cent of APMHR is 'vigorous' and is more appropriate for those who already have some basic fitness.

How to find your training heart rate (THR)

Table 7.4 provides an exercise training heart rate *range* only; it cannot tell you exactly what your THR should be. All one can say is that if you are 50 years old, your THR lies somewhere between 113 to 148 beats/min — a

Table 7.4 Exercise training heart rate (THR) ranges by age

		Target Heart Rate Range (beats/min)			
		Moderate		Vigorous	
AGE	**APMHR***	65 – 75%	(10 sec)	75 – 85%	(10 sec)
20	198	129–148	(21–25)	149–168	(25–28)
25	194	126–145	(21–24)	146–165	(24–27)
30	190	124–142	(20–24)	143–162	(24–27)
35	186	121–139	(20–23)	140–158	(23–26)
40	182	118–136	(20–23)	137–155	(23–26)
45	178	116–133	(19–22)	134–151	(22–25)
50	174	113–130	(19–22)	131–148	(22–25)
55	170	111–127	(18–21)	128–145	(21–24)
60	166	108–124	(18–21)	125–141	(23–23)
65	162	105–121	(17–20)	122–138	(20–23)
70	158	103–118	(17–20)	119–134	(20–23)

* APMHR = Age Predicted Maximum Heart Rate, based on APMHR = 214 − (0.8 × Age)
From this table you can find your THR range during exercise (select the age nearest to your own). If you are sedentary start in the 'moderate' intensity range (65–75 per cent) of APMHR. For a 50-year-old (male or female) this means that your heart rate during exercise should be 113–130 beats/min, or 19–22 beats over a 10-second count.
   If you already have a basic level of fitness you can move into the 'vigorous' THR range.

very broad range. The intensity of effort during physical activity is highly individual. Some people find that they can exercise quite comfortably at 80 per cent of their APMHR, whilst others need a much lower training intensity — closer to 65–70 per cent. This doesn't mean that those who exercise at a higher percentage of their APMHR are 'better' — it simply means that this is the level which suits them best. The aim is to increase your heart rate above the lower (65 per cent APMHR) threshold for your age — in this case 113 beats/min. Once you are at or above this you will be improving your health and your cardiorespiratory fitness. The point between 113 and 148 beats/min at which you feel most comfortable is a subjective evaluation which you should make for yourself.

   In general, aim for an intensity that you would subjectively rate as 'moderate' to 'hard'. A simple practical check is that when you are exercising you should be capable of holding a conversation of a few sentences. If you find it impossible to say more than a word or two, you are working too hard and should ease up. When you find the level that feels right for you, stop and check your pulse rate. By repeating this procedure a few times, you will find your exercise THR which will be somewhere in the THR range referred to earlier.

   As a final example, suppose that you are a sedentary 50 year old and have decided that brisk walking/jogging is to be your preferred form of activity. Referring to Table 7.4 you find that your THR range is 113–148 beats/min (19–25 per 10-second count). Armed with this information you start your programme by walking/jogging until you feel you are exercising comfortably at a moderate to hard intensity. At this point you would stop for a moment and check your pulse rate. Repeat this a few more times, and you should have an accurate figure for your exercise THR.

Using your exercise THR

By keeping your pulse rate around your exercise THR, you will ensure that the intensity of your chosen activity is between 65 and 85 per cent of your APMHR — the range required for cardiovascular and health benefits. Incidentally, you may be wondering whether there is any advantage at working above the 85 per cent APMHR threshold. The short answer is *no*. Athletes often work at much higher intensities, 90 per cent and more, but they are looking for relatively small additional improvements in performance — important if you want a gold medal, but not if you just want to stay healthy. In health terms there is no advantage in exercising above the 85 per cent upper limit shown in Table 7.4. You may, however, wish to extend the length of your exercise session to 45 minutes or even longer. There is no harm in this, provided you feel comfortable and since you will be burning more calories it may be beneficial if you are trying to lose weight.

We have discussed type, frequency, duration and intensity. To complete this section we need to address some practical questions.

How to take your pulse

Since you are using heart rate to measure exercise intensity, you obviously need to be able to take your pulse accurately — a procedure which requires a little practice. There are two places in which the pulse can be felt without difficulty — see Figure 7.1.

1. **The wrist**. Turn the left hand palm upwards, and with the fingertips of the right hand gently feel the pulse on the outer aspect of the wrist.
2. **The neck**. Feel the Adam's apple in the front of the neck. Move your fingers approximately 1–1.5 inches either side of this and you will feel the pulse. (Never compress both sides at once.)

Using whichever you find the easiest, count the number of beats over 10 seconds, and multiply by 6 to give you the number of beats per minute. If your 10-second pulse count is 27, your heart rate is 6 × 27 = 162 beats/min. Beyond 15 seconds the pulse slows rapidly, and so counting it over this time cannot be a reliable indicator of what it was during exercise proper.

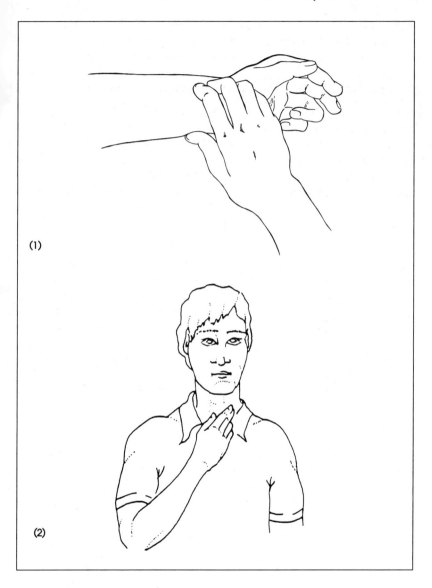

(1)

(2)

Figure 7.1 How to take your pulse

What if I have been sedentary for many years?

If you are starting exercise for the first time, or after a long sedentary period, you must start gently. I would recommend that you start with a programme of brisk walking on the flat, and look for an exercise THR around the 65 per cent APMHR threshold. After a few weeks you will be much fitter, and in order to get your pulse rate into the training range, you will probably have to start some walking up a gentle incline. With continuing improvements in fitness, you will be able to move into a walking/jogging programme, and try other forms of exercise if you wish.

Should my THR vary with different types of exercise?

Generally speaking, your exercise heart rate should be the same, whatever type of exercise you are involved in. The heart does not discriminate between different types of exercise — it simply responds to the increased metabolic load placed upon it. One exception is swimming, where because of the horizontal position of the heart, your THR should be 10–12 beats lower than it would be for upright exercise.

What happens to my THR as I become fitter?

One of the advantages of using the THR approach is that it automatically accounts for improvement. As you become fitter, your cardiovascular system undergoes a number of adaptations, including a reduction in heart rate for any given level of work. If you take your pulse first thing in the morning, you will find that it becomes slower as you become fitter. An average pulse rate at rest is about 70 beats/min, but a top-class athlete may have a rate as low as 35–40 beats/min. The reason for this is that the heart has become so efficient that it can pump the same volume of blood as an ordinary (untrained) heart, in only about half the number of beats. You may think that as you become fitter your THR will be easier to achieve, but paradoxically because your heart is more efficient (can accomplish the same work in fewer beats), you actually have to work harder to achieve the same THR.

Let's suppose, for example, that you complete a 2.5 mile jog/walk in 30 minutes with a THR of 130 beats/min. After a few weeks (assuming that you continue to take 30 minutes to complete the distance), you would find that your heart rate during exercise is well below your THR — perhaps only around 115 beats/min. This is obviously because you are much fitter, and your heart is able to accomplish the same amount of work, with significantly fewer contractions. If you continued to cover the same distance in the same time, you would not improve because the exercise is not of sufficient intensity for you to reach your THR. By increasing your effort to achieve your THR, you will be working at a higher intensity and, consequently, the *time* taken for you to complete the distance will fall accordingly. So the THR adjusts automatically to your increased cardio-respiratory capacity.

The essential elements of exercise are summarized as follows:

```
KEY NOTE — A SUMMARY OF EXERCISE

T = Type — The exercise must be regular, rhythmical and
    utilize major muscle groups. Examples are given in
    Group A of Table 7.3.
F = Frequency — Three or four times per week.
D = Duration — 20 to 30 minutes per session.
I = Intensity — Find your THR range for your age from Table
    7.4. To find your specific THR, exercise at an intensity
    which you would regard as moderate to hard. When
    you find the exercise level at which you feel comfor-
    table, find the heart rate which corresponds to it. This is
    your THR.
```

Warming up and cooling down

Stretching the limbs and the muscles prior to exercising is good practice, and will reduce the likelihood of muscular strains during the exercise session proper. Always start your exercise very gradually, never launch suddenly into a maximum effort. You wouldn't jump into a nice new Ferrari on a cold winter's morning and put your foot flat on the accelerator. Treat your body with the respect it deserves and increase the intensity gradually.

Cooling down is equally important. Never stop vigorous exercise suddenly — take a few minutes to cool down to allow your system to return to normal. So if you have been running for 20 to 30 minutes, walk for a further two or three more minutes to aid recovery. The reason is that during hard physical exertion there is tremendous pooling of blood in the muscles of the limbs, and if you suddenly stop you may well feel dizzy, or faint. This is due to a temporary drop in blood pressure, which can be made even worse if you walk straight into a hot shower. The cool down period greatly facilitates movement of blood back to the heart, thus helping to avoid any sudden drop in blood pressure.

Always take time to cool down properly.

When to exercise

This is very much a matter of personal preference, and will depend upon work and family commitments as well as the availability of the necessary facilities where required, eg a swimming pool or tennis court. Some people may be concerned about press reports suggesting that early morning exercise may be more hazardous than evening sessions. It is quite true that between the hours of 6 am and 10 am you are more likely to suffer a heart attack or stroke than in the late evening. But there is no evidence that exercise is more hazardous in the morning than at other times. Indeed, whilst it is true that exercise can precipitate a heart attack in a susceptible individual, in general sudden death due to a disturbance in heart rhythm or an acute heart attack is 60 per cent less likely in people who exercise regularly than in couch potatoes and 'weekend warriors'.

Whatever time of day you choose, always warm up gradually and cool down properly. Never exercise on a full stomach or after consuming alcohol, and make sure you stick to your training heart rate (THR). Finally, listen to what your body is telling you — if it doesn't feel right, *don't do it*.

Monitoring your progress

It's a good idea to keep an exercise diary, in which you record what sort of exercise you did and how well you feel the exercise session went. This provides you with a psychological incentive to persist with the programme, and also a useful record to look back on. Remember that the most important thing about exercise is **consistency**.

Exercising regularly is certainly going to make you feel and look better, but to give you a more objective measure of your improving physical condition, I would suggest that you repeat the baseline fitness test (either the 1.5 mile time or the 12 minute distance) at 4, 8 and 12 weeks respectively.

A note about exercise electrocardiography (ECG)

Many executives nowadays undergo regular health screening, usually as part of a company health package which includes private health insurance. One of the tests normally employed by the screening organization is a resting 12-lead electrocardiogram (ECG). Essentially, this is recording of the electrical activity of the heart, and in certain circumstances eg an acute heart attack, the ECG will show a specific diagnostic pattern. The problem is that as a screening tool in an apparently healthy population, the resting ECG has serious limitations. Most patients with angina, for example, will have a normal resting ECG. Whilst an abnormal resting ECG may indicate the presence of underlying heart disease, a normal resting ECG can neither confirm nor exclude the presence of coronary disease.

A much more useful test is the Exercise Electrocardiogram (or Exercise Stress Test). Vigorous exercise in patients with coronary artery disease produces changes in the electrocardiogram. The test is usually performed on a treadmill or a stationary bicycle, with the subject connected to an electrocardiogram, and with blood pressure monitored carefully throughout. This allows a continuous ECG tracing to be obtained at each level of exertion. Some screening organizations will also include measurement of maximum oxygen consumption (VO$_2$Max) as a routine procedure, but this requires expensive technology, as well as experienced laboratory personnel.

The point about the exercise test is that because it places the heart under load, underlying abnormalities of the heart muscle or coronary arteries which are not apparent at rest, may be revealed during physical exertion. Some people have quite extensive coronary disease but have no symptoms — the medical term for which is *silent ischaemia,* and because they are pain free, they may be at risk of a heart attack or sudden death. In expert hands, the exercise electrocardiogram can be a powerful diagnostic instrument for identifying this high-risk group.

Not everyone needs to have an exercise test prior to embarking upon a regular exercise programme. However, if you are aged 40 years and over, with two or more conventional coronary risk factors, eg a strong family history of heart disease or high blood cholesterol, it's well worth considering. This is, in fact, the recommendation of the American Heart Association. The problem is that access to high quality exercise stress testing facilities in the UK is very limited, and you will almost certainly have to pay for the test privately.

Key note — Some final do's and don'ts

DON'T:

- ignore symptoms during exercise. If you experience chest pain, dizziness, unusual breathlessness or feel unwell, stop immediately and talk to your doctor.
- be over-ambitious in your exercise programme. Progress is not smooth — there are always good days and bad ones. If the exercise really doesn't feel right, then leave it and go home. The key word is consistency — three or four exercise sessions per week.
- be afraid to vary your exercise programme. If you like to run, then why not do some swimming or cycling as well? Trying different types of exercise adds some interest to your routine, and it's useful to have both an indoor and an outdoor activity so that you can continue exercising even in severe weather.
- exercise after meals, alcohol, or on an empty stomach. You should avoid exercising for two to three hours after eating a heavy meal and you should reserve the glass of beer for after the workout, **not** before it. Conversely, exercising on an empty stomach can make you feel

weak and light headed, due to a low blood sugar. If you're an early morning exerciser, have some cereal or a roll and some orange juice before you start.

DO:

- use the correct equipment and clothing. A good quality tracksuit is an excellent investment and nowadays you'll be spoilt for choice. Seek the advice of a good quality sports shop for advice concerning exercise bicycles, rowing machines and running shoes etc.

- be careful of vigorous physical activity in hot weather. Jogging/running or cycling on a hot day can produce huge fluid losses — up to two or three litres an hour. It's virtually impossible to replace this sort of fluid on the move, so you invariably become water depleted. The body is able to compensate to some extent, but if you continue you run the risk of developing heat cramps, heat exhaustion or — most seriously of all — heatstroke. If you want to exercise in warm weather, the key points to avoiding the consequences of dehydration are as follows:

  - Choose the cooler times of the day — early morning or evening.
  - Always prehydrate by drinking water 15–20 minutes before starting.
  - Drink regularly — about 1 cup of cold water every 20 minutes.
  - **Don't** assume that because you're not thirsty, you don't need the fluid. Thirst is a poor indicator of your fluid requirements.
  - Wear cool clothing, and if you have access to cold water sponges — use them!
  - Weigh yourself before and after exercising. More than 5 per cent weight loss means that you are water depleted.

- begin your exercise gradually — always warm up with a few stretching exercises, and begin the exercise session proper at a low intensity, building up gradually over a few minutes. Warming down is equally important.

- **something!** Even if you find it difficult to motivate yourself to jog, cycle or swim, at least try brisk walking. It really is an excellent exercise and one that you can easily share with family and friends. You don't have to be a marathon runner or a 'fitness fanatic' to benefit from exercise. On the contrary, there is convincing scientific evidence to suggest that important health benefits accrue from quite modest levels of activity.

SO WHY EXERCISE?

If you have read through this section carefully, you should have become convinced of the power of exercise. If you have, then I have achieved my aim. The evidence is compelling, the goals are achievable and well worth achieving. Dr Stephen Blair from the Aerobics Institute in Dallas sums it up admirably:

> It is clear that moderate levels of fitness offer considerable health benefits. The key is moving from the unfit category — some 30 to 40 million people in this country — to the moderately fit category. By beginning programmes of moderate, regular exercise — half an hour each day, three times a week — anyone can join this group, and markedly lower their death rates from all-cause mortality, cancer, and cardiovascular disease.

Chapter 8

SENSIBLE DRINKING

Do you enjoy a drink? There is absolutely no reason why you shouldn't. After all, the pleasurable effects of alcohol have been known for thousands of years and its consumption (and presumably abuse) has been a major feature in the cultures of our ancestors and an integral part of our social and religious traditions. For those of us who enjoy a drink — and that includes the author — the challenge is to find a healthy and enjoyable drinking pattern that allows us to enjoy the positive benefits, whilst avoiding the potentially harmful effects. Most of us manage to achieve this reasonably well, but an increasing number of us are consuming far too much alcohol, and as a society we are paying an increasingly heavy price for the privilege. Alcohol is our most popular drug, but it is also our most dangerous one.

What is alcohol?

Alcohol is a drug and as with any other drug, it has certain side-effects and is potentially addictive. In fact, alcohol can create both a physical and a psychological dependence and has a well defined (and sometimes dramatic) withdrawal syndrome. In large enough doses, it can cause damage to virtually every organ in the body.

The secret is to use the correct dosage to achieve the desired effect, whilst avoiding the undesirable effects of overdosage.

In common with other drugs such as barbiturates, regular use of alcohol gives rise to an increased *tolerance*, so that over time the drinker needs to drink gradually more to obtain the same effect. This tolerance is a manifestation of the body's adaptation to alcohol, and is accompanied by specific biochemical changes in the liver and other body organs.

Who develops alcohol related problems?

It is a very common misconception that there are two types of drinker; those who drink 'socially' or 'normally' and those who are alcoholics. The popular image of the alcoholic is someone who is dirty, unkempt, drunk most of the time and who sleeps under bridges in cardboard boxes or on park benches. There are indeed many unfortunate individuals who do live this way and who at the same time have serious alcohol dependency problems. But the vast majority of individuals with drink problems are in regular gainful employment — a fact which clearly has enormous implications for industry. Some occupations appear to have a much higher incidence of alcohol-related problems than others. As might be expected, publicans have by far the highest rate of alcoholic liver disease and therefore the highest death rates from cirrhosis, but alcohol dependency is a problem which can afflict anyone, irrespective of income, social class, occupation, sex or age. Moreover, there is growing concern about the scale of the problem in young people, particularly young women. Recent evidence suggests that anyone who drinks heavily enough for a sufficient period of time can become alcohol dependent. But there is also evidence that some of us may be more at risk than others.

A person who uses alcohol primarily for its drug effects, eg to cope with financial worries or domestic problems, may be particularly vulnerable to addiction. We also know that an individual whose friends drink heavily or whose leisure activities are mainly focused around drinking, is at increased risk. There may be a genetic factor involved too; the children of alcoholics, even when they are not brought up by their biological parents, are more likely to develop alcohol addiction than the children of non-alcoholics. The debate about whether alcohol addiction is a disease, or whether it is merely a manifestation of an underlying personality disorder, has continued for many years. It is still not known for certain whether a specific alcoholic personality exists, but it is clear that alcoholics do develop certain personality characteristics as a *result* of alcohol dependence. These include emotional instability, a low tolerance to stress, feelings of insecurity, isolation and depression (all of which can also occur in people who are not addicted to alcohol).

What is an alcoholic?

Someone once said that an alcoholic can be defined as an individual who drinks more than his doctor. However, the term 'alcoholic' has never been adequately defined and is potentially misleading. It is part of the mistaken view that there are only two classes of drinkers — normal drinkers (like you and me) and alcoholics (someone else). Moreover, alcoholics are thought of as individuals with a condition which is entirely self inflicted, and that therefore carries a strong social stigma. For these reasons, the term 'dependent drinker' is preferred.

To understand the nature of alcohol addiction, it is essential to realize that there is no clear distinction between the social drinker and the heavy drinker, between the heavy drinker and the problem drinker, or between the problem drinker and the dependent drinker. These terms are merely convenient points of description along a continuum of alcohol consumption and its related problems (Figure 8.1).

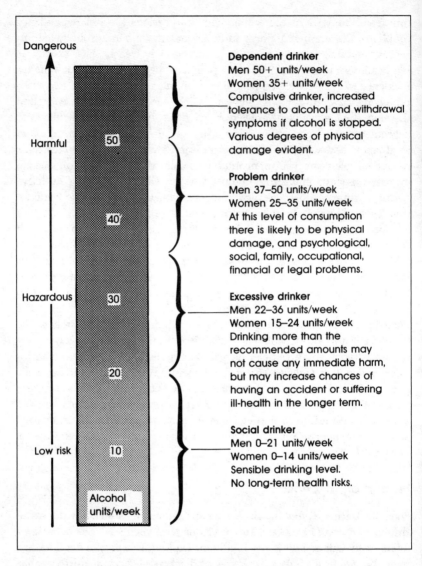

Figure 8.1   Alcohol problems related to consumption

So what is safe alcohol consumption?

One of the difficulties in suggesting safe levels of alcohol consumption for both men and women, is that individuals vary enormously. There is now a general consensus on safe levels of consumption, but you must bear in mind that the more you drink, the more likely you are to suffer from alcohol related problems.

In order to make alcohol consumption more easily quantifiable, the concept of the standard 'unit' has been introduced. A standard unit will contain roughly one half ounce (or 8–10 grammes) of pure ethyl alcohol.

The basic rule is:

One standard unit = one half pint of beer
                        one single measure of spirit
                        one glass of wine
                        one measure of vermouth, sherry etc.

So if you drink two pints of beer and one gin and tonic, you will have consumed a total of five units. If you do this seven nights a week, your weekly consumption will be 35 units.

Using the guidelines given in Table 8.1, you can quite easily estimate your daily and weekly consumption. Sensible limits of drinking are as follows:

Men — not more than 21 units a week including two or three days without any alcohol.
Women — not more than 14 units a week including two or three days without any alcohol.

Drinking at this level, for both men and women, does not appear to be associated with any long-term health hazards.

Incidentally, the reason why the limit for women is lower than for men, is purely physiological. In the first place, women tend to weigh less than men, so that a given amount of alcohol will result in a much higher blood alcohol concentration in the average woman, compared with the average man. The other reason is that women, especially younger women, have a lower proportion of their total body weight in the form of water; for men it is around 60 per cent, but for women 50 per cent. Therefore, since the body fluid is proportionally less in women, the alcohol concentration tends to be higher for any given amount of alcohol consumed. Thus, not only do women reach a higher blood alcohol concentration (BAC) for the same amount of drink, they also reach it sooner than do men. The converse of this is that women actually eliminate alcohol faster than men — their alcohol metabolism is more efficient. So, although women get drunk more quickly, they also sober up more quickly too.

These physiological differences need to be taken into account when considering blood levels of alcohol (see later).

WHAT HAPPENS WHEN WE DRINK?

When we drink, alcohol passes virtually unchanged from the mouth into the stomach; about 20 per cent is immediately absorbed into the bloodstream through the stomach wall; the remaining 80 per cent passes

Table 8.1 Alcohol content of various drinks in units.
Alcohol strength shown in ( ) is the percentage of alcohol by volume (the figure given on most wine labels) and should not be confused with 'proof' levels.

Drink	Amount	Units
Beer and lager		
Ordinary strength bitter or draught lager (3–4%)	1 pint	2
	½ pint	1
Special draught bitter (5%)	1 pint	3
	½ pint	1½
Strong lager (eg Carlsberg Special: 7%)	1 can	4
Cider		
Ordinary strength cider (4–5%)	1 pint	3
	½ pint	1½
Strong cider (eg Strongbow: 5%)	1 can	3
Spirits eg whisky, rum, gin, vodka etc.		
1 pub measure of spirits (38%)	⅙ gill	1
1 small home measure of spirits (38%)	¼ gill	1½
1 bottle of spirits (38%)	1 bottle	30
Wine and champagne		
Low strength table wine (8%)	1 glass	1
	1 bottle	6
Ordinary strength table wine (12%)	1 glass	1½
	1 bottle	9
Strong table wine (16%)	1 glass	2
Champagne or other sparkling wine (12%)	1 glass	1½
	1 bottle	9
Sherry and fortified wine eg port, vermouth etc		
Sherry (16%)	1 glass	1
	1 bottle	13
Vermouth (eg Martini, Cinzano: 15%)	1 glass	1
	1 bottle	11
Port (20%)	1 glass	1
	1 bottle	15

into the small gut where it is absorbed into the bloodstream. The alcohol then passes to the liver where it is broken down into waste products. After the liver has removed some of the alcohol, the remainder passes around the body where it can affect virtually every organ with which it comes into contact.

The amount of alcohol in the bloodstream at any one time depends upon a number of factors:

- **The amount of alcohol which has been drunk:** Obviously the more you drink, the higher the blood levels of alcohol.

- **The weight of the drinker**: The same amount of alcohol has a greater effect on a light person than a heavy one. This is obviously because the concentration of alcohol in the bloodstream is greater in a smaller person.
- **The sex of the drinker**: For reasons given earlier, a given amount of alcohol has a greater effect on a woman than on a man.
- **Eating food**: The presence of food in the stomach tends to slow down the rate of absorption of alcohol into the bloodstream. This is why drinking on an empty stomach is not a good thing.
- **Speed of drinking**: Obviously, the faster the alcohol is taken the more rapidly the blood level of alcohol will rise.

Blood Alcohol Concentration (BAC)

Blood alcohol concentration (BAC) is measured in milligrammes of alcohol per 100 millilitres of blood (mg/100mls). As the level of alcohol in the blood rises, it begins to exert a depressant effect on the brain, producing disturbances in thought, physical co-ordination, memory, judgement and sensation. Even relatively small amounts of alcohol can exert a negative impact on these brain functions which is why, after only a few drinks, people begin to slur their speech and stagger and driving may become dangerous.

You may be surprised that alcohol is a depressant; the common perception is that it is a stimulant. The explanation is to be found in the way in which alcohol affects brain function. Alcohol tends to affect what are known as the 'higher centres', allowing the functions of the lower brain — centres which are responsible for more primitive impulses and emotions — to express themselves. This produces a lack of control, aggression and lack of inhibition which may give the impression that alcohol is having a stimulating effect.

As the level of blood alcohol rises, the differing effects on behaviour can be observed (see Table 8.2).

How quickly is alcohol removed from the bloodstream?

One unit of alcohol increases the blood alcohol level within the first hour by about 15 mg per 100 mls in a man, and by around 20 mg per 100 mls in a woman. In a healthy person, alcohol is removed from the body by the liver at a rate of about 15 mg per 100 mls per hour.

This would mean that if you went to bed at midnight with a blood alcohol level of 200 mg/100 mls (having drunk, say, seven pints of beer) and then you drive to work at seven o'clock the next morning, you are likely to have a blood alcohol level well over the legal limit — 80 mg/100 mls. This is because in the seven hour period, your body will have removed about 105 mg/100 mls of alcohol, leaving you with as much as 95 mg/100 mls still in your bloodstream. Moreover, for the first few hours of your

Table 8.2   Blood alcohol concentration: effects and consequences

BAC (mg/100ml)%	Effects and consequences
30	No obvious outward effects, but increased likelihood of an accident.
50	Relaxed and happy, but less vigilant, poorer judgement and more accident prone.
80	Confident, talkative, more emotional and less inhibited. Slower reaction times and twice as likely to have a road accident. Loss of driving licence if caught.
120	Much less inhibited, over-confident, more impulsive as intermediate centres express themselves. Five times more likely to have a road accident.
150	Loss of self-control, slurred speech, impaired thinking and reasoning more evident. Aggressive and over-emotional. Ten times more likely to have a road accident.
200	Slurred speech, staggering, memory loss, belligerent or depressed and self-pitying. Over twenty times more likely to have a road accident.
300	Extremely drunk, difficult to remain upright, speech very difficult. Consciousness now threatened.
400	Oblivion, sleep, lower centres of brain seriously threatened. Dangerous situation.
500	Lower centres controlling breathing and heart rate now affected. Death possible.
600	DEATH PROBABLE

working day, you are much more likely to be involved in an accident and your overall judgement would be poorer than normal. It would be well after noon before the residual alcohol is finally removed from your bloodstream.

WHAT DAMAGE DOES ALCOHOL DO TO THE BODY?

There is scarcely any organ or system in the body which is not affected by long, heavy alcohol intake. Although the body may have a remarkable capacity to recover from the acute effects of alcohol, with high intake over a sufficiently long period of time, damage is progressive and may become irreversible. Most of us are aware of the potential damage done to the liver, and those individuals who have had a serious alcohol dependency for more than ten years or so have about a 10 per cent change of dying from cirrhosis. In advanced cases, an individual may get drunk on relatively small amounts of alcohol because the damage to the liver is such that most of the alcohol passes through without being removed from the blood. But remember, alcohol can have a direct effect on almost every organ, including the brain, the heart and the nervous system. It is also often associated with malnutrition.

Women and liver disease

Heavy alcohol consumption can cause liver damage in both men and women, but it does appear that women have a greater chance of developing liver disease than men drinking the same amount. Precisely why this should be the case is not known for certain, although there is some evidence that it is before the menopause that women are more in danger, and that it may therefore have something to do with the female sex hormones. Women may also be more susceptible to brain damage, certain cancers of the head and neck, and ulcers. Whatever the reasons, we can be certain that the death rate in female excessive drinkers is significantly higher than in men. Everybody who drinks too much is risking shortening their lifespan but, for women, these risks appear to be even greater than for their male counterparts.

Alcohol and cancer

Any form of alcohol intake in large amounts increases the risk of cancer, particularly in smokers. Heavy drinkers have a significantly greater risk of developing cancer of the mouth, the throat, and the gullet. Liver cancer, as a major complication of cirrhosis is not uncommon, and recent evidence would suggest that heavy drinkers may be as much as three times more likely to develop cancer of the pancreas.

Alcohol and pregnancy

Excessive consumption of alcohol in pregnancy can permanently damage the unborn child. This damage is usually manifest in terms of low birth rate, abnormal growth, mental retardation and a variety of other abnormalities including heart, kidney and skeletal defects. This combination of abnormalities is sometimes referred to as *foetal alcohol syndrome.*

Women who drink heavily have about a two-fold increase in the risk of spontaneous abortion. There is some evidence that even very small amounts of alcohol during pregnancy may have a detrimental effect upon the developing child. For this reason, and until further research clarifies the situation, it is probably sensible for women who are pregnant or plan to become pregnant, to abstain from alcohol or at least to restrict their consumption to an occasional drink, especially in the first three months of pregnancy.

Alcohol and the heart

Alcohol has a direct effect on the heart, reducing the strength of the heartbeat and sometimes causing disturbances in the rhythm of the heart.

Heavy and continued alcohol consumption may cause specific disease of the heart muscle, leading to heart failure. High alcohol intake is also an important and common contributor to raised blood pressure, which usually reverts to normal on cessation of alcohol. As noted earlier (see page 56), regular moderate alcohol consumption may have some cardioprotective effect on the heart, although the word 'moderate' in this context is critical!

The effects of malnutrition

Alcohol abuse is often associated with malnutrition. This is because the alcohol-dependent individual often has reduced food intake, impaired digestion and absorption of food, and inadequate intake of essential vitamins. Vitamin deficiencies can lead to serious nerve and brain damage, including dementia.

Obesity and alcohol

One gin and tonic contains approximately 140 calories (about the same as a large ice-cream) and one pint of beer has more than twice as many calories as this (see page 189). Clearly, therefore, alcohol is a very efficient producer of calories, but it does not supply vitamins, proteins or other necessary nutrients. In other words it is nothing other than empty calories. This is why heavy drinkers may become very fat, and yet be undernourished at the same time. Not everyone who drinks heavily becomes fat, and the effects of alcohol on weight and nutrition are very complicated. Nevertheless, if you are trying to lose weight, then drinking huge amounts of unwanted calories is hardly likely to help. Even low-sugar diet beers, while they may have less sugar, are usually rich in calories because they often have more alcohol and thus more calories.

SELF-ASSESSMENT

There are **two** very simple components of the self-assessment for alcohol consumption.

1. Calculate the number of units of alcohol you drink in an average week. To do this, simply estimate your consumption for each of the last seven days, and add up the total in units. Use the conversion table on page 142 to help you.
2. Ask yourself the following *yes* or *no* questions:
   — Have you ever decided to stop drinking for a week or so, but only lasted for a couple of days?
   — Have people annoyed you by criticizing your drinking?
   — Have you ever switched from one kind of drink to another in the hope that this would keep you from getting drunk?
   — Have you ever had a drink in the morning during the past year to steady your nerves?

— Do you envy people who can drink without getting into trouble?
— Have you had problems connected with drinking during the past year?
— Has your drinking caused trouble at home?
— Have you ever felt bad or guilty about your drinking?
— Do you tell yourself that you can stop drinking any time you want to, even though you keep getting drunk when you don't mean to?
— Have you missed any days from your work because of your drinking?
— Do you have loss of memory following a drinking bout?
— Have you ever felt that your life would be better if you did not drink?

INTERPRETATION OF RESULTS

1. **Consumption of alcohol per week**
   Men: If your grand total for the week is more than 35 units, **you are drinking too much**. Between 21 and 34 units means that you should consider cutting down a little.
   Women: If your grand total for the week is more than 20 units, **you are drinking too much**. If between 14 and 19 units, you should consider cutting down.
   Please bear in mind, however, that these are only guidelines to safe drinking. The simple fact is that the more you drink, the more likely you are to suffer from the adverse effects of drinking.
2. **Questionnaire results**
   If you have answered 'yes' to four or more of the twelve questions, the probability is that you already have a significant problem or you are developing one. If you answered 'yes' to *any* of the questions, then this may well indicate that you are beginning to develop alcohol problems, and should seriously consider ways of cutting down. The following section will help you to achieve this.

ACTION PLAN

Let's be clear, the aim of this section is not to coerce you into giving up alcohol. It's simply meant to help you to cut down on your drinking, or to exert a much greater level of control. You may have been under the impression that the only solution to an alcohol problem is to give up drinking completely, but this is not true. There is very good evidence that most problem drinkers can reduce their consumption to amounts which no longer do them harm.

However, if you have already received treatment for alcohol related problems, or you have already suffered permanent damage from excessive

excessive drinking, then complete abstinence is probably the only safe course of action for you. Alcohol dependency is a serious and complex problem, and dealing with it is clearly well outside the scope of this book.

There are three major components to the Action Plan:

1. Monitoring and self-awareness — your drinking diary.
2. Your drinking 'rules'.
3. Helpful hints to reduce your alcohol consumption.

MONITORING AND SELF-AWARENESS — YOUR DRINKING DIARY

Clearly, before you can break a habit completely you have to be aware of it. Sometimes drinking behaviour is habitual, and you may not be fully aware of the pattern of your drinking or of the circumstances in which you are likely to drink to excess. Keeping a drinking diary will give you detailed information about your drinking habits, the circumstances in which you are likely to drink more than you would wish etc. From this information you will be able to derive some drinking 'rules', (see page 150) that will help you to avoid situations where you may be likely to drink to excess. An example of a typical weekly drinking diary is given in Figure 8.2. You should try to keep an accurate diary for the next **four weeks.**

After this initial period, you need not record the details of your daily drinking, but **do** record the number of units each day, so that you can calculate your weekly total. You can then monitor your weekly alcohol consumption over the next twelve weeks. This will give you added incentive to make sure that the target you have set for yourself is achieved during that time.

YOUR DRINKING 'RULES'

When you have been monitoring your drinking habits for four weeks, a pattern will begin to emerge and you will begin to achieve a much better understanding of the circumstances in which you tend to drink to excess. You will then be able to draw up your own drinking 'rules'. Simply look at the main circumstances in which you tend to drink to excess, and adopt rules accordingly. An example of some drinking 'rules' for a particular individual are given below in Figure 8.3.

You will note that the first rule states that you will not drink more than a certain number of units per day and a specific total for the week. This is important, and whatever your other drinking rules should be, you must have a daily cut-off point for your drinking in terms of a number of units.

Drinking Diary

Day	Time	Hours spent	Place	Who with	Other activities	Money spent	Consequences (if any)	Units

Total for week

Figure 8.2 A drinking diary

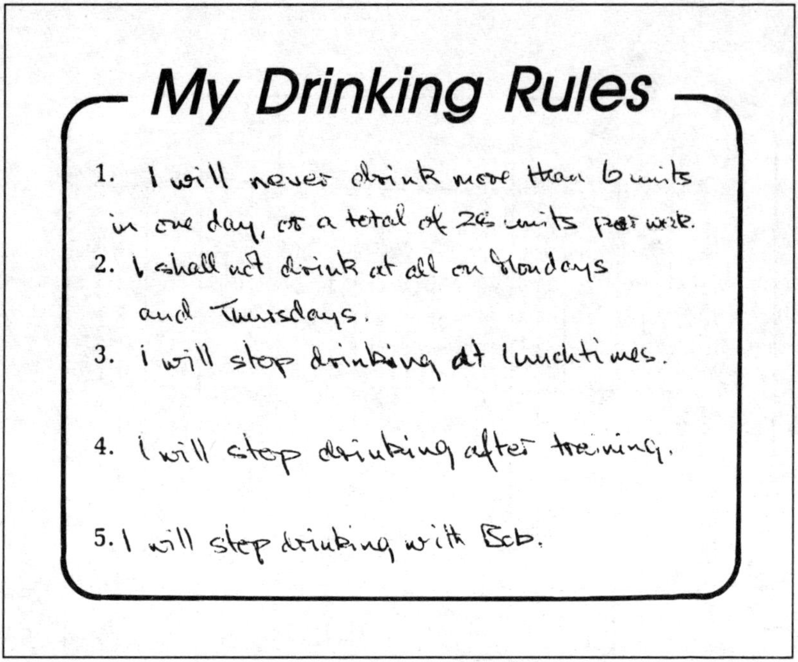

My Drinking Rules

1. I will never drink more than 6 units in one day, or a total of 26 units per week.
2. I shall not drink at all on Mondays and Tuesdays.
3. i will stop drinking at lunchtimes.
4. I will stop drinking after training.
5. I will stop drinking with Bob.

Figure 8.3   Your drinking rules

The other rather obvious point is that your cut-off **must** represent a significant reduction in your current drinking habits.

If you are male, I would recommend that your cut-off point is around four to six units per day.

If you are a woman, I would recommend that your cut-off point is between three to five units per day.

I don't mean that you should drink this amount every day without fail — it's not a prescription. Indeed, the second rule in the example says that you will have two or three days a week when you abstain. *Whatever else your own rules may contain, one and two should always be included.*

Setting realistic targets

The recommended number of units per week is 21 for men and 14 for women, and (strictly speaking) this is what you should aim for. However, if you are working through this section in detail, you are obviously drinking considerably more than this, and reducing to the recommended levels immediately may be unrealistic. Your drinking rules actually imply slightly different limits which will be easier to achieve. The cut-off if you are a male is 4–6 units per day, but we shall also assume that you will have at least two alcohol free days each week. This means that your target weekly consumption is 20–30 units.

For a woman the target consumption is 3–5 units per day, or 15–25 units per week (assuming two alcohol-free days).

Some helpful hints on reducing your alcohol consumption

Here are some points which will help you to enjoy alcohol, whilst avoiding any of the potential negative effects. Try to bear these in mind over the following twelve weeks as you monitor your alcohol consumption and do your best to stick to your drinking 'rules'.

1. Sip your drink slowly and drink smaller measures. Don't try to keep up with other drinkers. Your own sensible drinking limits may be substantially lower than theirs.
2. Avoid drinking alone.
3. Put your glass down between sips. If the drink is in your hand, it's going to end up in your stomach a lot quicker!
4. Choose low alcohol drinks occasionally, and alternate them with standard alcoholic drinks.
5. Don't drink beer and spirits together. If you do, you will take in alcohol very much faster.
6. If you drink spirits, dilute them. The longer the drink, the slower the rate of alcohol ingestion.
7. Use 'spacers' rather than 'chasers'. A spacer is a non-alcoholic drink which you take in between alcoholic ones — this enables you to space your alcohol consumption over a much longer period of time. In this way, you are obviously slowing down your rate of alcohol consumption. A chaser could equally well be a non-alcoholic beer.
8. Try not to use alcohol as a reward. For many people, a stiff gin and tonic at the end of the day is almost a reflex action, and you should do everything possible to break this habit.
9. Ask yourself occasionally why you decide to have a drink. It may help you to decide not to.
10. Working out how much alcohol costs you every month may provide an additional stimulus to cut down. Deciding that you could buy something much more useful with the cash you have saved, may give added incentive to cut down.
11. Pace yourself. Try to decide beforehand how many units of alcohol you intend to consume, and over what period of time you intend to consume them. Try to answer these questions *before* you start drinking. You may decide to set a specific period of time (for example 8 till 10.30 pm) and agree to drink 6 units (3 pints of beer) during that period of time. There is, of course, no reason why you should not add other (non-alcoholic) drinks during this two and a half hour period.

Key note — action plan summary

- Start to document your drinking habits in your drinking diary. After a period of some three to four weeks you will have enough information about your drinking habits to be able to set out your own set of drinking rules. These may change over time, but rules one and two will remain constant.
- After the first four weeks, you need not keep a detailed diary (unless you wish to), but you should record your daily alcohol consumption in units. This will allow you to calculate your weekly total and monitor your reduced consumption over a 12 week period.
- You should reduce your weekly consumption to no more than 30 units (male) or 25 units (female). But remember the recommended 'safe' drinking limits are below this.

As you work through the 12 week period, you will find the hints given above helpful in reducing your alcohol consumption to a level where it will no longer pose a threat to you or your family.

Remember: The aim is for you to *enjoy* your drinking, not to be completely abstinent.

Let's finish off this section with one or two questions and answers about alcohol.

Questions and answers about alcohol

1. **Is drinking beer less harmful than drinking spirits?** No. It's the *amount* of alcohol (in units) which is the important thing. So if you drink one half pint of beer or one measure of spirits, the actual alcohol content is the same.
2. **Does alcohol help to keep you warm on a cold day?** No. Because alcohol dilates the blood vessels in the skin and increases the pulse rate, body heat is actually lost and the temperature will fall. A St Bernard dog with a small barrel of brandy around his neck may be a welcome sight, but he isn't going to do your body temperature much good.
3. **Can alcohol help to prevent heart disease?** There is some recent evidence that regular, moderate consumption of alcohol may help to

prevent heart disease. Set against this, we have to be aware that in large enough doses alcohol may have a direct toxic effect on the heart muscle, and produce a specific type of alcohol-related heart disease. Heavy alcohol consumption is also a major risk factor for stroke. The message is **moderation**. Heavy alcohol consumption is almost always harmful.

4. **Does alcohol cause impairment of the sex drive?** Men who are heavy drinkers have more sexual problems than men who are not. To paraphrase Shakespeare, 'Alcohol increases the desire but ruins the performance'. What is less well known are the longer-term side effects. Evidence shows that heavy drinking reduces the level of sex hormones in the blood, in both men and in women. Prolonged heavy drinking may have a direct effect on the ovaries and the testes, but may also damage certain parts of the brain producing a marked reduction in sex drive. Of course some men and women drink heavily because of sexual difficulties, and in this case drinking is only likely to make matters worse. In other words, sexual problems may be both a cause *and* a result of heavy drinking.

5. **Can alcohol help to control anxiety and depression?** Alcohol is a depressant drug, which has some tranquillizing properties. However, heavy drinking makes many people anxious and tense, although this may not be obvious to them because they may feel a calming effect whilst actually drinking. Suicide is about 60 times more common among alcohol abusers than it is generally. Alcohol is not, therefore, a safe or recommended means by which to control either anxiety or depression.

6. **Doesn't the fact that I never touch spirits mean that I am at a lower risk?** No. A lot of drinkers have consoled themselves with this self-deluding assurance.

Key note

The only thing which determines how intoxicated, addicted or ill you become after drinking is how much alcohol you drink. Myths about mixing drinks, or drinking only beer or wine, are self-deluding rationalizations. All that matters is the number of alcohol units. So far as your liver is concerned, a drink is a drink is a drink.

Chapter 9

STRESS AND INSOMNIA

Ask any group of adults today what they would consider to be the major health hazards of modern living, and the majority would use the word 'stress' at some point in their reply. There is a widespread perception that stress is a major contributor to many forms of illness and that stress-related problems are on the increase. There is also a view that stress is something 'out there' which happens to us, and over which we can have very little control. Unlike smoking or eating too much, we can (at last) blame some-one else — usually the Government, the airline, the boss or British Rail.

Being under pressure of some kind is a normal and necessary part of everyday living. We encounter it in the hustle-bustle environment and in social situations; we have deadlines to meet and meetings to attend; we have to drive on crowded roads, travel in crowded buses, trains and planes; we have normal worries about money and about our families; and nowadays we may even worry about worrying because we are told incessantly that stress will damage our health.

The stress 'industry' has thrived on the widespread fear that stress can damage people and organizations, and therefore has important economic as well as medical consequences. Not surprisingly, the word stress — rather like cholesterol — has a very negative press. How often do you hear of the stress epidemic and how many billions of pounds it's now costing British industry?

This is a curious phenomenon, given that the word itself is not amenable to definition, and there is no absolutely reliable method of measuring it. It's also interesting that even though we cannot define it, we all feel absolutely confident that we know what it is. But do we really? In fact, stress is difficult to define precisely because it is perceived differently by different people. What may cause deep anxiety in me — a publishing deadline, for example — may be an exciting challenge and a necessary motivation for you. We are all individuals, with different experiences and varying perspectives on the world. Hence our reactions to any given stressful event may differ widely. As Emerson has said, 'We boil at different degrees'.

Moreover, most of us also recognize that there is a positive type of stress and a negative stress, and we can usually differentiate between the two quite easily. For example, the stress of sitting in a traffic jam when we are already twenty minutes late for a crucially important business appointment, is very different from the stress a man might experience when waiting for his first child to be born, or the stress we normally experience a few minutes before a key presentation to a large audience. These qualitative differences in stress are very important, and serve to emphasize that some types of stress may be hazardous to health, but other stressful situations provide the impetus and determination to succeed in a particular venture or project. Some of the most rewarding moments in our lives are moments of great pressure; pressure acts as a catalyst to our ambition and our drive to achieve and adds immeasurably to the quality of our lives. It is only when the resulting stress becomes unduly severe or prolonged that problems can arise.

But whatever our individual makeup, there are two things which are certain. Firstly, stress affects *all* of us — it is one of the great hazards of twentieth century living. Secondly, although we can avoid smoking, take regular exercise and avoid fattening or otherwise damaging foods, we cannot avoid stress. We are not in a position to opt out. Whatever we say, we are going to experience stress to a greater or lesser extent in many areas of normal everyday living. Learning how to deal with stress will become increasingly important to our physical and mental wellbeing.

Stress versus pressure

Imprecise though it may be, some sort of working definition of stress is very useful — and there are plenty to choose from. Rather than getting too hung-up on the definition, a more useful approach is to use the words stress and pressure to label different parts of the stress reaction.

Stress: I shall use this word to describe the various physiological and biochemical reactions which occur in the body as a response to external stimuli, eg increased pulse rate, dilated pupils, sweaty palms etc and which, taken together, make up the stress response.

Pressure: This is the term we use to describe all the events, conditions and circumstances that we face in our day to day lives. Pressure can be physical (eg running for a train); mental (eg meeting deadlines) or emotional (eg demands of family and other relationships). These various forms of pressure are also referred to as 'stressors'. Pressure may or may not produce a stress response.

So according to this model, pressure from external events (stressors), elicits a complex series of physiological and biochemical responses which we refer to as 'stress' (see Figure 9.1).

It's very important to understand that the amount of stress produced by a given amount of pressure, is highly individual, ie we all have an individual stress *threshold*.

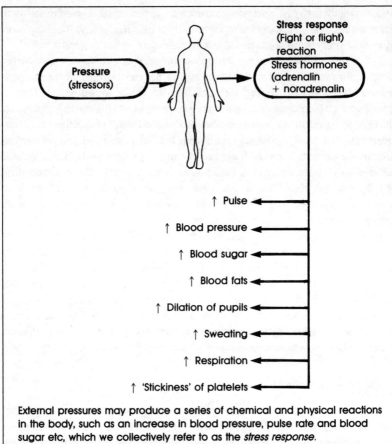

External pressures may produce a series of chemical and physical reactions in the body, such as an increase in blood pressure, pulse rate and blood sugar etc, which we collectively refer to as the *stress response*.

Figure 9.1   The pressure–stress model

The stress response

Let's have a closer look at the physiology of the stress response outlined in Figure 9.1.

Imagine the following situation. You have fallen behind on some important project and have decided to go away for a week on your own, to try and catch up. You have rented a small cottage in a remote part of Wales, and one night after dinner you are standing at the sink washing the dishes. It's been raining all day, and now a strong wind is blowing the rain against the windows. Although it's pitch dark outside, the cottage itself is warm, and you are looking forward to relaxing with a book prior to going to bed. As you turn away from the sink, you suddenly see a face pressed up against the window.

At the moment this happens, striking physical changes are set in motion in your body. Because you had just finished eating dinner, and relaxed, blood was being diverted to your gut to aid digestion (therefore less blood is being sent to your brain). Your breathing was relatively slow, your heart rate was quite slow and regular, and your skin was dry and warm.

Now, digestion has stopped. Blood is being shunted rapidly away from your gut to your brain, which is now highly aroused, and particularly to your muscles which are preparing for action. Your heart rate and blood pressure have increased dramatically, and your skin (as the blood is diverted away from it to feed the brain and muscles) becomes cool and clammy. The palms of your hands are becoming moist and your pupils dilate. From your nervous system a message has been sent to the adrenal glands to secrete the stress hormones, ie adrenalin and noradrenalin. These hormones increase the force and speed of contraction of the heart and they also enlarge the airways so that more air can reach the lungs more quickly. Blood sugar (glucose) is released from storage in the liver into your bloodstream in preparation for action. This is an extra supply of fuel that can be burned rapidly. Your blood has also become 'stickier' and more likely to clot should you be injured.

The perceived threat (the essential component in all stressors), has produced a highly complex series of biochemical and psychological reactions (summarized in Figure 9.1), which Walter Cannon of Harvard described as the 'fight or flight' reaction'. This sequence of bodily changes is genetically programmed into each of us and links us to our prehistoric ancestors. Of course, you don't need to go to a remote cottage in Wales to experience all this. A near miss on the motorway can produce exactly the same (although less severe) pattern of changes.

Today, most of the stressors we face are not solved physically by either fighting or fleeing, so the body's stress response has no way to dissipate. Modern man has retained his primitive hormonal and chemical defence mechanisms, but a twentieth century lifestyle does not allow a physical reaction to the stress agents we face. Physically attacking our boss, or running from what we find to be an acutely stressful business meeting (however much we may relish the thought), are not socially acceptable reactions. Our long evolved and ancient defence mechanisms prepare us for dramatic and rapid action, but find little outlet. We have to repress them. It is the inappropriateness of the normal biological stress response in the context of modern living which is potentially harmful.

WHY IS THE STRESS REACTION HARMFUL?

The stress reaction was originally designed to be a life saving mechanism, to be activated occasionally. However, if this stress response is evoked repeatedly, thus putting the body into a high state of arousal for long periods, the mechanism can be life threatening. How this happens is not fully understood, but evidence would suggest that the human body weakens as a result of being bombarded by stimulation and stress related chemicals over long periods. And as stress begins to take its toll on the body and mind, a variety of symptoms can result (see later). The body will begin to show signs of wear and tear and, if the stress is sufficiently prolonged, the system may eventually break down completely.

The stress threshold

Pressure is only harmful to the degree that it elicits the stress reaction. Not all pressure is harmful; many people have an enormous capacity to deal with severe, unremitting pressure without adverse consequences because they have highly developed coping skills which keep the stress reaction to a minimum. Some types of personality may also be more vulnerable to pressure than others, and experience all the symptoms of stress from pressures which many others would regard as trivial. So how do pressure, ability to cope and personality modify the individual stress reaction? In the series of diagrams (Figure 9.2), I have tried to illustrate how pressure, coping skills and personality type can determine the degree of the stress response in any one individual.

There is a considerable individual variation to external pressures which depends not merely on the pressure itself, but also on coping skills and personality structure. This highlights two key points:

1. The fact that you may be under great pressure is not in itself the critical factor. What matters is your ability to deal with it because it is this which determines the amount of stress which you experience.
2. The stress reaction is not harmful in itself. It is simply a series of physiological and biochemical reactions which occur quite naturally; it is only when the reaction becomes unusually severe or prolonged that it may be harmful. There is therefore a stress 'threshold' for every individual, above which the symptoms and signs of stress become apparent and the risk of ill-health (both mental and physical) increase.

Pressure, stress and performance

When pressure increases, our performance tends to improve — up to a point. When we exceed our individual threshold, the adverse effects of stress begin to influence our behaviour and efficiency.

This balance between the beneficial and deleterious effects of stress on performance and efficiency were first described in 1908 by Dr Robert M Yerkes and Dr J D Dodson of the Harvard Physiology Laboratory. These investigators demonstrated that as pressure increases so do efficiency and performance. However, this relation persists only to a certain level. If stress continues to increase, the resulting anxiety results in a *reduced* performance and efficiency (see Figure 9.3).

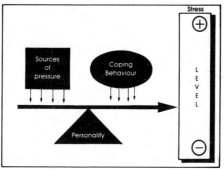

A. In this example pressure is matched by coping skills, so that the stress reaction is held below the harmful threshold.

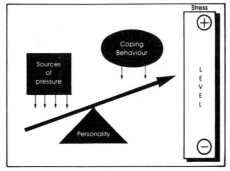

B. Here the pressure exceeds the ability to cope, and the elicited stress reaction rises above the harmful threshold.

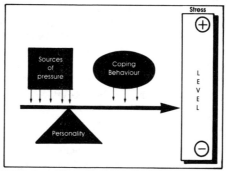

C. An example of a more 'stress-resistant' personality, able to cope with a large amount of pressure even though coping skills may not be particularly highly developed.

Reproduced with permission of Stephen Williams, Resource Systems, Harrogate.

Figure 9.2 The stress model

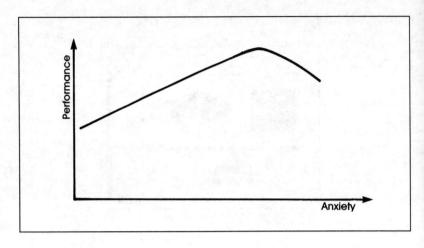

Source: A Melhuish, *Executive Health*, 1978

Figure 9.3   Effect of anxiety on performance: Yerkes–Dodson law

SO WHAT ARE THE SYMPTOMS?

When unremitting pressure elicits the stress reaction, and the stress 'threshold' is exceeded, symptoms and signs of overload will become apparent. It's useful to consider these in terms of physical symptoms, and mental or behavioural symptoms. These are shown in Table 9.1.

Table 9.1   Symptoms of stress

Physical symptoms of stress	Mental (behavioural) symptoms of stress
Loss of appetite	Constant irritability
Craving for food when under pressure	Feeling unable to cope
Indigestion/Heartburn	Loss of interest in life
Constipation/Diarrhoea	Constant or recurrent fear of disease
Insomnia	Indecisiveness
Fatigue	Feelings of anxiety, tension and fear
Excess sweating	Loss of interest in other people
Nervous twitches	Loss of a sense of humour
Recurrent headaches	Dread of the future
Cramps and muscle spasms	A sense of failure
Palpitations	Difficulty in concentrating and poor memory
Nausea	Inability to show true feelings
Breathlessness without exertion	
Impotence or frigidity	
Frequent crying	
Nail biting	

What are the signs?

The physical and mental symptoms of stress are listed in Table 9.1, but how might one recognize stress in other people? The signs may include the following:

- Reduced performance.
- Increasing absenteeism.
- Excessive consumption of alcohol, and cigarettes.
- Irritability.
- Rapid and inappropriate mood changes.
- Indecisiveness.
- An appearance of fatigue, nervousness and/or depression.

Insomnia

About one person in five suffers from insomnia, with about half having problems every night. A recent survey of 2500 people found that 21 per cent had problems sleeping, 36 per cent suffered two or three times a week, and 48 per cent almost every night. The main cause appeared to be stress of various kinds, often related to problems at work or at home. Since this is such a common problem, I shall be discussing insomnia in more detail at the end of this section.

WHAT ARE THE LONG-TERM CONSEQUENCES?

In the longer term, the individual who suffers chronic, unremitting stress, may be placing himself at risk of serious disease or even death. Scientific evidence suggests that under prolonged stress, the body's immune system is depressed, thus making us more susceptible to infections. This explains why we may get cold sores and other minor infections during periods of prolonged stress.

Stress is also thought to contribute to many other conditions, including asthma, colitis, rheumatoid arthritis, ulcers, some skin disorders, high blood pressure, cancer and heart disease.

Heart disease and stress

Despite a widespread perception to the contrary, the precise relationship between stress and heart disease remains controversial. One of the difficulties is that stress is very difficult to measure directly; unlike your cholesterol concentration, there is no blood test available which will give us an accurate and precise measure of your stress level. Consequently, the independent contribution made by stress to the development of coronary disease is uncertain.

However, there seems little doubt that it does represent a significant 'trigger' factor in individuals who may already have evidence of coronary disease. For example, a group of Canadian physicians published a study on the immediate antecedents of heart attacks in 102 active men, between 30 to 60 years of age. On the day of the attack, 24 of the men had experienced an unusual annoyance; 27 had had to face an unusual business problem; 12 had been bothered by an unusual social or domestic problem; and 4 had an unusual financial problem. During the Gulf war, there was a significant increase in the heart attack rate in Israel as a result of the Scud missile threat.

The likely explanation is that the diseased heart is electrically unstable, and a sudden stressful event producing an increase in levels of adrenalin and noradrenalin, may be sufficient to provoke a life-threatening disturbance in the normal rhythm of the heart.

Cancer and stress

Although there is no convincing evidence that stress can itself lead to cancer, there is some evidence that it may influence the course of cancer once it has occurred. Some studies have shown that women with breast cancer are nine times more likely to have a recurrence of the disease if they are experiencing stressful life events.

WHO GETS STRESS RELATED PROBLEMS?

There is a widespread belief that stress related problems are more common in executives and senior managerial groups than in other people, and that this helps to explain why heart attacks occur so frequently amongst those in managerial and executive positions. In fact, the reverse is true. Social class trend data demonstrate that coronary disease is more prevalent in blue collar groups, manual workers and the unemployed. Results from the Whitehall study of civil servants showed that it was the lowest employment grades who were the most likely to be affected by stress-related diseases.

A study of employees of the Bell Telephone Company revealed that senior executives actually have a *lower* risk of heart disease than other employee groups, and many other studies from various parts of the world have confirmed this observation. It follows that if stress is a risk factor for heart disease, then from a public health perspective it must be at least as important a problem in blue-collar workers, as it is in managers and executives.

The fact is that stress is for everyone — including babies.

Stress and personality

In a variety of studies and experiments, scientists have attempted to describe certain personality 'types', which may be more susceptible to the effects of stress than others. The concept of the 'coronary personality' has been with us for many years, and was first propounded in the 1930s and 1940s by Franz Alexander and Helen Flanders-Dunbar. The idea was subsequently taken up by two Californian cardiologists, Mayer Freedman and Ray Rosenman. They described two forms of behaviour pattern in the subjects involved in their study, and these were designated 'Type A' and 'Type B'.

1. **The Type A personality** is characterized by intense ambition; competitive drive; constant preoccupation with deadlines; impatience with delay; time conscientious; irritability and hostility. A specific characteristic feature of the hostility is that it is *inwardly* directed ie the individual finds it difficult to express anger externally. The importance of the Type A construct is that the specific behaviour pattern with which it is associated has been shown in some studies to be associated with an increased risk of heart disease.
2. **The Type B individual** contrary to popular belief is not simply the converse of Type A. On the contrary, the Type B personality may well be strongly achievement orientated and ambitious, but he/she is more consistent and tends to have greater application and concentration than their Type A counterpart.

The Type A, Type B hypothesis gained a strong following in the 1970s but has become much less generally accepted of late.

Exactly how personality type may influence the development of heart disease is not well understood; it may, for example, influence the brain to produce increased levels of stress hormones which are known to elevate blood pressure and blood lipids (fats) Some studies have indeed shown that Type A individuals tend to have higher blood pressures and cholesterol levels, and may also be inclined to smoke more and exercise less than their Type B counterparts, thus increasing their susceptibility to coronary disease. It may also be that the Type A individual tends to seek out stressful situations as a natural side effect of intense ambition and competitive drive.

SELF-ASSESSMENT

Two questionnaires make up this self-assessment section:

1. Stress and Coping Skills.
2. Type A Behaviour.

The stress and coping skills questionnaire on pages 164–66 is designed to give an assessment of your current stress levels and your ability to deal with them. You will have completed this as part of the initial Health Risk Appraisal carried out in Part I, Chapter 3. It also contains one or two questions which are related to Type A behaviour.

PERSONAL QUESTIONNAIRE
ASSESSMENT OF TYPE A PERSONALITY, STRESS AND COPING SKILLS

For each of the questions, please indicate whether the item is true for you or not by circling YES (if it applies) or NO (if it does not). We realize that you may have reservations about a clear-cut YES or NO, but we would like you to indicate which comes closest to describing yourself.

Please answer *all* questions and work through from first to last without going back over your answers.

Award yourself 0, 1 or 2 points as appropriate.

				Points
1.	I can take a measured look at a job to be done without feeling an urge to rush into action before getting the thing properly sorted out.	YES 0	NO 1	☐
2.	I have recently had to give up an important personal relationship	YES 2	NO 0	☐
3.	I often need understanding friends to cheer me up	YES 2	NO 0	☐
4.	I can control my temper, when I lose it, this is calculated, I don't go beyond what I intended to say or do.	YES 0	NO 1	☐
5.	I find it easy to get along with and accept people who hold different points of view to my own.	YES 0	NO 1	☐
6.	My mood often goes up and down.	YES 2 ?	NO 0	☐
7.	Having to tolerate delays of any kind is very irritating to me.	YES 2	NO 0	☐
8.	I prefer to assume complete responsibility rather than sharing it with others.	YES 2	NO 0	☐
9.	Recent events in my life have forced an important change in my social relationships.	YES 2	NO 0	☐
10.	I do not suffer fools gladly.	YES 2	NO 0	☐
11.	I can focus on one thing when necessary and clear my mind of other things to be done.	YES 0	NO 1	☐
12.	I take pride in getting the job done faster than most.	YES 2	NO 1	☐

		Points
13.	I sometimes feel 'just miserable' for no good reason.	YES 2 ? NO 0 ☐
14.	My feelings are rather easily hurt.	YES 2 NO 0 ☐
15.	Deadlines are very important to me.	YES 2 NO 0 ☐
16.	I can say 'no' to people who make an unreasonable demand without them being too upset.	YES 0 NO 1 ☐
17.	My sexual needs are largely unsatisfied	YES 2 NO 1 ☐
18.	I usually try to deal with problems systematically and in an organized way.	YES 0 NO 1 ☐
19.	I have plenty of battles on my hands at work.	YES 2 NO 0 ☐
20.	I have suffered considerably from constant arguments at home and at work.	YES 2 NO 0 ☐
21.	I have very real financial problems.	YES 2 NO 0 ☐
22.	I am often troubled by feelings of guilt.	YES 2 NO 0 ☐
23.	I can get over disappointments without getting too upset; I recognize that one cannot have everything the way one wishes.	YES 0 ? NO 1 ☐
24.	I would call myself tense or highly-strung.	YES 2 NO 0 ☐
25.	I can immerse myself in constructive activity as a way of taking my mind away from a problem	YES 0 NO 1 ☐
26.	I have recently had serious problems in a close relationship.	YES 2 NO 0 ☐
27.	I can usually get other people to see all sides of a problem.	YES 0 NO 1 ☐
28.	I can unwind quickly on a holiday and begin to enjoy myself from the start.	YES 0 NO 1 ☐
29.	I enjoy competing at work and elsewhere.	YES 2 NO 0 ☐
30.	I feel I am as good as the next man.	YES 2 NO 1 ☐
31.	When confronted with a problem I usually remain optimistic about the outcome.	YES 0 NO 1 ☐
32.	I get impatient and angry with incompetence and inefficiency.	YES 2 NO 0 ☐
33.	I get attacks of shaking or trembling.	YES 2 NO 0 ☐
34.	I work long hours from choice.	YES 2 NO 0 ☐

		Points

35. I or members of my family, have recently experienced problems due to illness.   YES 2   NO 0   ☐

36. I am an irritable person.   YES 2   NO 0   ☐

37. I drive myself harder than most.   YES 2   NO 0   ☐

38. I can usually break down a problem into manageable chunks.   YES 0   NO 1   ☐

39. I worry about awful things that might happen.   YES 2   NO 0   ☐

40. I would call myself a nervous person.   YES 2   NO 0   ☐

41. I can count on the support of my family and friends.   YES 0   NO 1   ☐

42. I have to spend too much time away from home.   YES 2   NO 0   ☐

43. I am very ambitious.   YES 2   NO 0   ☐

44. I am easily hurt when people find fault with me or my work.   YES 2   NO 0   ☐

45. I sometimes have to assume responsibility for events over which I have no control.   YES 2   NO 0   ☐

46. I am troubled by feelings of inferiority.   YES 2   NO 0   ☐

47. Someone close to me has recently died.   YES 2   NO 0   ☐

48. At times I have more work than I feel able to cope with.   YES 2   NO 0   ☐

49. I am able to tell other people what I feel and think; I do not simmer privately or explode.   YES 0   NO 1   ☐

50. I tend to get involved in many different ideas and projects.   YES 2   NO 0   ☐

51. I suffer from sleeplessness.   YES 2   NO 0   ☐

52. I have to work with others of unpredictable and uncertain temperament.   YES 2   NO 0   ☐

53. I feel dissatisfied at work due to eg blocked promotion, threat of redundancy, excessive demands of superiors, etc.   YES 2   NO 0   ☐

Total Points   26

The second questionnaire (Figure 9.4) in this section is meant to assess your Type A behaviour quite specifically.

INTERPRETATION OF RESULTS

1. STRESS AND COPING SKILLS QUESTIONNAIRE

0–24 points
In terms of stress, coping skills and personality, you appear to be in a low risk category. Whatever pressures are present do not appear to be provoking a harmful stress reaction.

25–50 points
You evidently have some pressure, but in general manage to cope. Your levels of stress are acceptable for most of the time and are not generally at levels where it is likely to cause you any harm. Much of the pressure which you experience is productive and should not, therefore, be viewed negatively.

51–70 points
You are now moving into a category where the stress response to whatever pressure you are experiencing could be harmful to your health. Sometimes the stress can make you uncomfortable and you may find it difficult to cope adequately. You tend to feel 'stretched' or 'pushed' a lot of the time, although you may sometimes find this enjoyable. You are probably prone to fairly marked fluctuations in mood. With scores at this level you may run the risk of ill-health if the pressure (and the stress which results) continues unremittingly.

More than 70 points
This is high risk category. Levels of stress are far too high, and may increase your susceptibility to various illnesses. In combination with a high Type A personality score (see (2) below), you are likely to be in the 'coronary prone' group. You may be experiencing problems sleeping and your alcohol consumption may also have increased. You may also be using various forms of tranquillizers and sedatives and have the constant feeling that you are unable to cope. Continuing to live at this sort of intensity may well result in eventual breakdown both physical and mental. You need to do something — fast.

2. Type A behaviour

As was indicated previously, the Type A individual tends to seek out stressful situations and there is some evidence that the individual scoring high in terms of the Type A trace, may well be more prone to coronary disease than his Type B counterpart. The following scoring will give you

Circle one number for each of the statements below which best reflects the way you behave in your everyday life. For example, if you are generally on time for appointments, for the first point you would circle a number between 7 and 11. If you are usually casual about appointments you would circle one of the lower numbers between 1 and 5.

Casual about appointments	1 2 3 4 5 6 7 8 9 10 11	Never late
Not competitive	1 2 3 4 5 6 7 8 9 10 11	Very competitive
Good listener	1 2 3 4 5 6 7 8 9 10 11	Anticipates what others are going to say (nods, attempts to finish for them)
Never feels rushed (even under pressure)	1 2 3 4 5 6 7 8 9 10 11	Always rushed
Can wait patiently	1 2 3 4 5 6 7 8 9 10 11	Impatient while waiting
Takes things one at a time	1 2 3 4 5 6 7 8 9 10 11	Tries to do many things at once, thinks about what will do next
Slow deliberate talker	1 2 3 4 5 6 7 8 9 10 11	Emphatic in speech fast and forceful
Cares about satisfying him/herself no matter what others may think	1 2 3 4 5 6 7 8 9 10 11	Wants good job recognized by others
Slow doing things	1 2 3 4 5 6 7 8 9 10 11	Fast (eating, walking)

Figure 9.4   Type A behaviour

Easy-going	1 2 3 4 5 6 7 8 9 10 11	Hard driving (pushing self and others)
Expresses feelings	1 2 3 4 5 6 7 8 9 10 11	Hides feelings
Many outside interests	1 2 3 4 5 6 7 8 9 10 11	Few interests outside work/home
Unambitious	1 2 3 4 5 6 7 8 9 10 11	Ambitious
Casual	1 2 3 4 5 6 7 8 9 10 11	Eager to get things done

Scoring

Below 70	70–90	90–110	110 upwards
Type B	Type B+	Type A−	Type A

Source: Watts and Cooper, *Dealing with Stress*. Reproduced with permission.

Figure 9.4 continued

some idea as to whether you tend towards the Type A or the Type B construct.

Obviously, the higher the score obtained on this questionnaire the more firmly you can be classified as Type A. Anything above 110 would certainly be regarded as Type A, whereas anything below 70 would certainly be Type B. However, please understand that there are no distinct divisions between the two types; rather, people fall somewhere on a continuum leaning more towards one type than the other. An average score would be around 84.

Above 110

Type A: If you find yourself in this category, you could be regarded as 'coronary prone'. This is particularly true if you are over the age of 40, smoke cigarettes and have other coronary risk factors such as hypertension, high blood cholesterol etc. It is extremely important that you should make every effort to modify your behaviour, and some advice with regard to this is given in the next section.

90 to 110 points

Type A−: You still tend towards the 'coronary prone' personality, but your risk is clearly not as high as the Type A group. Nevertheless, you should pay careful attention to the advice given to all Type As in the next section.

70 to 90 points
Type B+: Your behaviour is certainly on the less 'coronary prone' end of the spectrum. You are generally relaxed and you are able to cope adequately with stress. However, you may have the potential for slipping into some forms of Type A behaviour and you should recognize this.
Below 70
Type B: You tend to the extreme of the non-coronary-prone personality. Your current behaviour expresses few of the reactions associated with coronary disease.

ACTION PLAN

Your Action Plan for managing stress consists of two distinct sections:

1. General strategies for managing stress and Type A behaviour
2. The Relaxation Response.

1. GENERAL PRINCIPLES — MANAGING STRESS AND TYPE A BEHAVIOUR

If you have scored high on the stress and coping skills questionnaire, the chances are that you will also rate quite highly on the Type A questionnaire. The following principles are meant to help you to manage stress more effectively, and also to modify specific Type A traits which may be present. Since we are all individuals, each of these principles will have differing importance depending upon our own personality type and predispositions etc. Much of what is contained here has been adapted from the work of Freedman and Rosenman in *Type A Behaviour and your Heart*. In this they recommend a number of 'drills against hurry sickness' which, they maintain, are effective for their Type A patients.

1. **Stop trying to be the centre of attention by talking all the time**. Make yourself *listen* to others and stop interrupting or finishing their sentences.
   If you still find yourself talking unnecessarily, ask yourself:
   — *Do I really have anything important to say?*
   — *Does anyone really want to hear it?*
   — *Is this the best time to say it?*
   If the answer to any of these three questions is **no**, then you should stop talking.
2. **Develop strategies designed to help you slow down.** Slow your speech when you talk; drive more slowly; stop battling with the clock. More importantly, try to assess the causes of your 'hurry sickness'. Are you in a hurry because rushing is really essential to the success of a

particular goal, or is your time-dominated behaviour nothing more than a need to feel important? Is it designed to avoid or impress some particular individual? Freedman and Rosenman offer this specific advice when dealing with obsessive time orientation:

> 'Never forget when confronted by any task to ask yourself the following questions:
> a. Will this matter have importance five years from now?
> b. Must I do this right now or have I enough time to think about the best way to accomplish it?'

3. **Organize and Prioritize**. Poor organization lies behind a great deal of completely unnecessary and avoidable pressure and anxiety. Review what sources you have at your disposal and see if you are utilizing them to your full potential. Delegate. Good organization implies detailed forward planning and a clearly defined set of goals and objectives, with an appropriate scale of priorities.

4. **Manage your time more effectively**. Time is the most precious (and non-renewable) resource you possess. Learning to value your own time will also help you to avoid wasting that of other people. Once you have decided upon your priorities, do one thing at a time. Focus all your effort on one task and only when you have achieved this, move on to the next. Be realistic about your time allocation to various projects and the setting of deadlines both for yourself and for others. Where possible, avoid making unnecessary appointments or deadlines. The more deadlines you make for yourself, the worse your 'hurry sickness' will become. If a meeting is necessary, make it as short and to the point as possible. President JF Kennedy would often open a meeting with the words, 'please be brief'.

5. **Learn to protect your time and to say no.** If you don't learn how to do this, nobody is going to do it for you. The older you get, the more important this becomes.

6. **Self-awareness and monitoring**. It is important to recognize signs of exhaustion and stress in yourself and you should not ignore obvious symptoms such as irritability, insomnia, depression and anxiety. Family, friends and colleagues may be far better judges of this than you are. Indeed, it is characteristic of many highly stressed individuals that they are really not aware of the extent to which stress is damaging their lives. If people around you are telling you that your behaviour is unusual and that your outbursts of temper are uncharacteristic, you must not simply dismiss them. These may well be early warning signs that you will ignore at your peril.

7. **Relaxation**. Having periods for relaxation and the development of new leisure interests is of the greatest importance. Many intensely work orientated individuals suffer a real sense of guilt at taking time for relaxation and rest. But hobbies and interests outside the

workplace are essential to the development of a balanced personality and they are extremely effective 'buffers' against the continuing stress of working life.

8. **Regular exercise**. This is an extremely important ingredient in effective stress management. Regular exercise not only promotes physical health and wellbeing, it has a highly beneficial psychological impact.

9. **Keep a sense of perspective**. A characteristic feature of individuals under continuing, unremitting pressure is that they begin to lose their sense of perspective. They live as though the only important thing in the world is their job, and that all else must be subservient to it.

I vividly recall a patient some years ago who had been diagnosed as having a life-threatening heart problem, and who needed admission to hospital for urgent surgical intervention. I explained this to him very carefully and he nodded his head in all the right places, suggesting that he had understood. After I had finished speaking, he took out his diary and began flicking through the pages, telling me about his impending visit to Japan etc, and eventually concluded that it would be at least four to five months before he could even contemplate finding the time to come into hospital. I remember staring at him in complete disbelief — in fact I recall him asking me if *I* felt alright. It took me another 30 minutes of blunt speaking to finally get the message through, so completely had he lost his sense of perspective.

It's a good idea to remind yourself of what really is important by recalling some major event in your life which you lived through and overcame, or in fact anything which left a deep impression upon you. We all have our triumphs and tragedies. A colleague of mine thinks about the time when his six year old daughter was seriously ill with a bone disease and doctors feared for her life. Fortunately, she made a full recovery, but he often uses this memory as a means of getting other apparently important or difficult issues into perspective. Another friend thinks of Mahler's 'Resurrection' Symphony while another recalls the unforgettable silence of the Grand Canyon. The essential point of this strategy is that there is a comparison being made ie comparing whatever is worrying you now, with something else which has much more significance for you in the grander scheme of things. Work is but one component of your life, and by no means the most important. As Bertrand Russell once said: 'One of the signs of impending madness is the belief that one's work is important. If I were a medical man, I should prescribe a long holiday to anyone who believed that his work was important'. Believe it or not, the company will be there long after you have disappeared.

10. **Pay attention to your diet**. When people are working under constant pressure, it's quite common for eating habits to deteriorate.

The tendency is to resort to eating 'fast food' or 'junk food', which is always high in calories, and often has relatively little nutritional value. This can lead to deficiencies of important vitamins and trace elements, factors which may themselves adversely influence mood. One of the common dietary consequences of prolonged stress is excessive coffee consumption. The average cup of brewed coffee contains about 140 mg of caffeine, so if you drink ten cups of coffee a day your total daily intake is around 1400 mg. (Bear in mind that tea also contains significant amounts of caffeine, although rather less than coffee.) Caffeine may produce anxiety, restlessness, insomnia, headaches, an increase in pulse rate, blood pressure and palpitations. It is true that caffeine heightens physical performance, but its effect on mood and intellectual performance is (contrary to popular belief) much less predictable. If you are a heavy coffee or tea drinker, you would be well advised to reduce your consumption, or change to decaffeinated.

11. **Be careful about your alcohol and cigarette consumption**. Prolonged stress often leads to an increase in cigarette and alcohol consumption. Drinking may become an escape mechanism, a way of avoiding having to face stressful situations. It's remarkably easy to slip into regular and excessive alcohol and tobacco use as a response to long term stress. The need to find temporary respite from stress or life events may also lead to an increased dependence on prescribed drugs like tranquillizers, or a temptation to use non-prescribed drugs.

12. **Get adequate sleep**. People vary enormously in the amount of sleep they require. Some feel refreshed after as little as five or six hours, while many others may need a minimum of 9 or 10. The quality of sleep and not merely the quantity, is also an important factor and there needs to be a balance between dreaming sleep (known as REM sleep because it is accompanied by Rapid Eye Movements) and deep (non-REM) sleep. Insomnia is discussed in more detail shortly.

2. THE RELAXATION RESPONSE

Apart from the general principles of managing stress and your personality type more effectively, what can be done about everyday situations that lead to stress and its harmful consequences? Since we cannot always control the external circumstances which may give rise to stress, we have to devise strategies which will help us to cope with it more effectively. One way of achieving this is to practice regular relaxation.

Like the fight or flight response, the relaxation response is also present in man. Until recently, the relaxation response has been produced primarily by meditational techniques — transcendental meditation (TM) is perhaps the best known example. But the benefits of meditation do not need to be allied to any specific religious philosophy or system of beliefs. The relaxation response is a simple technique which utilizes the essential principles of meditation, and results in reductions in blood pressure, heart rate, stress levels and even in body temperature.

The basic technique for producing the relaxation response is extremely simple. Its elements have been known for centuries and are present in many cultures throughout the world. As was indicated previously, the relaxation response has usually been elicited in a religious context, via specific systems of meditation. Nevertheless, four basic elements are common to all these practices:

1. **A quiet environment.** You need to choose a quiet, calm environment with as few distractions as possible. Even background noise may prevent or impede the elicitation of the response. Any quiet room (even the office) will suffice.

2. **A mental device.** The meditator employs the constant stimulus of a single syllable sound or word. This is repeated silently or in a low, gentle tone. In some systems this word is referred to as a *mantram* (or the more familiar variant *mantra*), and I suppose to many of us it conjurs up exotic images of flowing robes, garlands and incense. However, the mantram — under other names to be sure — has been known in the West for centuries and there is actually nothing secret or occult about it. The purpose of repeating a single word is simply to free oneself from logical, externally orientated thought by focusing solely on the stimulus. The word 'Mantra', in fact, means 'the word that protects'. It is simply a means of calming the mind, and excluding the millions of distracting thoughts that jostle for position in our consciousness.

    Any number of different words and sounds can, and are, used in traditional practices. The selection of a word is important, and it is better to choose something that has particular personal significance for you. If the word you focus on has special meaning, it will not only be more effective in meditation, but you are more likely to become more deeply involved in practising the relaxation response. Perhaps you would prefer something associated with a particular religious or spiritual faith, eg 'Lord have mercy', or 'Allah'. Some, however, may prefer the word to be more neutral — 'One', 'Peace' or 'Ocean' etc. Whatever word you choose, it will become the focus of your meditation, and the key that will elicit the relaxation response. The only requirement is that the word or phrase should be short enough to coordinate easily with your breathing.

3. **A passive attitude.** The purpose of the response is to help one rest and relax, and this requires a completely passive attitude. You should not think about whether you are achieving the relaxation response or

scrutinize your performance in any way. When you allow distracting thoughts to enter the mind, you must learn to disregard them. The mental device indicated above will help you to do this.

4. **A comfortable position**. You should sit in a comfortable chair in as restful a position as possible. The purpose is to reduce muscular effort to a minimum but the head must be supported and the arms should be balanced and supported as well. I would suggest that you should remove your shoes and loosen all tight fitting clothing.

So now that you have found your quiet environment, decided which mental device — I have chosen the word 'One' here — and found a comfortable position, you can now go about eliciting the relaxation response.

To do this, follow these steps in sequence:

*   Close your eyes gently . . .
*   Now think about the whole of your body as one relaxed entity.
*   Become aware of letting go; of the silence and the gentle ebb and flow of your breathing.
*   Breathe in and out gently through your nose.
*   As you breathe out, say the word 'One' silently or quietly to yourself.
*   Breathe in once again gently, then exhale and as you do so repeat the word 'One'.
*   Continue to do this focusing on your breathing and the repetition of the word 'One'.
*   Try to empty your mind of all outward thoughts. Focus solely upon the gently rhythm of your breathing and the repetition of the word 'One'.

Don't worry about whether you are successful in achieving a deep level of relaxation — maintain a passive attitude and permit relaxation to occur at its own pace. Inevitably, distracting thoughts — 'mind-chatter' — will occur, but whenever you find your mind beginning to wander, gently bring yourself back to your word and your breathing once again. Don't actively fight against the distractions; let them enter your mind and leave again as your concentration returns. It's perfectly normal to lose your mental focus — everyone does. But with practice, you will find yourself able to achieve greater degrees of concentration, for longer periods. It also leads to a much greater awareness of the way your mind works; of its unceasing activity, endless wanderings and lack of discipline. The central point of the meditation process is that it is an effective way of training your mind to become more focused and, at the same time, more alert.

I would suggest that you should practise this technique for 20 to 30 minutes every day. Avoid practising within two hours after a meal, because the digestive processes appear to interfere with the elicitation of the physiological changes. In time, the relaxation response should come with remarkably little effort.

This is a useful and simple technique which really does help and you will become very efficient at it if you do it regularly. It does require some discipline and pre-planning to make the time available each day, but it will more than repay itself in terms of the potential benefits. If you can, try to set aside a specific time each day when you can go through this process — perhaps first thing in the morning or last thing at night. As Gandhi once said, 'Meditation is the key to the morning and the latch in the evening'.

INSOMNIA

We all have periods when we sleep badly. It may be due to a change in circumstances, such as a new baby, or examinations, or there may be no apparent reason. Usually these periods are short lived, and we are able to cope with them. But for some, occasional sleeping problems can develop into chronic insomnia. About 10 million individuals in this country have significant sleeping problems, although interestingly it is a subject which few people talk about very much. In the United States, up to 50 million Americans are said to have trouble sleeping. Experts who have studied insomnia attribute the problem to stress, evening socializing which is often required of executives, heavy travel schedules and general workaholism. There is also some evidence that the Type A personality may be more prone to sleeping problems.

What is insomnia?

There is no standard definition of insomnia, since the amount of sleep required for feeling rested varies enormously among individuals. Some may feel completely rested with as little as four hours of sleep while others require a minimum of ten.

Essentially, there are two kinds of insomnia:

1. **Sleep onset insomnia**: Difficulty in falling asleep, as defined by an average of at least 30 minutes to fall asleep; and
2. **Sleep maintenance insomnia**: Difficulty in staying asleep, as defined by an average awake-time, after falling asleep, of more than 30 minutes per night; or early morning awakening before the desired wake up time, with an inability to fall back to sleep.

The effects of sleep loss

The effects of sleep loss are subject to many popular misconceptions. The belief that everyone has to sleep eight hours a night is a myth. In fact, 20 per cent of the population sleep less than six hours per night. Another significant fact is that sleep time decreases with age.

Contrary to popular belief, our ability to tolerate lack of sleep is much greater than we think. Even one night of complete sleep deprivation may have remarkably little effect on work performance. In fact, evidence would suggest that most individuals can maintain their usual performance with 60 to 70 per cent of their normal sleep. If you are an eight hour sleeper, this means that your performance at work will not suffer significantly if you get only 4½ to 5½ hours of sleep. So for moderate sleep loss, the perception is as important as the amount lost. **Don't be afraid of insomnia. The less you fear it, the better you will sleep and the better you will feel the next day.**

Why do we sleep?

It is still not known for certain why we sleep, but in the past forty years or so we have learnt a great deal more about the basic physiology involved. Scientists distinguish between two types of sleep: the rapid eye movement (REM) variety — when beneath your eyelids your eyes are darting about — and the non-REM type also called 'orthodox', 'quiet' or 'slow wave' sleep. We dream during REM sleep. In the course of the non-REM type, your body seems to do more of the work of restoring itself.

At night-time, these two types of sleep alternate.

Sleeping better — practical strategies to improve your sleeping pattern

These practical steps can be conveniently divided into two groups:

1. Daytime preparation for sleep.
2. Night-time preparation for sleep.

Daytime preparation for sleep

- **Step 1.** Reduce your consumption of alcohol and caffeine. Contrary to popular belief, alcohol actually disrupts sleep and it should not be consumed within two hours of bedtime.

  Caffeine is a powerful stimulant and this should not be consumed within six hours of bedtime. Remember that many other foods and drinks contain caffeine besides coffee and tea.
- **Step 2.** Exercise regularly. People who have difficulty in sleeping tend to be more sedentary than good sleepers, and there is now good evidence that physical inactivity may contribute to insomnia. Conversely, regular aerobic exercise, even brisk walking, can make a significant contribution to healthy sleeping patterns.
- **Step 3.** Plan tomorrow's activities, and review your day's work early in the evening, so that in the immediate period before bedtime you can relax properly without mulling over the day's events. You may choose to read, listen to music or watch some television. A light carbohydrate snack during this wind down period may help you sleep, since carbohydrates appear to increase the production of certain chemicals in the brain which are responsible for sleep.

- **Step 4.** Make sure your sleeping environment is conducive to sleep. This is an intensely individual thing. Some people like to have complete silence, where others may require some background music or noise. Obviously you need to make sure the temperature of the room is comfortable and that the bed itself provides you with adequate support.
- **Step 5.** Drink as little as possible after 8 pm to reduce the likelihood of your having to get up during the night to pass water.

Night-time preparation for sleep

- **Step 1.** If you are taking sleeping pills you should gradually eliminate their use under the supervision of your doctor. Sleeping tablets may help you to get through a particularly difficult period for a short period of time, but they are not a long-term solution. They also reduce the amount of dream sleep and deep sleep, so that although you may fall asleep more rapidly than usual, your sleep will be of poorer quality. Moreover, people also tend to develop a tolerance for most types of medication and therefore need increasingly larger doses. The result is that physiological or even physical dependence can develop if the medication is used for extended periods. Moreover, when you stop using them you may experience a temporary increase in your insomnia which may be even worse than the initial insomnia. The advice must be that if you have to take a sleeping pill, then you should limit this to one per week.
- **Step 2.** Schedule your sleep properly. You should aim to reduce your time in bed to no more than six to seven hours. One of the most common mistakes made by people who suffer from insomnia is to spend too much time in bed. Reducing the actual amount of time spent in bed is important, even if it means delaying bedtime by an hour or so.
- **Step 3.** Try to ensure that you get up at about the same time every day (including weekends), even if you have had a poor night's sleep. This helps to maintain a consistent circadian rhythm — the 24 hour internal body rhythm or cycle that keeps humans awake during the day and asleep at night. With time, the hour that you will become drowsy and ready for sleep will become more consistent.
- **Step 4.** Don't take naps any longer than one hour, particularly late in the day, because sleeping for this length of time will make you less sleepy at bedtime. However, taking a short nap of less than one hour, particularly in the afternoon, may be helpful in compensating for a sleep deprived night. A short nap can satisfy this immediate need for sleep and will usually not affect your sleep onset at night.
- **Step 5.** Use the bedroom only for pleasurable relaxing activities and sleep. Don't use your bedroom for any stressful activities such as working or studying. The goal is to associate your bedroom and bed with relaxation and sleep only.

- **Step 6.**   Go to sleep only when you are drowsy, even if that time comes later than your new delayed bedtime. The important thing is to begin to associate bedtime and your bed with drowsiness.

- **Step 7.**   When you are drowsy, go into bed and relax for 15 to 20 minutes by reading, listening to music or even watching television until you are *very* drowsy. Then turn out the lights with the intention of going to sleep. If you are unable to sleep after about 20 minutes or so, *stop trying to sleep*! The harder you try, the more difficult you are going to find it.

  Instead, open your eyes and read for a while or else watch television until you are drowsy again, then turn out the lights a second time. You can repeat this procedure as often as necessary. You may also find it beneficial to go through the relaxation response which we discussed in an earlier section. If you are absolutely wide awake, you may find it better to get out of your bed and leave the bedroom entirely. Engage in a quiet relaxing activity such as listening to music or reading until you begin to feel drowsy again, and then return to your bedroom with the intention of going to sleep.

Practising proper sleep hygiene is essential if you are going to get over your insomnia problem. If you consistently implement the principles outlined above, the chances are that you will impove your sleeping pattern even if you do not manage eight hours a night! Most of all, **don't worry** about sleep deprivation. As I said previously, even a completely sleepless night is unlikely to significantly affect your work performance the next day, and the more you worry about not getting sleep, the less you are actually going to get.

Finally, take some time to organize your sleep preparation properly. I know it's something else that needs organizing, but after a while you won't actually have to think about it any longer. It will simply become second nature. According to some experts, the biggest problem in treating sleepless executives is their unwillingness to take time to improve sleeping habits.

Chapter 10

THE FAT PROBLEM

In most industrialized countries obesity is a major public health problem and the chronic diseases with which it is associated are major killers.

In the UK, despite growing concern about the importance of obesity and a much clearer understanding of the mechanisms by which it contributes to poor health, the problem of overweight is more widespread today than ever before. One survey in 1980 showed that between the ages of 16 and 64 years, about 6 per cent of men and 8 per cent of women were obese, but the recently published Allied Dunbar Fitness Survey (ADFS) showed that the prevalence has increased to 8 per cent and 13 per cent for men and women respectively.

The problem of overweight (see later) is even more widespread. The ADFS revealed that 48 per cent of men and 40 per cent of women over the age of 16 are overweight, including about 15 per cent of those in the 16–19 age range — good evidence that this is not simply a question of 'middle-aged spread'. In the USA the position is similar. Not only are Americans getting fatter, but they are also getting fatter earlier.

Not that we are unaware of the problem. Losing weight (particularly in women), has become something of a national obsession supported (and many experts would say created) by an enormously profitable slimming industry. Estimates suggest that about two-thirds of adult women and about one-third of adult men are trying to slim at any one time — big business by any standards. Everyone who has ever dieted (and that means most of us), soon hears that 95 per cent of people who lose weight on diets will put it back again sooner or later. In other words, the problem is not one of losing weight, but of bringing about *sustained* weight loss.

Most of us know what the remedy is — eat less and take more exercise — but we also know that many other factors play a part, many of which are poorly understood.

If you have a weight problem, (and at least 20 million people in this country do), then reading through this chapter and applying the principles outlined here, will give you a much greater chance of getting the weight off and keeping it off.

WHY IS OBESITY IMPORTANT?

Over a period of years, being overweight or obese can have a significant impact on your health and will make a number of diseases more likely. The US Surgeon General's report on Nutrition and Health in 1988 pointed out that obesity is an important risk factor for the development of diabetes, hypertension, high blood cholesterol, coronary heart disease, stroke, gallbladder disease and certain types of cancer — of the bowel and prostate in men and of the breast and uterus in women. Of course obesity is also associated with a sedentary lifestyle — itself a major independent risk factor for heart disease.

Other ailments include arthritis and various respiratory problems, making the obese individual a much greater anaesthetic risk during surgery. These risks become much greater for those who are seriously obese, but it is important to remember that even moderate degrees of overweight can be significant.

Apart from these problems, general fatigue is an extremely common complaint amongst overweight people and whilst it most often does not indicate anything serious, it does substantially reduce the **quality** of life for many individuals. Moreover, back problems including slipped discs are much more liable to be a problem in the overweight and obese.

Finally, it is important to stress the potential psychological consequences of being overweight. For many fat people, the need to lose weight becomes almost an obsession and their continued failure to do so leads to feelings of guilt, inadequacy and sometimes real depressive illness. These negative feelings are reinforced by the activities of the slimming industry which has a vested interest in promoting the idea that to be slim is to be healthy, successful, desirable and (above all else) sexy. Fat people — by implication — are none of these things. The constant striving for unrealistic weight loss targets and the failure to achieve them, can be physically and psychologically damaging.

Some experts believe that obesity is fundamentally a psychological rather than a physiological problem, ie that fat people over-eat for a reason, and this is certainly true for a proportion of overweight individuals. For example, some studies in grossly obese women reveal a high frequency of rape and other forms of sexual abuse during childhood and early adult life. In other cases the source of the psychological distress may not be so clear-cut, although many people indulge in 'comfort eating' as a response to a difficult emotional problem or use food as a reward in much the same way that others use alcohol. It's the old conundrum: do we eat because we feel depressed, or are we depressed because we over-eat and get fat? The situation is made even more complex by the fact that the process of dieting itself may cause changes in mood, emotional instability, anger and depression.

For all these reasons, obesity should be accorded the seriousness it deserves and not dismissed as being simply the result of gluttony and a lack of willpower.

How is obesity measured?

The definition of obesity as being a condition in which there is an excess of body fat is rather arbitrary. Visual inspection of ourselves and others gives a subjective but fairly accurate estimate of the degree of overweight, but we usually rely on somewhat more objective measures such as height–weight tables, weight related indices such as Body Mass Index (BMI), and other anthropometric measurements.

You are almost certainly familiar with the height and weight charts in magazines and books which are supposed to tell you what your desirable weight is, based on your height and your frame size. Most of these tables are derivatives of those originally developed by the Metropolitan Life Insurance Company. In the 1950s, Metropolitan's statisticians studied the height and weight records of several million individuals with life insurance policies. By comparing mortality rates in the different weight ranges, they were able to produce a table of 'desirable' weights for each height, which was published in 1959 and 1983. However, with the benefit of more evidence it is now clear that acceptable weight ranges are identical for **both** sexes and this is reflected in the unisex table used later on in this chapter.

Another method for deciding whether someone is too fat (or too thin) is to use a number derived from the height and weight, known as the Body Mass Index (BMI). This is calculated as follows:

Body Mass Index (BMI) = Weight (Kg)/[Height (Metres)]^2
or BMI = Weight (lbs)/[Height (ins)]^2 × 703

This has the great advantage that it gives a single number and is the measure most often used in long-term prospective research. It is sometimes referred to as *Quetelet's Index*. A BMI of 30 or more is a commonly used criterion for defining obesity in both sexes, even though at equal BMI women are consistently fatter than men. Body fat percentages are discussed in more detail later (see page 190).

Weight and age

One of the many criticisms of the Metropolitan Life tables is that they do not take age into account, ie they assume that there is no reason for anyone to gain weight after 25. But experience tells us otherwise. The fact is that most people *do* gain weight as they get older because age is a fattening process. Young and old people of comparable body weights are not comparably obese; young people have a much greater lean body mass than older people.

Recent research from Dr Reubin Andres and his team in the USA suggests that a little weight gain over the years is both natural and healthy. In other words, the pattern should be one of leanness in the twenties followed by a very moderate weight gain as one gets older. Moreover, Dr Andries has been able to demonstrate that this gradual increase in weight is associated with the lowest mortality in both males and females. Accordingly, the height/weight tables which we shall be using later in this chapter will also be age-related.

Weight ranges and health

Most people who decide to try and lose weight will have some fixed idea of what their ideal or 'goal' weight should be. Organizations such as Weight Watchers use this sort of approach by prescribing a 'target weight' for each of the programme participants. All efforts are then directed towards the achievement of this particular number, with success (usually short-lived), being marked by a sort of graduation ceremony. But from a health perspective there is good reason to question the common notion that everyone has a **single** ideal weight for health. Recent evidence suggests that we each have a **range** of weights that are healthy for us and sticking obsessively to a predetermined target is unnecessary and maybe unrealistic. The most important thing is that you should be comfortable with the way you look, and provided that you fall within the acceptable weight range you really should not be too concerned about a few pounds either way.

The truth is that a large part of what determines our shape, our metabolism and fat distribution, is genetically programmed. Setting totally unrealistic weight targets or attempting to attain a fundamentally different body shape by 'spot-reducing' is not merely doomed to failure — it may well bring you into conflict with your biological makeup. For all sorts of reasons, women are especially vulnerable to dieting propaganda, a fact which may help to explain the worrying increase in eating disorders such as anorexia and bulimia in young females.

WHAT CAUSES OBESITY?

There is no doubt whatever that genetics has a large part to play in determining our risk of obesity. Whatever the genetic mechanism might be, if one of your parents was obese you have a 40 per cent chance of becoming obese yourself; if both of your parents were, your risk is about 80 per cent. Conversely, if both your parents were slim, your risk is less than 10 per cent. Studies on twins suggest that up to 70 per cent of differences in obesity can be attributed to genetic influences, with the remaining 30 per cent due to environmental factors, including diet and exercise.

But the simple fact is that most people are overweight because they have a total calorie intake which is substantially higher than their energy expenditure — ie they eat too much. A number of studies have shown that overweight people invariably underestimate their food intake (by 35–54 per cent), and overestimate their calorie expenditure via exercise. They are probably not doing this intentionally, however, a fact which underscores the complex nature of the problem.

The simplified basic facts are these:

- If the food you eat provides the same amount of energy (calories) as your body utilizes, then your weight will remain unchanged.
- If you eat fewer calories than your body utilizes, then you will have an energy deficit and you will lose weight.
- If you eat more calories than your body requires, then this energy surplus will be stored and you will put on weight.

Key note

Our energy needs are measured in kilocalories (kcal), more usually referred to simply as 'calories'. I have used the terms interchangeably throughout the text, so remember that 'calories' and 'kcals' mean exactly the same thing.

Exercise, obesity and metabolic rate

One of the most important mechanisms which determines how much weight you will carry is your metabolic rate, or basal metabolic rate (BMR). The metabolic rate is measured by the number of calories your body 'burns up' to take care of its basic physiological needs: breathing, heartbeat, maintaining body temperature, repair of body tissues and the billions of chemical reactions that keep you alive and functioning. In most adults, BMR accounts for about 50–70 per cent of daily energy expenditure, with much of the rest spent in physical activity. Dieting and exercise can influence the metabolic rate, either decreasing or increasing it.

The essence of dieting is that you should create an *energy deficit*, ie you have to burn up more calories than you take in. In theory, then, if a reduction in your calorie intake is less than that required by your BMR (assuming that you are sedentary), you would lose weight. But this assumes that your metabolic rate remains constant. The problem is that as you diet, your metabolic rate starts to slow down and because your body's energy requirements are less, you need fewer calories. This is why after a while, cutting your calories becomes a less effective means of losing weight. The thermostat becomes set at a lower level, and therefore your energy requirements are less. Each time you cut the calories in an effort to lose weight, the thermostat becomes set at a lower point and the rate at which you burn energy becomes less. In fact the more often you diet, the more quickly your body will respond by lowering the metabolic rate which may eventually become slowed down permanently. Because you are constantly trying to stay ahead of the game, you have to cut your diet back to the point where it no longer becomes sustainable. At this point you will probably give up and return (with a vengeance) to your old eating habits, including fat consumption. Obese individuals have a natural (most likely genetic) preference for fatty food, and since fat is by far the richest dietary source of calories, the fat weight begins to accumulate rapidly.

This phenomenon may well help to explain why it is that so many fat people claim that they actually eat very little. Many of these people have been chronic dieters, and have presumably set their metabolic rates at a permanently low level. Because their energy requirements are so low, in order to create an energy deficit they have to make really savage cuts in their calorie intake to produce any noticeable effect on their body weight, and most find that they simply cannot sustain this. A number of recent studies confirm that many women really do maintain their weight on as little as 1500 kcals a day, simply because they have such low metabolic rates. Moreover, those with the lowest metabolic rates are those who had been on the most diets.

Another factor which tends to exacerbate the situation is that dieting invariably results in some loss of muscle tissue. In fact regular dieting leads to cumulative changes in body composition, characterized by an increase in the ratio of fat to lean body tissue. The net result of a diet in a sedentary individual may be a loss of weight, but the body of such a dieter may actually contain a much greater proportion of fat. If you regain weight after a period of dieting you are bound to be fatter than before, simply because you will have replaced heavier muscle with lighter and bulkier fat.

Yet another important consequence of this change in body composition is that the larger the proportion of fat in the body, the lower the metabolic rate. Conversely, the greater the proportion of lean body tissue, the higher the metabolic rate. So whilst dieting itself reduces metabolic rate, the changes in body composition which occur as a result of dieting in the sedentary individual contributes to a further lowering of BMR.

Although most of us believe that fatness comes from eating too much, there is good evidence that it is just as easily caused by inactivity. Whatever makes an individual overweight, exercise can usually play a major role in helping them to lose weight and an even more significant role in maintaining that weight loss. By helping to preserve lean body tissue, regular exercise prevents the inevitable reduction in metabolic rate which normally accompanies dieting in the sedentary individual. Of course it also contributes to weight loss by burning calories and thereby helping to create an energy deficit.

At first sight the calorie expenditure involved in most forms of physical activity, even vigorous physical activity, is not all that impressive. A mile of jogging, for example, burns only about 100 to 120 kcals, roughly the number in a large apple or two biscuits. However, as we shall see later, even modest increases in caloric expenditure can lead to long-term differences in caloric balance, provided exercise is performed on a regular basis. For example, a daily increase in energy expenditure of only 300 kcal over a period of 12 weeks, would lead to weight loss of around 7 pounds (3.3 Kg).

There are other advantages also. For example, exercise is an effective appetite suppressant so that if you eat within a couple of hours of vigorous exercise, you will tend to eat less. Another great benefit is that it tends to burn calories from the kind of tissue you really want to get rid of, ie from fat, and not from muscle. Conversely, as we have seen above, dieting alone tends to bring about destruction of lean body tissue and adverse effects on overall body composition. For all these reasons, exercise will be the cornerstone of the weight reduction programme outlined in the Action Plan later.

Body fat distribution

The problem with diagnosing obesity from height and body weight tables, or calculating body mass index, is that these measures do not take into account the distribution of fat. Recent research in the United States and Sweden suggests that **where** your body stores fat may be even more important to health than your overall body weight.

There are two main types of fat distribution in the obese. The first is the so-called 'android' or male type, in which the fat is deposited centrally, ie over the belly. This is also called truncal obesity. The second is the 'gynoid' or female pattern in which the fat is deposited peripherally, ie over the hips, buttocks and thighs (see Figure 10.1). It's important to understand that male pattern fat distribution can occur in both men and women, as can the female or 'gynoid' distribution.

This difference is important because there is good evidence that the male pattern of fat deposition, mainly over the belly, is associated with a significantly increased risk of diabetes, heart disease and stroke. This is true irrespective of whether it occurs in a woman or a man. Conversely, the female pattern of fat distribution is not associated with any increase in risk. In other words, a pot belly is bad news, irrespective of whether you are male or female and pear-shaped people are at a lower risk than apple shaped people. That's the bad news.

The good news is that high risk abdominal fat is much easier to lose, because the abdomen seems to store it by expanding fat cells, which can also be shrunk. Fat stores around the hips and thighs are made up of a larger number of much smaller fat cells, which don't shrink very much and are therefore much more difficult to get rid of. Women spend an enormous amount of time, money and effort trying to lose fat from the thighs and hips — usually without success. But from a *health* point of view, these fat stores are metabolically inert and are of no importance.

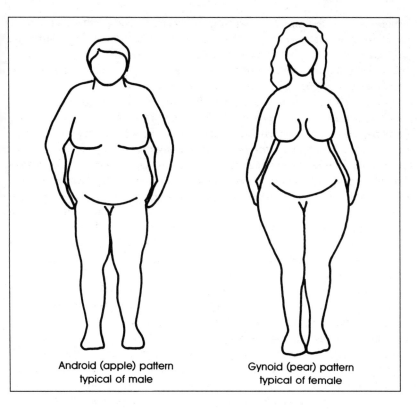

Android (apple) pattern
typical of male

Gynoid (pear) pattern
typical of female

Figure 10.1 Body fat distribution

A simple way to get an idea of your own fat distribution is to divide your waist measurement by your hip measurement, ie the waist/hip ratio. Ratios for men should not exceed 1.0 and for women 0.8. So a man with a waist measurement of 42 inches and a hip measurement of 38 inches has a waist/hip ratio of 1.1 which indicates truncal or central obesity and an increased risk. A woman with a 24 inch waist and 36 inch hips has a waist/hip ratio of 0.6 — well within the acceptable range. However, if her hips remained the same but her waist increased to 34 inches, the ratio would be 0.94 which indicates truncal fat distribution and an increased risk of obesity-related diseases.

The waist/hip ratio will be used in the self-assessment section later.

Fat children and fat adults

About 80 per cent of fat children become fat adults and a significant part of this tendency is due to genetic factors. Evidence would suggest that we are genetically programmed to carry a certain number of fat cells and minimal amount of body fat, and this obviously varies considerably from one individual to the next. Many of the fat cells are deposited before birth, but there is a further addition during the second year of life and during adolescence. Moreover, once these fat cells are set down they cannot be removed. As you would expect, therefore, a number of studies have shown that children and adults with large numbers of fat cells have a very hard time losing weight.

In adult life, weight gain is primarily due to an increase in the *size*, rather than number, of the cells. In fact, the body will only begin to manufacture additional cells when those already present are unable to store any more fat, usually when the degree of obesity exceeds 30 per cent of the desirable weight. With an excess of calories, the fat cells swell (*hypertrophy*) to accommodate increased fat stores. Conversely, dieting removes fat from the cells which therefore become smaller. However, since the number of cells remains constant, there is always the risk that if energy intake exceeds energy requirements, they will begin to accumulate fat again.

But whilst the luck of the genetic draw undoubtedly makes some of us more prone to obesity than others, genetics is not destiny. The number of fat cells may be largely out of your control, but there is still considerable scope for us to control the amount of fat which they hold — by adopting sensible exercise habits and a prudent diet. Establishing healthy behaviour patterns must be done as early as possible. which is why the current lack of emphasis on nutritional education in our schools is so lamentable. Fat children must be recognized as having a substantially increased risk of becoming overweight in adult life, even if they slim down during late childhood. Health surveys carried out on British children make depressing reading; in general they are much too fat and exercise far too little. Unfortunately they are often merely adopting the same pattern of behaviour as their parents, but this is not a popular public health message.

Finally, do bear in mind that a genetic tendency to obesity may not be expressed until middle-age. If you're thin at 30, you may well become fat at 45. Constant vigilance will be required to keep your weight under control and this is why adopting healthy habits early on is so important — it will become a normal and integral part of your life, rather than something else which has to be taken care of.

Smoking cessation and weight gain

Despite the well publicized adverse health effects of tobacco and the declining prevalence of smoking both in the UK and the United States, about one-third of adults in this country and one-quarter of adults in the USA continue to smoke cigarettes. Some smokers may be reluctant to stop smoking because they are concerned about weight gain.

A major study recently published in the *New England Journal of Medicine* suggests that while major weight gain can be a consequence of smoking cessation, it only occurs in a minority of individuals. For most people, the expected weight gain is quite small and the associated risk is irrelevant when compared with the risks of continuing to smoke.

Table 10.1 Calorific values of alcoholic drinks

Drink	Calories (kcals)
1 pint of beer	300
1 glass of wine	80
1 gin and tonic	140
1 whisky	90
1 vodka and orange	130

■ Remember: 3500 extra calories (kcals) will produce 1 pound of fat.

Alcohol and obesity

Alcohol is a rich source of calories — one gin and tonic contains around 150 calories, roughly the same as a large ice-cream (see Table 10.1). So if you're serious about losing weight you will have to watch your alcohol intake very carefully. Don't be deceived by the low-sugar diet beers either — they may have less sugar, but their higher alcoholic content means more calories.

SELF-ASSESSMENT AND INTERPRETATION OF RESULTS

Before turning to specific measures, it's worthwhile pausing for a moment to ask yourself whether you have a genetic tendency to weight gain. Are your parents or other members of your immediate family overweight or obese? If so, then you will need to be especially vigilant both for yourself and for your own children.

We shall use four measures to evaluate your present weight and body composition.

1. **Your desirable weight range**

    Table 10.2 will give you a rough initial estimate as to whether you fall within the acceptable weight range for your height and age. Please note that these values are based upon weight without clothes and height without shoes.

    When you have measured your body weight, you should enter it into the first box in Table 10.6 on page 196.

2. **Body Mass Index (BMI)**

    This measurement takes into account your weight and your height, but has the advantage of expressing them in a single number. If you turn to the Body Mass Index chart (Table 10.3) you will be able to find your Body Mass Index without doing the calculation. Simply find your height on the horizontal axis, your weight on the vertical axis, and the point of intersection will give you your Body Mass Index. For example, if I am 5 feet 11 inches (1.8 metres) tall, and weigh 14 stone 4 pounds

Table 10.2   Weight range for men and women by age, in lbs.

Height (ft–in)	Age (years)†				
	25	35	45	55	65
4–10	84–111	92–119	99–127	107–135	115–142
4–11	87–115	95–123	103–131	111–139	119–147
5–0	90–119	98–127	106–135	114–143	123–152
5–1	93–123	101–131	110–140	118–148	127–157
5–2	96–127	105–136	113–144	122–153	131–163
5–3	99–131	108–140	117–149	126–158	135–168
5–4	102–135	112–145	121–154	130–163	140–173
5–5	106–140	115–149	125–159	134–168	144–179
5–6	109–144	119–154	129–164	138–174	148–184
5–7	112–148	122–159	133–169	143–179	153–190
5–8	116–153	126–163	137–174	147–184	158–196
5–9	119–157	130–168	141–179	151–190	162–201
5–10	122–162	134–173	145–184	156–195	167–207
5–11	126–167	137–178	149–190	160–201	172–213
6–0	129–171	141–183	153–195	165–207	177–219
6–1	133–176	145–188	157–200	169–213	182–225
6–2	137–181	149–194	162–206	174–219	187–232
6–3	141–186	153–199	166–212	179–225	192–238
6–4	144–191	157–205	(171–218)	184–231	197–244

* Values in this table are for height without shoes and weight without clothes. To convert inches to centimetres, multiply by 2.54; to convert pounds to kilograms, multiply by 0.455.
† Data from Andres, R, Gerontology Research Center, National Institute of Aging, Baltimore, MD.
Reproduced with permission.

(90 kilograms) my Body Mass Index is 27.9. Acceptable ranges for BMI by age, derived from the weight table above, are shown in Table 10.4.

You can enter your BMI and the acceptable range for your age in box 2 in Table 10.6.

3. **Body fat percentage**
    Your body weight and BMI will give you a broad indication of whether you are within the acceptable range for your weight, according to your height and age, but they tell you nothing about your body composition, ie the amount of fat compared with lean body mass. Lean body weight (muscle, bone, tendon etc), is desirable weight, whereas fat clearly is not. It is quite possible to be well within the recommended weight range, but to be overfat. Equally, a very muscular individual may be well outside the acceptable weight range and yet only 10–12 per cent of this may be fat weight (remember that muscle is heavier than fat). So the important question may not be what you actually weigh, but what proportion of your total body weight is fat, and what proportion is lean body tissue.

To measure body composition accurately requires sophisticated equipment, but the charts in Figure 10.2 will allow you to perform a quick estimate of your own. For women this is based upon hip size and height, and for men weight and waist measurement. Healthy ranges are 17–20 per cent for males and 19–24 per cent for women, although younger people should obviously have a lower fat percentage than those in later life. Estimate your body fat percentage and enter it into box 3 in Table 10.6.

4. **Waist-hip ratio**

You have now determined your actual body weight, your BMI and an estimate of your total body fat percentage. The final measure is to gain some idea as to how this fat is distributed. This is the waist/hip ratio referred to earlier.

To obtain the ratio you simply divide your waist measurement (taken in a relaxed state!) by your hip measurement. Acceptable ranges are up to 1.0 for men, and up to 0.8 for women.

Enter your waist/hip ratio in box 4 in Table 10.6.

ACTION PLAN

In essence, the way to produce sustained weight loss is to combine a low fat diet with a programme of regular, moderate exercise.

Trying to lose weight by diet alone is very difficult. Relying on exercise alone is not very rewarding either — to lose one pound of fat you would need to run or walk about thirty five miles. The secret is to use a combination of diet and exercise. Let me explain why. Each pound of fat has an energy value of 3500 kcals. You can lose a pound of fat in one of three ways: dieting, exercise or a combination of diet and exercise. If you were to cut out a single slice of buttered bread from your diet each day (about 100 calories), you could lose one pound of fat in 35 days. Equally, you can burn about 100 kcals per day by jogging one mile (assuming that everything else remains constant). However, if you cut out the slice of bread *and* jog a mile each day, your energy deficit will be 200 kcals and you will lose your pound of fat in only half the time, ie seventeen and a half days. You can also speed the process up by increasing your exercise and reducing your food intake further.

Let's look at diet and exercise in relation to losing weight in more detail.

DIETING FOR WEIGHT LOSS

A weight-reducing diet should have **three** main characteristics:

1. It should reduce the food energy intake (calories) to below the amount necessary to maintain body weight. This calorie 'deficit' will result in weight loss.

Table 10.3 Body Mass Index (BMI) = weight (kg)/(height metres)^2 for specified height and weight, without shoes and clothes

Weight kg (lb)	Height m^2(in)																
	1.47 (58)	1.50 (59)	1.52 (60)	1.55 (61)	1.57 (62)	1.60 (63)	1.63 (64)	1.65 (65)	1.68 (66)	1.70 (67)	1.73 (68)	1.75 (69)	1.78 (70)	1.80 (71)	1.83 (72)	1.85 (73)	1.88 (74)
50(110)	23.0	22.2	21.5	20.8	20.1	19.5	18.9	18.3	17.8	17.2	16.7	16.2	15.8	15.3	14.9	14.5	14.1
52(115)	24.0	23.2	22.5	21.7	21.0	20.4	19.7	19.1	18.6	18.0	17.5	17.0	16.5	16.0	15.6	15.2	14.8
54(120)	25.1	24.2	23.4	22.7	21.9	21.3	20.6	20.0	19.4	18.8	18.2	17.7	17.2	16.7	16.3	15.8	15.4
56(125)	26.1	25.2	24.4	23.6	22.9	22.1	21.5	20.8	20.2	19.6	19.0	18.5	17.9	17.4	17.0	16.5	16.0
59(130)	27.2	26.3	25.4	24.6	23.8	23.0	22.3	21.6	21.0	20.4	19.8	19.2	18.7	18.1	17.6	17.2	16.7
61(135)	28.2	27.3	26.4	25.5	24.7	23.9	23.2	22.5	21.8	21.1	20.5	19.9	19.4	18.8	18.3	17.8	17.3
63(140)	29.3	28.3	27.3	26.5	25.6	24.8	24.0	23.3	22.6	21.9	21.3	20.7	20.1	19.5	19.0	18.5	18.0
65(145)	30.3	29.3	28.3	27.4	26.5	25.7	24.9	24.1	23.4	22.7	22.0	21.4	20.8	20.2	19.7	19.1	18.6
68(150)	31.4	30.3	29.3	28.3	27.4	26.6	25.7	25.0	24.2	23.5	22.8	22.2	21.5	20.9	20.3	19.8	19.3
70(155)	32.4	31.3	30.3	29.3	28.4	27.5	26.6	25.8	25.0	24.3	23.6	22.9	22.2	21.6	21.0	20.4	19.9
72(160)	33.4	32.3	31.2	30.2	29.3	28.3	27.5	26.6	25.8	25.1	24.3	23.6	23.0	22.3	21.7	21.1	20.5
74(165)	34.5	33.3	32.2	31.2	30.2	29.2	28.3	27.5	26.6	25.8	25.1	24.4	23.7	23.0	22.4	21.8	21.2
77(170)	35.5	34.3	33.2	32.1	31.1	30.1	29.2	28.3	27.4	26.6	25.8	25.1	24.4	23.7	23.1	22.4	21.8

79(175)	36.6	35.3	34.2	33.1	32.0	31.0	30.0	29.1	28.2	27.4	26.6	25.8	25.1	24.4	23.7	23.1	22.5
81(180)	37.6	36.4	35.2	34.0	32.9	31.9	30.9	30.0	29.1	28.2	27.4	26.6	25.8	25.1	24.4	23.7	23.1
83(185)	38.7	37.4	36.1	35.0	33.8	32.8	31.8	30.8	29.9	29.0	28.1	27.3	26.5	25.8	25.1	24.4	23.8
86(190)	39.7	38.4	37.1	35.9	34.8	33.7	32.6	31.6	30.7	29.8	28.9	28.1	27.3	26.5	25.8	25.1	24.4
88(195)	40.8	39.4	38.1	36.8	35.7	34.5	33.5	32.4	31.5	30.5	29.6	28.8	28.0	27.2	26.4	25.7	25.0
90(200)	41.8	40.4	39.1	37.8	36.6	35.4	34.3	33.3	32.3	31.3	30.4	29.5	28.7	27.9	27.1	26.4	25.7
92(205)	42.8	41.4	40.0	38.7	37.5	36.3	35.2	34.1	33.1	32.1	31.2	30.3	29.4	28.6	27.8	27.0	26.3
95(210)	43.9	42.4	41.0	39.7	38.4	37.2	36.0	34.9	33.9	32.9	31.9	31.0	30.1	29.3	28.5	27.7	27.0
97(215)	44.9	43.4	42.0	40.6	39.3	38.1	36.9	35.8	34.7	33.7	32.7	31.8	30.8	30.0	29.2	28.4	27.6
99(220)	46.0	44.4	43.0	41.6	40.2	39.0	37.8	36.6	35.5	34.5	33.5	32.5	31.6	30.7	29.8	29.0	28.2
101(225)	47.0	45.4	43.9	42.5	41.2	39.9	38.6	37.4	36.3	35.2	34.2	33.2	32.3	31.4	30.5	29.7	28.9
104(230)	48.1	46.5	44.9	43.5	42.1	40.7	39.5	38.3	37.1	36.0	35.0	34.0	33.0	32.1	31.2	30.3	29.5
106(235)	49.1	47.5	45.9	44.4	43.0	41.6	40.3	39.1	37.9	36.8	35.7	34.7	33.7	32.8	31.9	31.0	30.2
108(240)	50.2	48.5	46.9	45.3	43.9	42.5	41.2	39.9	38.7	37.6	36.5	35.4	34.4	33.5	32.6	31.7	30.8
110(245)	51.2	49.5	47.8	46.3	44.8	43.4	42.1	40.8	39.5	38.4	37.3	36.2	35.2	34.2	33.2	32.3	31.5
113(250)	52.3	50.5	48.8	47.2	45.7	44.3	42.9	41.6	40.4	39.2	38.0	36.9	35.9	34.9	33.9	33.0	32.1

Table 10.4 Acceptable ranges for body mass index (BMI) by age

Age (years)	25–34	35–44	45–54	55–64	65+9
BMI	17–23	19–25	21–26	22–28	24–29

2. It must, in all other respects, be nutritionally adequate in terms of vitamins etc.
3. The diet must be acceptable to the person trying to lose the weight.

1. Reducing total calorie intake

The key to this is to reduce the fat content of the diet. A low fat diet (which will automatically reduce the number of calories) is the absolute corner-stone of dietary treatment. The reason is quite simple, as shown in Table 10.5. As you can see each unit of fat contains more than twice the number of calories as protein or carbohydrate.

It follows that if you want to lose the calories, you have to lose the fat. You should familiarize yourself with the elements of a low fat diet which are outlined on pages 76–78. The principles, however, are as follows:

- Choose lean meats, and trim off the visible fat before eating.
- Eat more fish and poultry (remove skin from poultry).
- Eat less chocolate, cakes, pastries and biscuits.
- Try to use a frying pan less often. Use alternative methods of cooking such as grilling, baking or boiling. Microwave cooking is particularly helpful. If you do fry food, try to use a polyunsaturated vegetable oil such as olive oil, sunflower oil or safflower oil.
- Eat fewer eggs, and less cheese, cream and other dairy products which tend to be high in saturated fat.
- Drink less whole milk and use either semi-skimmed or skimmed milk.
- Eat more fresh vegetables and fruit and try to eat a purely vegetarian meal on one or two occasions per week.
- Use butter, margarine and other spreads sparingly.

Table 10.5 Comparative calorie values

Nutrient	Energy (kcal/gram)
Fat	9.00
Carbohydrate	3.75
Protein	4.00
Alcohol	7.00

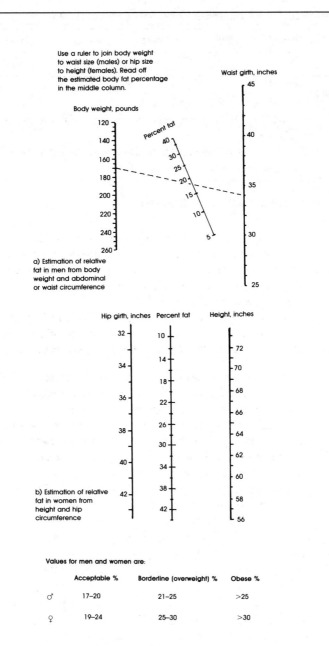

Use a ruler to join body weight to waist size (males) or hip size to height (females). Read off the estimated body fat percentage in the middle column.

Waist girth, inches

Body weight, pounds

Percent fat

a) Estimation of relative fat in men from body weight and abdominal or waist circumference

Hip girth, inches   Percent fat   Height, inches

b) Estimation of relative fat in women from height and hip circumference

Values for men and women are:

	Acceptable %	Borderline (overweight) %	Obese %
♂	17–20	21–25	>25
♀	19–24	25–30	>30

Source: *Sensible Fitness* (2nd edition) by JH Wilmore, Leisure Press, Champaign, IL (pages 30 and 31). Copyright 1986 by Jack Wilmore. Reprinted by permission of Human Kinetics Publishers.

Figure 10.2   Estimation of relative fat in men and women

Table 10.6   Your body weight/composition results

1	Body weight (without clothes) . . . . lbs
	Acceptable range for height and age . . . . lbs
2	Body Mass Index (BMI) . . . .
	Acceptable range for age . . . .
	Estimated body fat % . . . .
	♂ Acceptable range = 17–20%
	♀ Acceptable range = 19–24%
4	Waist measurement . . . . inches
	Hip measurement . . . . inches
	Waist/hip ratio . . . .

2. Ensuring the weight reducing diet is nutritionally adequate

Although low in fat, your diet must also have an overall balance in terms of
vitamins and other essential elements. This means that the construction of
your daily diet is of considerable importance. Examples of low fat dietary
programmes are shown in Tables 10.7, 10.8 and 10.9. They represent
1200, 1500 and 2000 kcals per day respectively, but also contain a good
balance between carbohydrate, protein and trace elements. Although the
basic structure of this diet should remain the same each day, by following
the guidelines in Table 4.4 on pages 78–9, you can obviously vary this quite
a lot by choosing foods to suit your own taste.

3. The diet must be acceptable

By 'acceptable' I obviously don't mean 'easy' or 'exciting'. In other words
you are going to have to compromise to some extent — this is self-evident. If
you are not prepared to make some effort to compromise, you might just as
well carry on with your normal diet and get fatter as a consequence.
Arguments about 'not having the willpower' are not going to cut any ice.
We all carry out tasks which we find boring, unpleasant or difficult.
Getting up to feed a hungry baby at night is not a question of willpower —
it's a basic necessity and we just have to do it. Getting up in the morning
and shaving before going to work is something we just do as a part of a
normal, daily routine. Watching our diet should be regarded in just the
same way. If you can convince yourself that losing weight is just one of the
number of daily tasks that just has to be done, the 'willpower' argument
becomes non-existent.

Table 10.7 Dietary programme — 1200 calories (kcals)
Suggested Meal Plan
This is only a *suggested* menu. For variety many meals can be adapted to fit in
with this plan. (Choose alternative foods from Table 4.4 on page 78.)

Breakfast	— ½ fresh grapefruit
	Choice of ONE of the following:
	— 1½ oz (37g) breakfast cereal (preferably wholemeal)*
	— 1 egg (not fried)
	— 1 small *lean* rasher of bacon
	PLUS
	— 3 small slices wholemeal bread
Mid-morning	Tea, coffee or low calorie drink
Mid-day	— Home-made clear soup
	Choice of ONE of the following:
	— 2 oz (50g) *lean* meat
	— 4 oz (100g) fish
	— 1 oz (25g) cheese
	— 4 oz (100g) cottage cheese
	— 6 oz (150g) baked beans
	PLUS
	— 3 small slices wholemeal bread
	— Large helping of vegetables or salad
	— One portion of fruit, fresh, stewed or tinned in unsweetened juice
Mid-afternoon	Tea, coffee or low calorie drink
Evening meal	Choice of ONE of the following:
	— 3 oz (75g) *lean* meat
	— 6 oz (150g) fish
	— 2 oz (50g) cheese
	Plus ONE of the following:
	— 6 oz (150g) Potato — preferably cooked with skins
	— 1½ oz (37g) Pasta
	— 1½ oz (37g) Rice (raw weights)
	PLUS
	— Large helping of vegetables or salad
	— One portion of fruit, fresh, stewed or tinned in unsweetened juice
Bedtime	Tea, coffee or low calorie drink

Daily allowance*
½ pt (300 ml) skimmed milk or ¼ pt (150 ml) whole milk (* and if you choose breakfast
cereal allow an extra ¼ pt)
1 oz (25g) low fat spread or ½ oz (12g) butter or margarine
No more than three eggs per week

Table 10.8　Dietary programme — 1500 calories (kcals)
Suggested Meal Plan
This is only a *suggested* menu. For variety many meals can be adapted to fit in
with this plan. (Choose alternative foods from Table 4.4 on page 78.)

Breakfast	— ½ fresh grapefruit Choice of ONE of the following: — 1 oz (25g) breakfast cereal (preferably wholemeal)* — 1 egg (not fried) — 1 small *lean* rasher of bacon PLUS — 2 small slices wholemeal bread
Mid-morning	— 1 digestive biscuit or 1 portion of fruit — Tea, coffee or low calorie drink
Mid-day	— Home-made clear soup Choice of ONE of the following: — 2 oz (50g) *lean* meat — 4 oz (100g) fish — 1 oz (25g) cheese — 4 oz (100g) cottage cheese — 6 oz (150g) baked beans PLUS — 3 small slices wholemeal bread — Large helping of vegetables or salad — One portion of fruit, fresh, stewed or tinned in unsweetened juice
Mid-afternoon	— 1 digestive biscuit or 1 portion of fruit — Tea, coffee or low calorie drink
Evening meal	Choice of ONE of the following: — 3 oz (75g) *lean* meat — 6 oz (150g) fish — 2 oz (50g) cheese Plus ONE of the following: — 8 oz (150g) Potato — preferably cooked with skins — 2 oz (37g) Pasta — 2 oz (37g) Rice (raw weights) PLUS — Large helping of vegetables or salad — One portion of fruit, fresh, stewed or tinned in unsweetened juice
Bedtime	— 1 digestive biscuit or 1 small slice wholemeal bread — Tea, coffee or low calorie drink

Daily allowance*:
1 pt (600 ml) skimmed milk or ½ pt (300 ml) whole milk (* and if you choose breakfast
cereal allow an extra ¼ pt)
1 oz (25g) low fat spread or ½ oz (12g) butter or margarine
No more than three eggs per week

Table 10.9 Dietary programme — 2000 calories (kcals)
Suggested Meal Plan
This is only a *suggested* menu. For variety many meals can be adapted to fit in with this plan. (Choose alternative foods from Table 4.4 on page 78.)

Breakfast	— ½ fresh grapefruit, if desired
	— 1 oz wholemeal cereal
	Choice of ONE of the following:
	— 1 egg (not fried)
	— 2 oz cottage cheese
	PLUS
	— 3 small slices wholemeal bread
Mid-morning	— 2 digestive biscuits
	— Tea, coffee or low calorie drink
Mid-day	— Home-made clear soup, if desired
	Choice of ONE of the following:
	— 2 oz (50g) *lean* meat
	— 3 oz (75g) cottage cheese
	— 4 oz (100g) fish
	— 1 oz (25g) fish
	— 1 oz (25g) cheese
	PLUS
	— 3 small slices wholemeal bread
	— Large helping of vegetables or salad
	— One portion of fruit and low fat yogurt
Mid-afternoon	— 2 digestive biscuits
	— Tea, coffee or low calorie drink
Evening meal	Choice of ONE of the following:
	— 3 oz (75g) *lean* meat
	— 6 oz (150g) fish
	plus one of the following:
	— 8 oz Potato preferably cooked with skins
	— 2 oz (50g) Pasta (raw weights)
	— 2 oz (50g) Rice (raw weights)
	PLUS
	— Large helping of vegetables or salad
	— One portion of fruit, or milk pudding (skimmed milk and sweetener)
Bedtime	— 1 small slice wholemeal bread
	— Tea, coffee or low calorie drink

Daily allowance:
½ pt (300 ml) whole milk or 1 pt (600 ml) skimmed milk and 1 oz (25g) low fat spread or ½ pt (12g) butter or margarine.
No more than three eggs per week.

Table 10.10   Calorie expenditure by activity

Activity	kcal/hour	Activity	kcal/hour
Aerobic dance	435	Running (8 mph)	660
Badminton	360	Sitting (desk work)	80
Cycling (10 mph)	410	Skating	435
Cycling (13 mph)	525	Skiing (cross country)	550
Driving a car	80	Skipping (rope)	650
Football (soccer)	545	Squash	800
Gardening	165	Swimming (continuous)	650
Golf	265	Table tennis	220
Hiking/backpacking	490	Tennis (singles)	450
Housework (general)	200	Walking (3 mph)	260
Jogging (5 mph)	550	Walking (4 mph)	400

Figures given represent average estimates in calories (kcals)/hour

Exercise and weight loss

Exercise has been discussed in detail elsewhere (see Chapter 7). It is an extremely important adjunct to a weight loss programme, but in itself is a remarkably ineffective means of losing weight. This is mainly because very fat people have such a low exercise tolerance that their ability to sustain exercise at a level which makes a meaningful contribution to total calorie expenditure is negligible. Table 10.10 shows the calorie expenditure for a variety of activities according to weight. To repeat, it is the combination of regular exercise with restriction of calorie intake via a low fat diet which will bring you the results you need.

Some experts have argued that although the number of calories used during the exercise phase itself is relatively small, because of its impact on Basal Metabolic Rate (BMR) the value of exercise in terms of the number of calories burned, is much greater. Because exercise raises the metabolic rate and keeps it up, so the argument goes, the active body keeps burning extra calories long after the exercise session is finished.

This view is wrong. Exercise does not cause an increase in BMR, except in elite athletes who are able to sustain very high work rates for long periods. However, exercise does appear to make an important contribution to *maintaining* weight loss once it has occurred.

What kind of exercise is more effective? In general terms, aerobic exercises are the best kind for losing weight. These are exercises that increase the heart rate over a sustained period of time, examples of which are jogging, cycling, swimming, brisk walking etc. All of this is covered in Chapter 7.

One or two additional points are relevant. Firstly, if you are very overweight, it is best to stick to non-weight bearing exercises, for example, using a stationary exercise bicycle, swimming etc. Brisk walking is also excellent. Using a non-weight bearing programme to start with will significantly reduce the danger of sustaining an injury and will be much less traumatic to your joints. Whatever you do, start gradually and build up your programme over time.

Finally, 'spot reducing' exercises which are supposed to trim your thighs or your hips, simply don't help. **You cannot spot reduce.** Although these exercise programmes may help to tone up muscles in a specific area, they are not going to reduce the fat there. The distribution of fat in your body is determined genetically and all you can expect to do is to lower your overall fat stores, although you may tend to lose the most fat from areas where you have the most to lose.

EFFECTIVE WEIGHT LOSS — AN OUTLINE PROGRAMME

Let's apply the principles outlined above and show how reducing fat intake in combination with a moderate exercise programme can produce weight loss of about 2 lbs per week. The arithmetic, I assure you, is simple. I will assume that you are an average male or female with a daily calories intake of 2800 and 2000 kcals respectively. If you are a male I would suggest the diet structure on page 199 (2000 kcals), and if you are a female the plan on page 197 (1200 kcals). This means that a male and female will each have an energy deficit of about 800 kcals per day, or 5600 kcals per week. If we now assume that you are prepared to walk/jog two miles per day, you will make an additional contribution of 200 kcals per day or 1400 per week. Thus, your total calorie saving/expenditure will be 7000, which is equivalent to a 2 lbs weight loss. This is summarized in Table 10.11.

Alternatively, if you are a woman and you cannot manage the 1200 kcal programme, you can switch to the 1500 kcal diet and still lose about one and a half pounds per week. If you are a male and you can tolerate the 1500 kcal diet, you can expect to lose about three and a half pounds per week. This would be excessive; but this example illustrates the principle. The point is that by adjusting your calorie intake via diet, and your calorie expenditure via exercise, you can construct your own programme to suit your own individual needs.

How much weight should I aim to lose?

Target weights for weight loss are influenced by age and height; younger, taller people can usually achieve more rapid weight loss than older, shorter ones.

The recommended weight loss is between one and two pounds per week (0.5 to 1 kilogram). It is important not to try and exceed this because more rapid weight loss involves excess loss of lean (muscle) tissue.

Table 10.11 Expected weekly weight loss on a recommended diet/exercise programme

Daily kcal intake to maintain present body weight	Recom-mended diet (kcals)	kcals saved per day & × 7 (weekly)	kcal expenditure via exercise per day & × 7 (weekly)	Total kcal reduction	Weight loss per week (lbs)
Male 2800	2000	800 (5600)	200 (1400)	5600 + 1400 = 7000	2 lbs (1kg)
Female 2000	1200	800 (5600)	200 (1400)	5600 + 1400 = 7000	2 lbs (1kg)

a) Recommended diet 2000 kcals (male) and 1200 kcals (female)

Daily kcal intake to maintain present body weight	Recom-mended diet (kcals)	kcals saved per day & × 7 (weekly)	kcal expenditure via exercise per day & × 7 (weekly)	Total kcal reduction	Weight loss per week (lbs)
Male 2800	1500	1300 (9100)	200 (1400)	9100 + 1400 = 10 500	3.5 lbs (1.6kg)
Female 2000	1500	500 (3500)	200 (1400)	3500 + 1400 = 4900	1.4 lbs (0.63kg)

b) Recommended diet 1500 kcals (male and female)

On the other hand, anything less than about a pound a week will be very demoralizing and will make your efforts difficult to sustain.

Why does it get more difficult with time?

People often complain that losing weight becomes more difficult the longer their weight loss programme continues. There are a number of reasons for this.

Initially, your weight loss may be quite rapid. In the first two or three weeks of dieting you may in fact lose much more than 1–2 lbs per week — perhaps twice this amount. This is because you are losing not only fat, but also *glycogen* (a muscle storage form of sugar) and water. Loss of glycogen and water causes a rapid weight loss and this is the basis of most crash diets (see later). Once this effect has been lost, you will settle into a much slower but steady rate of weight loss. This does not mean that your diet is not going to be effective; it simply means that you are entering into a different physiological phase. The other point to note is that as you lose weight, your energy requirements to maintain your weight becomes less and so if you stay on the same diet you will lose less weight.

So remember that as you lose weight it becomes more difficult to go on losing weight, and at some point (depending upon how much you want to lose), you are going to need to adjust your diet and exercise. You can make this adjustment quite easily by either:

- reducing your calories; or
- increasing your exercise; or
- preferably, a combination of both.

Do I need to count calories?

In the past, weight management programmes have focused on calories. Dieters memorized lists of 'fattening' foods and 'good' foods. It's a boring and tedious process but it's also disheartening and unnecessary. The most important thing is to understand what produces weight loss rather than slavishly following calorie counters. In the plan which I have outlined previously, you simply apply the principles of a low-fat diet within a 1200, 1500 and 2000 kcals per day programme and combine this with a regular programme of moderate exercise. That's all you need to do. You then judge the effects of the programme by measuring your weight loss over time, aiming for around one to two pounds per week. It's as simple and straightforward as that.

What about crash diets?

I mentioned the issue of crash diets a little earlier on. If I am recommending a weight loss of one to two pounds per week, what about those programmes that many of your friends might have tried which claim weight losses of up to one pound per *day*? How can one explain a weight loss of 10–15 lbs per week? The answer is related to what I described earlier, ie the loss of glycogen and water. Most rapid weight loss programmes have one thing in common — they allow only a moderate intake of carbohydrate. This means that the body starts to utilize its own carbohydrate stores in the liver and muscles. As the glycogen is mobilized, water begins to move with it, so the large losses of weight which occur in the first few weeks of a crash diet programme are mainly the result of lost glycogen and water rather than body fat. After this point, the weight loss slows down rapidly and very often the individual becomes disillusioned at the sudden loss of progress. They tend to revert back to their normal diets, the glycogen and water are rapidly replaced and they are back to where they started from. They then become candidates for the next 'wonder' diet which repeats the cycle all over again.

The other potential danger with crash dieting is that you will tend to lose lean body mass (muscle tissue) as well as fat, glycogen and water. Over time, your lean body (muscle) tissue will diminish and your body fat percentage will increase.

For all these reasons, it is actually much more sensible to aim for a weight loss of around one to two pounds per week and not to be seduced by the totally unsubstantiated claims of 'miracle' diets. It really is mass-marketing mythology. The efficacy of a weight loss programme should be judged over *months* and *years*, not days and weeks.

The effects of cyclical weight loss — 'Yo-Yo' dieting

There is quite good evidence that people whose body weights fluctuate widely over time, are more liable to heart disease than are people who manage to maintain a relatively constant body weight. Evidence from the Framingham Heart Study shows that the people whose weight repeatedly cycles up and down have a greater risk of heart disease than those who maintain a more stable weight — even if the stable weight is higher. Men appear to be at a slightly greater risk than women, and weight fluctuation is more strongly associated with health risks in the younger age groups, ie 30–44 years. This makes it all the more important to lose weight gradually, but also to keep the weight off once you have achieved your target.

What is my ideal weight?

There is no way of defining an 'ideal' weight. As we saw earlier, most recommendations for weight ranges are derived from Life Insurance Tables, usually the Metropolitan Life (1959 or 1983). The problem is that differing weight tables may give widely differing recommendations for acceptable ranges by age and sex. This is one of the reasons why I have chosen to use a number of different measures of weight and body composition (see the early part of this chapter).

In the end, your 'ideal' weight is the one where the recommendations I have set out in terms of the four measurements have been achieved and where you *feel* the most comfortable. So, if you have a weight range within the acceptable range given in Table 10.2; your Body Mass Index (BMI) falls within the range for your age (Table 10.4); you have an acceptable body fat percentage as estimated from Figure 10.2 and your waist/hip ratio is less than 1.0 (male) and 0.8 (female) — you really have no need to worry. As long as you are within these broad parameters, you can effectively select your own 'ideal' weight according to the way you look and the way your clothes feel.

How should I monitor my progress?

In the self-assessment section we describe four measures of weight and body composition, ie

1.   A recommended weight range.
2.   Body Mass Index.
3.   Estimated body fat percentage.
4.   Waist/Hip Ratio.

As you progress with your programme, you can monitor your progress by repeating each of these four measurements.

Make sure that you weigh yourself at the same time each week (but don't weigh yourself any more frequently). The other three measurements should be repeated monthly.

Key note — Implementing your weight loss programme

1. Apply the principles of a low-fat diet (page 194).
2. Adopt the 1200, 1500 or 2000 calorie diet framework (pages 197–9).
3. Take up a regular programme of moderate exercise (see Chapter 7).
4. Monitor your progress periodically. I would suggest weighing yourself once a week and repeat the other three measurements (ie BMI, waist/hip ratio and body fat percentage) each month. Over a 12-week period you can expect to lose up to 25lbs.
5. Aim for a weight loss of around 1–2 lbs per week.
6. Avoid crash dieting.
7. Adjust your calorie intake and your exercise levels over time, since your requirements will change as you lose weight.
8. When you have achieved the weight you feel comfortable with, monitor yourself by weekly weighing.
9. Maintain your achieved weight via adjusting your calorie intake and your calorie expenditure via your exercise programme.
10. **Be consistent** and don't look for any quick fix solutions — there aren't any.

Part III

DIET AND NUTRITION

Chapter 11

EATING FOR HEALTH

Eating is one of life's great pleasures. The bewildering variety of new foods now on the market along with the much wider availability of different ethnic foods, has given us a greater range of choices than ever before. Moreover, being adventurous about your eating is by no means inconsistent with eating healthily.

The key to healthy and enjoyable eating is knowledge. Being informed about food gives you control which in turn allows you to make informed choices about what you **want** to eat, as opposed to what the food manufacturers would **like** you to eat.

The science of nutrition has grown exponentially during the last decade, and constitutes a firm foundation upon which to make recommendations for healthy eating. The problem is that the amount of nonsense written about diet has increased at the same time. There are few areas of popular writing on health so replete with false hopes, fads, irrational fears, insupportable claims, over-simplification and plain quackery. What most people end up with is a long list of dos and don'ts, with very little understanding of the reasoning behind them. Furthermore, although a number of recent surveys have shown that there is generally a much greater awareness of the importance of healthy eating, it also confirms that equally large numbers of people are hopelessly confused about many of the most important nutritional issues.

Nutrition is a complicated business but fortunately the principles are not difficult to understand given a reasonable degree of application and interest. In any event, there are few areas of knowledge in which your effort will be rewarded with such rich returns. Paul Saltman from the University of California puts it in a nutshell:

> Without an adequate amount and proper balance of nutrients, you are simply not going to live as long or as healthily, look as good, or work as hard as you are genetically programmed to do. Neither will you be able to run as fast, resist infection as well, or overcome illness as easily.

It is now clear that just as poor nutrition will increase the risk of various diseases, so good nutrition can substantially reduce those risks. Of course proper nutrition, however scientifically based, is not going to allow you to live for ever. There will always be limits imposed by our genetic make-up and many other factors. But it can help you to live right up to that limit and, in the process, to enjoy a healthier more active and more productive life.

My aim in this chapter is to give the essential facts about good nutrition, so that you can get the most enjoyment and the most benefit from your diet. For the sake of clarity, I have divided it into **four** sections:

1. — Contains essential background information about the various components of a good diet.
2. — Deals with some common sources of confusion about diet.
3. — Eating to avoid heart disease and cancer.
4. — Reading a food label.

1. NUTRITION: THE ESSENTIALS

You will probably remember from your schooldays that there are five major components of a balanced diet:

- Proteins
- Fats
- Carbohydrates
- Vitamins, minerals and trace elements
- Fish oils.

Nothing very much has changed, except that our understanding of each of these components and the contribution that they make to good health or disease, is greater today than ever before. I think it is worthwhile reviewing these because they are absolutely fundamental to your ability to make informed choices.

Proteins

Proteins are required for the maintenance and repair of all body tissues.

The major dietary sources of protein are meat, fish, shellfish, eggs, milk, cheese, lentils, peas, beans, bread and cereal grains. All protein, whether it comes from animals, fish or vegetable sources is made up from the same basic building blocks — the amino acids. There are 22 amino acids, and each protein chain consists of different sequences of amino acids strung together like a string of beads. Different foods contain different types of protein, and so it is an advantage to eat a variety of foods so as to ensure that you are getting enough of each of these amino acids.

It used to be thought that meat, cheese and eggs were essential sources of protein to be eaten in abundance. Whilst there is no harm in these foods eaten sparingly, they do of course contain large amounts of fat; hence the recommendation from a number of expert committees that we should use fish, vegetables and cereals as alternative protein sources.

Fats

There is still much confusion about some aspects of healthy eating, particularly the importance of dietary fats.

There are several different types of fat ie saturated, monounsaturated and polyunsaturated, but they all contain the same amount of energy (calories), and are all composed of what chemists call **fatty acids**. There are about 20 different fatty acids in food, and they all have different properties. It is the relative proportion of the different fatty acids in a fat or an oil, which makes it solid or liquid; healthy or unhealthy.

Fatty acids

Each fatty acid is made up of a chain of carbon atoms, which are joined to each other by an attractive force, or **bond**, and the number of bonds in the structure determines the physical characteristics of the fats.

Key note

Fatty acids can be either saturated or unsaturated, with the unsaturated being further divided into monounsaturates and polysaturates.

- **Saturated** fatty acids have *no* double bonds:

$$- C - C - C -$$

- **Monounsaturated** fatty acids have *one* double bond:

$$- C = C - C -$$

- **Polyunsaturated** fatty acids have *more than one* double bond:

$$- C = C = C -$$

As a broad generalization, saturated fats tend to be solid at room temperature, whereas mono- and polyunsaturated fats tend to be liquid.

All cooking fats and oils contain saturated, monounsaturated and polyunsaturated fatty acids. None is made of one type alone. As we shall see later, it is the **proportion** of different fatty acids that is important for health. If saturated fatty acids predominate, it is called a saturated fat. Butter, for example, contains some unsaturated fatty acids, but because about 66 per cent of them are saturated, we regard butter as a highly saturated fat. If unsaturated fatty acids (mono- or polyunsaturated) predominate, the fat or oil is called unsaturated. Olive oil, for example, contains about 14 per cent saturates, but 70 per cent monounsaturates.

Saturated fats

Saturated fats tend to be solid at room temperature. Examples of fats and oils which are saturated are:

- **Dairy fats** — Butter, cheese, cream etc.
- **Meat fats** — Beef, mutton, pork, lard, dripping, suet etc.
- **Plant fats** — Coconut oil, palm oil.
- **Processed fats** — Many fats used in industry to make cakes, biscuits, pies, snacks, sausages and some blended vegetable oils and margarines.

Saturated fats are important because they are strongly associated with the development of premature coronary artery disease. There is a remarkably large and consistent body of evidence to show that populations on diets high in saturated fats have a high incidence of coronary artery disease. This is because a diet which is composed of large amounts of saturated fat, will usually bring about a substantial increase in the blood cholesterol level which, as we have seen previously, is a major risk factor for coronary disease (see Chapter 4).

Monounsaturated fats

The best known example of a monounsaturated fatty acid is Oleic acid, which is the main constituent (more than 70 per cent) of olive oil.

Monounsaturated fats are not associated with premature coronary disease. Indeed, there is some evidence that monounsaturates may actually *reduce* blood levels of the artery-clogging LDL cholesterol. This may explain why many Mediterranean countries, in which large amounts of olive oil are consumed, have relatively low death rates from heart disease. Major sources of monounsaturated fats are olive oil, canola oil, peanut oil, nuts and margarine.

Polyunsaturated fats

Polyunsaturated fats tend to be of liquid consistency. They also tend to be derived mostly from vegetable sources, including nuts and seeds, examples of which are:

- Sesame oil.
- Sunflower oil.
- Soya oil.
- Safflower oil.
- Corn (Maize) oil.
- Fish oils.
- Wheatgerm oil.
- Some margarines (see later).

In addition, all whole grain cereals (wheat, barley, oats, rye, rice, corn) and all fruits and vegetables contain small quantities of these essential oils.

As we shall see later, a number of expert committees have made specific recommendations about what proportion of fats in our diet should be saturated and what contribution should come from polyunsaturated fats. **But remember, all fats contain the same number of calories**.

Carbohydrates

There are three major groups of carbohydrates in food, ie sugars, starches and fibres.

Sugars

Sugars are the simplest form of carbohydrates. There are a number of different sugars in food, including glucose and fructose. Fructose is the sweetest known natural sugar, twice as sweet as sucrose. It is found in honey and some fruits and vegetables. Sucrose (white, packet sugar), is a chemical made of fructose and glucose sugars.

In the UK we have one of the highest sugar consumptions in the world. On average we each eat about 1.5 lbs of sugar every week, or around 80 lbs per year. This amounts to about 18 per cent of our total daily food energy (calories). The consumption of packet sugar has fallen substantially in recent years, which suggests that we are all becoming much more aware of the need to reduce our sugar consumption. However, total sugar consumption has not changed significantly. So where is all this extra sugar coming from?

The answer, of course, is that an enormous amount of it is 'hidden sugar'. Like saturated fat, sugar is an ingredient of a large variety of foods in which it is not obvious or expected. We know that food such as cakes and pastries have a high sugar content, but we might not realize that tinned soups, tinned vegetables, pizzas, frozen prawns, sauces, pickles, tinned meats, cereals and cornflakes all contain sugar. In fact, it's quite difficult nowadays to find *any* processed food which does not contain at least some sugar.

The point about sugar is that it has no nutritional value whatsoever. It's nothing but empty calories. No vitamins, no minerals, no fibre, no protein — nothing but energy. This is true irrespective of whether the sugar is white or brown, whether it comes wrapped up in biscuits, cakes or fizzy drinks, or is simply spooned into your tea or coffee.

Everyone knows that sugar is a direct cause of tooth decay, but by far and away the most important potential effect of eating too much sugar is obesity (see Chapter 10). Sugars are digested and absorbed very rapidly, and because of this they can disrupt the body's metabolism. Eating starch is a much better way of building up glucose reserves because starch is digested much more slowly, and is absorbed in a healthy and controlled way rather than the very rapid absorption in the case of simple sugars. Sugar is not the evil substance that some people seem to believe, but it is not essential to a balanced diet either. Sweet food occasionally will do you no harm — again it is a question of moderation. Here are some tips on how to reduce the amount of sugar in your diet.

- Use less packet sugar in tea, coffee, with breakfast cereals and when cooking. Use an artificial sweetener instead.

- Beware of 'hidden' sugars, in foods like cakes, pastries, some breakfast cereals, biscuits, chocolates and so on. Examine the food labels carefully to see how much sugar you are actually taking. Don't let the language fool you: syrups, glucose, fructose, fruit sugar, cane sugar, brown sugar, dextrose, invert sugar, lactose, maltose, maple syrup etc are **all** sugars. Honey too has no magical qualities: it's nothing other than a mixture of glucose and fructose (although the flavour comes from the aroma of flowers).

- Many fizzy drinks such as Coca Cola, Pepsi Cola, squashes and some juices contain enormous amounts of sugar. Again, check the label before you buy it. There are a number of unsweetened fruit juices on the market, but a lot more have had sugar added to them.

- Try to cut down on jam, marmalade, honey, canned pie fillings and tinned fruit in syrup. All these foods contain large amounts of sugar. Did you know, for example, that jam *must* be 60 per cent sugar in order to be called jam.

Starch

Until recently starch had become the forgotten nutrient, because for most of this century the British population has been told that starchy carbohydrate foods such as bread and potatoes were inferior to animal products. Bread and potatoes were considered 'energy' foods, in contrast to meat, milk, eggs, cheese etc which were regarded as high protein foods essential for normal growth. In the last ten to twenty years our attitude towards the humble starch food has changed dramatically. Starch too is made up of glucose sub-units, but unlike simple sugars does not dissolve in water and needs cooking in order to be digested (for example, potatoes and flours). Cooking helps to break starches down into smaller molecules which can then be more easily used as an energy source by your body.

But if both sugars and starches are forms of carbohydrates, why is eating starch so much better for you than eating sugar?

The reason is that starches are *complex carbohydrates*. This means that it takes these compounds longer than simple sugars to break apart in the digestive system. Not only that, starches are found in foods that often contain substantial amounts of fibre, which can also help to slow down the rate of absorption. So the glucose units in most complex carbohydrates move into the bloodstream more slowly than the glucose in most simple sugars. This allows the body to process the sugars more effectively and store them in the form of glycogen rather than fat, within the muscles and liver.

But the nutritional advantages that complex carbohydrates have over simple sugars as a source of energy also derive from the amount of fibre and other nutrients which tend to be found in the major sources of starch (grains, beans, cereals etc). Here are some tips on increasing the amount of complex carbohydrate in your diet:

1. Eat more cereal foods of all kinds, especially the whole grain varieties.
2. Eat more bread, particularly wholemeal bread.
3. Spread butter and margarine thinly.
4. Eat pasta, rice and jacket potatoes.
5. Eat beans, peas and lentils — they are excellent sources of complex carbohydrates and fibre.

Dietary fibre

Fibre is a special form of carbohydrate which used to be called 'roughage'. It is a substance which forms the cell walls of plant foods and is therefore the main structure component of all plants, vegetables, fruit, seeds etc. It is not actually one substance which is common to all plants; it varies greatly from one food to another. But the important fact about dietary fibre is this: it is the part of our food *not* digested by the body.*

Throughout human evolution our daily diet came mainly from plants, unrefined cereals, pulses, root vegetables and fruits, all of which contain large amounts of fibre. For our ancestors, meat and fish were delicacies. By comparison, our modern day diet contains little dietary fibre. In fact, between 1880 and 1960, there was a 90 per cent decline in the volume of fibre in the British diet. Not only does a great part of our diet contain no fibre at all, but we also eat less cereals, and much of the bread and cereals which we do eat have had most of the fibre refined out of them. Average daily intake of fibre in this country is between 11–13 grams/day.

In Britain about 50 per cent of dietary fibre is provided by vegetables, and 40 per cent by cereals. Fibre comes in two basic forms: those that are soluble in water, and those that are not:

1. **Insoluble fibre:** This is required for a normal, smooth and regular bowel movement. It tends to promote the growth of bacteria, and makes a soft bulky stool. Breakfast cereals, whole grain breads (eg wholemeal), nuts, brown rice and bran products, are good sources of insoluble fibre. Vegetables, which contain more moisture than cereals, have a lower total fibre composition, but the proportion of insoluble and soluble fibre is approximately equal. By keeping things moving in the intestine, insoluble fibre may help to prevent a range of bowel disorders, including colon cancer. The theory is that potential carcinogens (cancer causing agents) in the gut have much less time to cause damage if they are passed out of the body more quickly.

2. **Soluble fibre:** There are two main types: *gums*, found particularly in oat products, eg oatmeal (porridge), oatbran, beans, lentils and peas, and *pectins*, found in apples, citrus fruits, bananas and some vegetables. Soluble fibre dissolves in water and forms a gel in the gut,

---

* Recently, the term 'dietary fibre' has been dropped by nutritionists, and replaced by 'Non-starch Polysaccharide' or 'NSP'. The reasons for this are complex and need not concern us here. I mention it only because you may come across the term from time to time.

and appears to lower levels of blood cholesterol, especially the harmful LDL-C form. (This cholesterol lowering effect is, however, relatively modest.)

Increasing fibre intake

The current recommendation from the Committee on Medical Aspects of Food Policy (1991), is that we should aim for a fibre consumption of around 18–20 g/day.

Please bear in mind that any increase of fibre in your diet should be gradual; this will help you to avoid bloating and discomfort which may otherwise occur.

To increase your daily dietary fibre consumption:

- Eat more bread, especially wholemeal bread which contains twice as much fibre as white.
- Eat more cereals, wholewheat pasta, brown rice, oats including porridge and rye bread.
- Eat more vegetables, especially peas, beans, lentils but also leaf and root vegetables.
- Eat more fresh fruit which is an important source of dietary fibre, particularly 'soluble fibre'.

The key is to eat a **mixture** of these different foods to make sure you get a balanced intake of the various types of fibre.

Vitamins, minerals and trace elements

These are sometimes known collectively as *micronutrients*. There are more than 30 micronutrients essential for health (see Table 11.1).

Vitamins, minerals and trace elements are essential in your diet so that your body can use the rest of your food effectively. They assist with the absorption and the breakdown of various dietary components, and also with the repair and rebuilding of body tissues.

The vitamins are divided into two types; the **fat soluble** vitamins which are found mainly in fatty foods, and the **water soluble** vitamins which occur in both fatty and non-fatty foods.

1. **Fat soluble vitamins** (A, D, E and K) are found in meat, fish, dairy products and vegetable oils, although green and yellow vegetables are also sources of vitamins A and K. These vitamins travel in fat, which makes them less fragile than their water soluble counterparts, so they are better able to survive the cooking pot and processing plant.
2. **The water soluble vitamins** include vitamin C, plus eight B vitamins. They are much less hardy than their fat soluble relatives. Because they are vulnerable to heat, they are often broken down in cooking and processing, and some can also be destroyed by light. Fortunately, they are relatively easy to replace. With few exceptions

Table 11.1 Micronutrients

Vitamins	Minerals
Fat soluble	
Retinol and carotenoids (Vitamin A)	Calcium
Calciferols (Vitamin D)	Chlorine
Tocopherols (Vitamin E)	Magnesium
Phylloquinones (Vitamin K)	Phosphorus
	Potassium
	Sodium
	Sulphur
Water soluble	**Trace elements**
Thiamin (Vitamin B1)	Chromium
Riboflavin (Vitamin B2)	Copper
Nicotinic acid	Fluorine
Pyridoxine (Vitamin B6)	Iodine
Cobalamins (Vitamin B12)	Iron
Folic acid	Manganese
Biotin	Molybdenum
Pantothenic acid	Selenium
Ascorbic acid (Vitamin C)	Zinc

(like vitamin B12), the water soluble vitamins are present in a wide variety of foods, either naturally or as synthetic fortifiers.

Minerals and trace elements have a vast array of complex biochemical interactions, both with themselves, normal dietary constituents and the various vitamins. It is not possible to go into the various actions of each of these micronutrients — it would take at least one large volume on its own!

From a practical point of view, you need only to know that a well balanced diet should provide you with all the micronutrients you need. Some people take the view that if a little is good, then a great deal must be even better. This is not true, and whilst 'megadosing' on some vitamins, for example vitamin C, will do no harm, some of these micronutrients (vitamins A and D for example), in massive doses, can produce serious illness. As always, the word to remember is 'moderation'.

If you feel that there are some elements of your diet that are not well covered, or your eating patterns or lifestyle do not allow you to achieve the balanced diet you would like, you may wish to consider taking vitamin supplements. There are many of these available, and you should choose one from a reputable manufacturer and follow the recommended dose.

Salt

Salt (sodium chloride) is, of course, essential to life. All the cells that make up your body are bathed in a fluid which contains sodium and chloride in solution, in other words a salt solution. The importance of salt, and sodium in particular, is in relation to high blood pressure and I have already covered this in detail on page 89 (Chapter 5). The principles of reducing salt consumption, however, bear repeating here:

- Avoid adding salt during cooking or at the table. Use a salt substitute (eg *Lo-salt*) if necessary.
- Be careful about the salt contained in processed and canned meats, bottled sauces, fish canned in brine etc. Check the label.
- Beware of the sodium which may exist in another chemical form, eg sodium bicarbonate.

Fish oils

Although the Eskimos of Greenland can apparently put away large amounts of seal and whale meat, blubber, and some fish, they have a death rate from heart disease which is only a fraction of that found in most Western developed countries. Moreover, Danish researchers have found that Eskimos have lower levels of total cholesterol and LDL-cholesterol, and higher levels of HDL-cholesterol, than Danes in all age groups and both sexes. But even though the Eskimo diet is rich in fat from whales and fish, this fat is unique in that it contains a large amount of fatty acids of a type not commonly seen in Western diets. These are known as the *Omega-3* fatty acids. (The bulk of the polyunsaturates in the typical Western diet are derived from vegetable sources, and these are the *Omega-6* type.) The two most important Omega-3 fatty acids are eicosapentanoic acid (EPA), and docosahexanoic acid (DHA). Fish oils contain large amounts of these substances, and have two important effects:

1. They reduce blood levels of total cholesterol and LDL-cholesterol, whilst raising the protective HDL-cholesterol.
2. They reduce the clotting tendency of the blood.

These important effects help to explain why Eskimos have such a low rate of heart disease. Interestingly, those Eskimos who have migrated to Denmark and adopted a Western diet, have the same level of risk for heart disease as the native Danes, confirming that the important factors are dietary rather than genetic.

White fish such as cod, coley and haddock, contain about one per cent of fat by weight. Oily fish, such as mackerel, herring, trout and salmon contain 5–25 per cent, providing 2–3 times more Omega-3s than white fish. (see Table 11.2). As you might expect, fish oil supplements have become very popular in health-food stores and heavily promoted as a means of preventing heart disease. Some may well benefit from them, but most of us will do just as well by eating fish rich in Omega-3s as part of our normal diet: twice a week should be the aim. [It's also much cheaper this way!).

Table 11.2   The Omega-3 fatty acid content of several common marine foods

Species	Omega-3 fatty acids (g/100g*)
Mackerel	2.5
Trout, lake	1.6
Trout, rainbow	0.5
Herring, Atlantic	1.6
Sardine, canned	1.7
Tuna, Albacore	1.3
Salmon, Chinook	1.4
Salmon, Atlantic	1.2
Oyster, European	0.5
Crab	0.4
Cod, Atlantic	0.3
Lobster	0.2

* Number of grams of Omega-3 fatty acids per 100g of the raw, edible portion of the food source. (Adapted from Hepburn *et al.*)

2.   SOME SOURCES OF CONFUSION

Low fat spreads and margarines

There is probably no other food product in the average supermarket that has such complex nutritional labelling as do low fat spreads, cooking oils and margarines. Very few people really understand what they mean and manufacturers seem determined to make informed choice as difficult as possible. After all, what does the statement that a particular product is 'rich in cis-linoleic acid' mean to the average shopper?

Now that you understand a little about the biochemistry of fats, particularly the difference between saturated and polyunsaturated fats, it will make choosing much easier. The essential point is that whatever spread you buy should be:

Low in saturates and high in unsaturates (mono- and polyunsaturated fatty acids).

Flora is a good example. This is the labelling on the lid:

FLORA

SUNFLOWER MARGARINE

HIGH IN ESSENTIAL POLYUNSATURATES

LOW IN SATURATES LOW IN CHOLESTEROL

The fact that the spread is also low in cholesterol is helpful, but is not as important as the fact that it is low in saturates (see later). You may ask what does 'high in polyunsaturates' mean? If you turn to the labelling on the side of the Flora tub, you will find the following additional information about the fat content per 100 grams:

Fat _____	80g
(of which polyunsaturates _____	40g
and saturates _____	14g)

So, of the total fat content, about 50 per cent is in the polyunsaturated form, and only about 17 per cent saturated. (The remainder is mainly monounsaturated fat.)

Unfortunately, not all spreads or oils are labelled quite so clearly. Some of the common sources of confusion, together with a word of explanation, are given below.

1. *Labels reading 'soft' margarine but not accompanied by 'high in polyunsaturates'.* The fact that the margarine is soft doesn't mean anything; soft margarines can also be high in saturated fats.

2. *Labels reading 'low in cholesterol' but* **not** accompanied by 'high in polyunsaturates' A spread may well be low in cholesterol, but it can equally well be high in saturated fat. Moreover, it is the **saturated fat**, rather than the cholesterol content, which is the important factor.

3. *Labels with the statement 'contains hydrogenated vegetable oils'* When oils become hydrogenated (or hydrolyzed), hydrogen atoms are added to the molecular structure, causing mono- or polyunsaturated fats to become saturated. All vegetable margarines have to contain *some* saturated fat, otherwise they could not be solid at room temperature. Lightly hydrogenated oils, such as those commonly used in salad dressings, are no problem since they will remain far less saturated than coconut oil, lard, butter, and other saturated alternatives. Heavily hydrogenated oils become highly saturated and are commonly used in baking as shortening.

    So — avoid margarines which list hydrogenated oil as the first ingredient.

    Heating cooking oil to a high temperature converts it to a saturated fat. Try it for yourself. Take a good quality oil, and heat it in a frying pan — **carefully** — until it *just* begins to smoke. Leave the pan overnight, and you will see that the oil has become a solid white — saturated — fat. It follows that when you use oils for cooking, the correct temperature is very important.

4. *Labels reading 'made of 100% vegetable oil', but* **not** *accompanied by 'high in polyunsaturates'.* Even if they are made with 100 per cent vegetable oils, they may well be very high in saturated fats.

5. *Labels with the statement 'made with 100% sunflower oil'.* The product may well contain sunflower oil, which is 100 per cent pure. But the sunflower oil may only constitute a very small part of the total fat content. The remainder of the fats may well be highly saturated. Strictly speaking, of course, the label is accurate, but it is certainly misleading and may well make the potential purchaser believe that the product is healthier than it actually is.

These are just some of the misleading statements that make informed choices for these sorts of fats and oils very difficult. Nevertheless, if you remember that the essential point to look for is that the product should be low in saturates, and high in mono- and polyunsaturates, you will manage perfectly well.

The same principles apply to cooking oils. Don't go for vague labels such as 'vegetable oil' because again you don't know exactly which oils it contains. Named vegetable oils are the ones to choose, such as:

- Olive oil.
- Safflower oil.
- Sesame oil.
- Maize (or Corn) oil.
- Sunflower oil.
- Rapeseed oil.

Make sure the oil contains only the named oil, and if it contains other 'vegetable oils', avoid it.

Red meat

There is a mistaken idea that in order to reduce the amount of fat in your diet, it is necessary to exclude red meat completely. This is not true. There are many sources of saturated fat in the diet, and whilst red meat may be one of them it is not necessarily the most important. Moreover, it contains a number of very important nutrients which are essential to a balanced diet, the most important of which is iron. Iron deficiency anaemia is one of the commonest nutritional disorders in the world, and a significant section of the population in the UK are known to be iron deficient. Not only does red meat offer an extremely valuable source of iron, but it also increases the absorption of it from other foods. Thus if you exclude red meat completely from your diet, you may well not be getting sufficient iron for your requirements. This is particularly true in women, who do of course lose a certain amount of iron each month as part of the normal menstrual blood loss.

Remember, it is meat **fat** which you need to cut down on, not necessarily red meat itself. As long as the meat is lean and you trim off the visible fat, it should remain an important part of a balanced diet. If you wish to exclude it completely from your diet for some other reason, whether religious, moral or otherwise, you would be well advised to take iron supplements to ensure that you are achieving your minimum daily requirements.

Dietary cholesterol

If a high level of blood cholesterol is recognized to be a major risk factor for heart disease, then it seems reasonable to assume that cutting down on dietary cholesterol will result in lower blood cholesterol levels. Unfortunately, this is not true — or not quite.

Because of the complex way in which fats are handled by the body, the major determinant of blood cholesterol levels is **saturated** fat. Cholesterol contributes a little, but not very much. This is why dietary recommendations designed to reduce the risk of heart disease have been directed towards the reduction of saturated fat, ie a cholesterol lowering diet, rather than a low cholesterol diet.

Many food manufacturers believe that simply by putting the words 'low in cholesterol' on their products, the potential purchaser will regard this as a seal of approval. At least you will not be one of them!

Cholesterol is found only in animal products; a fact which often causes confusion, since many people appear to believe that foods like avocado pear and coconut are rich in cholesterol. In fact avocado contains about 20 per cent total fat, although only 4 per cent is saturated. Dessicated coconut, on the other hand, contains 62 per cent total fat, and 55 per cent saturated fat. So avocado is comparatively innocent.

Key note

Both dietary cholesterol and saturated fat will tend to elevate blood cholesterol levels, but the amount of **saturated** fat is the most important determinant. It follows that if you wish to reduce your cholesterol levels, you should first focus upon reducing the total saturated fat content of your diet, rather than trying to reduce dietary cholesterol. 'Low in cholesterol' on food labels is largely irrelevant.

Dietary balance and nutritional guidelines

As we have seen, the basic nutrients required for good health are proteins, fats, carbohydrates, micronutrients (vitamins, minerals and trace elements) and water. Fibre, though not strictly a nutrient, is also very important.

Because different foods contain many different types of nutrients in different proportions to each other, no *single* food can provide you with all the nutrients you require for a balanced diet. This is why variety in your diet is so important: it allows you to obtain different nutrients from a wide variety of sources, so that a correct balance is achieved. There are many ways to combine foods into a healthy diet to take into account individual food and eating preferences. Foods are not in themselves 'good' or 'bad'. Despite the concern about so called 'junk' food nowadays, **no** food is devoid of nutritional value, although some are clearly more nutrient packed than others. Variety is the best way to ensure that you are getting all the nutrients you require. You can achieve this quite simply by using the four basic groups of foods in the correct proportions. Because some foods have higher concentrations of nutrients than others, it is useful to group them according to the main nutrients which they provide. The meat group, for example is high in protein, while the grain group is rich in complex carbohydrates.

- **Grains**: This large group includes cereals, bread, rice oats, wholemeal pasta etc. These foods are rich in complex carbohydrates (starch), as well as vitamins, fibre and minerals.
- **Fruit and Vegetable Group**: Fruits and vegetables are important sources of vitamins, fibre, potassium and beta-carotene (see later).
- **Dairy Group**: Including milk, cheese, yoghurt etc. These foods are rich in calcium, protein and phosphorus. You can avoid the butterfat in normal dairy products by choosing the low-fat varieties. Skimmed and semi-skimmed milk actually contains *more* calcium than ordinary milk, but only a fraction of the saturated fat.
- **Meat and Fish Group**: This includes poultry, fish, meat, eggs, beans, peas and nuts. These foods are important principally because of their protein, and many micronutrients such as iron, copper and zinc. What about shellfish? Despite the popular perception, all shellfish have a low fat content. The concern normally centres around the amount of cholesterol they contain, because original analyses suggested that this was quite high. In fact, as was discussed earlier, the main determinant of cholesterol levels is not cholesterol, but saturated fat. More sophisticated analytical methods show that shellfish are not particularly high in cholesterol, with the exception of shrimp which are better avoided if you are trying to lower your blood cholesterol level.

In general, a well balanced diet should consist of the following daily quantities:

- Six servings of grain products.
- Three servings of vegetables and two of fruit.
- Two servings from the meat and fish group.
- Two servings from the dairy group.

The quantities involved will obviously vary according to age, sex, body weight, exercise habits and calorie requirements. So long as your calorie

Table 11.3 Recommended values for food intake as a percentage of daily total energy (calorie) intake. (Figures in brackets are those for non-drinkers.)

Total Fat	33% (35)	(of which no more than 10% as saturated fat)
Carbohydrate	47% (50)	
Protein	15% (15)	
Alcohol	5% (0)	

intake is matched to your calorie expenditure, you will maintain a healthy body weight. To vary your calorie intake, you simply reduce or increase the size of those servings, **without changing the proportions**. In this way your diet will stay balanced.

The recommended daily allowance (RDA) for the main nutrients can also be expressed as a proportion or percentage of your total energy intake. The latest recommendations from the Committee on Medical Aspects of Food Policy (1991) for the UK, suggest a dietary composition for each of the major nutrient groups, as a percentage of energy intake as shown in Table 11.3. (The panel recognized that many people will derive some energy from alcohol, which is assumed to contribute about 5 per cent to total daily energy intake. Those who are teetotal will derive all their energy requirements from food sources alone.

Key point — Summary of the seven basic principles for healthy eating

1. Balance your calorie intake and energy expenditure to maintain a healthy body weight.
2. Eat a variety of foods from the four main groups.
3. Choose a diet which is basically low in saturated fat and high in fibre.
4. Eat plenty of fresh fruit, vegetables and grain products.
5. Be careful about your sugar intake; use in moderation only.
6. Keep a careful eye on your salt (sodium) intake.
7. Control your alcohol consumption to within the recommended safe drinking limits.

---

3. EATING TO AVOID HEART DISEASE AND CANCER

The aim of this short section is to bring together a concise summary of the dietary information concerned with avoiding cancer and heart disease, much of which is scattered throughout the text.

EATING FOR A HEALTHY HEART

Heart disease

Much of this book is to do with the prevention of heart disease. Many physicians (including myself) believe that heart disease is fundamentally a nutritional disorder. There is impressive evidence that dietary modification, particularly of saturated fat, can contribute much to heart attack prevention. Not only is there evidence that dietary intervention can prevent the progression of the fatty deposits which are the hallmark of coronary artery disease, recent research suggests that regression (reversal) of this process by reduction of dietary fat intake may also be possible. This is very exciting and offers new opportunities for treatment and prevention of coronary disease.

Key point — Eating to avoid heart disease

Let's summarize how to eat for a healthy heart:

- Reduce your total fat consumption, and saturated fats in particular. The saturated variety should constitute no more than 10 per cent of your total fat intake.
- Avoid foods which are very high in cholesterol (eg shrimp, liver and eggs) if your own cholesterol level is raised. Although dietary cholesterol makes only a very small contribution to blood levels, it is best avoided if you are trying to lower it.
- If you are overweight, reduce your calorie intake and exercise more regularly to promote weight loss.
- Increase your consumption of fish. Marine oils are rich in Omega-3 fatty acids and these will help to reduce total and LDL-cholesterol, as well as reducing the blood clotting tendency.
- Reduce your salt consumption. Salt is strongly linked to the development of high blood pressure, which is in itself a major risk factor for heart disease and stroke.
- Increase your consumption of fibre, particularly soluble fibre. Again, this may help to reduce your cholesterol concentration, either directly or because it will result in your consuming less saturated fat. Increased dietary fibre may also help to lower blood pressure.
- Eat more garlic. There is some evidence that garlic may act in a similar way to fish oils, although less dramatically. If the odour bothers you (or particularly other people!) you can help this by consuming garlic with parsley and salad greens, or aromatic seeds such as aniseed.
- Choose a good quality oil for cooking; olive oil preferably.
- Consume regular (but moderate) amounts of alcohol.

EATING TO AVOID CANCER

Evidence of a link between some aspects of our diet and heart disease started to accumulate in the early 1960s and has been growing stronger ever since. Only in recent years have we heard so much about diet in relation to cancer, from fibre and calcium, to antioxidants and selenium. More recent studies suggest that excess calories or fat may increase cancer risk substantially in some susceptible individuals.

There will be a tremendous growth in our understanding of the relationship between diet and cancer during the next decade. This is clearly of some importance because, although some cancers are on the decline, the overall incidence has been increasing since the 1950s. As it stands at the moment, almost one in four of all deaths in this country are caused by cancer and about one in three of us can expect to develop cancer at some point in our lives. The best current estimate is that about one third of all current cancer deaths might be prevented by changes in diet.

What happens when a cell becomes cancerous?

The process by which a normal cell becomes a cancer cell always starts with damage to the cell's DNA, the special nucleic acid which carries the body's genetic code. As a result of this initial damage, the cell begins to multiply in an uncontrolled way and continues to divide rapidly. After a variable period of time, there may be a large enough number of these abnormal cells to form a tumour.

There are lots of agents that can cause damage to the cell's DNA and thus initiate a cancer. In some cases it's known that viruses damage the DNA and trigger tumour growth. The same process can be initiated by radiation, which is why ultra-violet rays like those present in sunlight, can produce skin cancer. Various chemical agents can also damage the cell's genetic code. Even though there are scores of different types of cancer, they all start with damage to the cellular DNA, leading to uncontrolled growth. Some chemicals in food are known to be strongly carcinogenic (cancer causing). *Aflatoxin*, a mould which grows on contaminated peanuts, is a powerful carcinogen and is known to cause liver tumours in some parts of Africa where peanuts are a dietary staple. But most diet-cancer connections are nowhere as clear.

Some components of our diet may not actually cause genetic damage, but may promote the growth of cells which have *already* mutated.

Antioxidants, free radicals and cancer

The chemical process by which we burn fuel in our body is called **oxidation**. Although oxidation is obviously essential, it does have a potentially undesirable side effect — the accumulation of products known as **free radicals** which can damage various tissues, particularly cellular DNA. In this way the free radicals may produce mutations that can eventually lead to cancer. They may also be involved in the ageing process.

Interestingly, polyunsaturated fatty acids are an important dietary source of free radicals, whilst saturated fats are not. This is why polyunsaturates may increase the risk of cancer, at least in experimental animals. It is also the reason why, if you are seeking to reduce your risk of heart disease, you should reduce the **total** amount of fat in your diet, and not simply substitute the saturated fat with polyunsaturated fats.

But if the body produces these free radicals, does the body have any way of defending itself? In fact the body has special substances called **antioxidants** that can help to limit the damage caused by free radicals. High levels of some naturally occurring antioxidants in the diet may help to prevent cancer.

Vitamins E, C, and **A** are potent natural antioxidants, and this may explain why there is such good scientific evidence that a diet rich in certain fruits and vegetables can reduce the risk of some kinds of cancer. (Antioxidants may also have a part to play in the prevention of heart disease.)

In particular, a great deal of work has been carried out on the **carotenoids**, which are special pigments related to vitamin A and which give orange, yellow and green vegetables their colour. One carotenoid in particular — beta-carotene — appears to have particularly strong cancer preventing properties. (Vitamin A is produced from beta-carotene and other carotenoids.) Carotenoids are found in all brightly coloured vegetables such as pumpkins, sweet potatoes, apricots, carrots, peaches, tomatoes, red peppers, yellow peppers and spinach. They are also found in high levels in vegetables such as broccoli, Brussels sprouts, cauliflower, turnips and cabbage.

Dietary fats and calories

There is a growing body of scientific evidence to suggest that diets which are high in fat may increase the risk of certain types of cancer — particularly breast and colon cancer. Of course diets which are high in fat have a higher calorie content than other diets, and tend also to be strongly associated with obesity. So it becomes difficult to know whether it is the fat in the diet and the high calorie intake, or the obesity which increases cancer risk in some susceptible individuals.

In practical terms, the question of whether it is the fat in the diet, the calories, or the obesity is not desperately important, because they are all clearly related. If you reduce the total fat content of your diet, you will reduce your calorie intake and you will lose weight — and in the process you will reduce your cancer risk substantially.

Fibre

This has been discussed elsewhere (page 215), and the general view is that a low intake of dietary fibre may increase the risk of certain types of cancer, particularly bowel cancer. The evidence for this link stems from work carried out in Africa by a number of British physicians, including Dr Dennis Burkitt. They observed that Africans ate much more fibre than Westerners, resulting in much more frequent bowel movements and bulkier stools. This was thought to account for the fact that Africans have an extremely low incidence of colon cancer as well as a whole range of other bowel disorders, including constipation and diverticular disease.

However, although the idea has won popular acceptance, the link between fibre and cancer protection is still not proven. People who eat high fibre diets also tend to eat low fat diets, so it still isn't clear whether the reduced risk of bowel cancer is due to more fibre, less fat or a combination of the two.

Of the two main types of fibre (soluble and insoluble), it's the insoluble fibre that works best as a bulking agent, making the stools larger, softer and facilitating more regular bowel movements. If you eat a diet which is high in fibre, it will almost by definition be low in fat. Lower fat means fewer calories and fewer calories means a lower body weight. For all these reasons, increasing fibre in your diet is an important dietary strategy which will reduce your risk of cancer.

Other dietary factors

Some other dietary factors may also contribute to an increased cancer risk:

- **Smoked, Pickled and Salt Cured Foods**
  Cancers of the stomach and oesophagus (gullet) are far more common in countries where large amounts of these foods are consumed, particularly in Japan and Iceland. Although Japan has a low rate of heart disease, it has the highest death rate from stomach cancer in the World. In practical terms, most of us eat relatively small amounts of these types of food, and raw herring and similar products are occasional delicacies, rather than part of our staple diet.
- **Alcohol**
  The relationship between alcohol and the diet and various forms of cancer is well known. It is particularly potent when combined with cigarette smoking, and substantially increases the risk of developing cancer of the gut, stomach and liver.

Key note — Eating to avoid cancer

- Reduce your total fat consumption to no more than 33 per cent of total calorie intake. This should apply not only to saturated fats (which increase the risk of heart disease), but also to polyunsaturated fats, which are an important dietary source of free radicals.
- By eating plenty of fruit, vegetables and whole grains you will reduce your intake of fat and calories, both of which are associated with an increased risk of cancer.
- Foods rich in carotenoids — the brightly coloured vegetables and fruits — can reduce the risk of some kinds of cancer, as can vegetables containing large amounts of vitamin C.
- Limit your consumption of smoked, pickled and salt cured foods.
- Increase your consumption of fibre, especially insoluble fibre (found in vegetables and bran) which will help to protect you against bowel cancer. It will also lower your intake of fat and calories which will provide other health benefits as well.
- Control your calorie intake, maintain a healthy body weight, and exercise regularly. This will help to keep your weight within acceptable levels and reduce the risk of various types of cancer known to be strongly associated with obesity and inactivity.

4.   READING A FOOD LABEL

The key to healthy and enjoyable eating is knowledge. Moreover, understanding the basic principles of good nutrition puts *you* in control, not the food manufacturer or retailer. Not that you will always adhere strictly to the ground rules; there will always be days when you indulge yourself a little bit, and there is no reason why you shouldn't. The point is that knowledge gives you greater flexibility, because it allows you to compensate for today's indiscretions by altering the balance of your diet tomorrow. If overall knowledge is the key to enjoying food, then balance and variety are the most important principles. Having worked through this chapter you will now be in a much better position to make informed choices, and there is one immediate area in which that knowledge can be put into practice, ie reading food labels.

Most of the products in your local supermarket or shop have some nutritional information printed on the label or the packet, although the amount of detail is highly variable. Before placing an item in your shopping basket, quickly scan the nutritional information on the label. The food manufacturers are very smart, and they know exactly how to use words, colours, pictures etc to entice you. Because we are all becoming much more aware of the importance of diet, the food industry has wasted no time in jumping on the bandwagon by making nutritional claims in their advertising and on food labels. Some of these assertions are valid, but others are definitely misleading. A good example of this is the growing tendency to label a product as 'cholesterol free', even though it contains large amounts of saturated fats which are far more important in terms of their ability to raise blood cholesterol levels. The label is not wrong; it's simply that there is an implicit assumption that the average shopper will associate 'cholesterol free' with 'healthy'.

With your new found nutritional knowledge, you should find no serious difficulty in negotiating the food label hurdle; you'll probably enjoy rooting out the facts from the fiction.

I have chosen four labels from commonly consumed foods, and given a brief commentary on each.

Manufacturers list the values for each ingredient according to the amount per average serving, or per 100 grams(g). The latter is generally more useful, because it provides a degree of standardization which assists comparison with other food products. Amounts per serving are valuable, provided you remember that what you may put on a plate as a serving, may be more than the amount suggested as a serving on the label.

Label 1 — Comment

You can see that each 100g of baked beans provides 70 kcals (calories), and the average serving about 159 kcals. This is not a particularly calorie rich food — 100g of sweet biscuits would provide more than 500 kcals.

Working down the first column you will see that there are 5g of protein, and 12.7g of carbohydrate. However, 5.6g of the total carbohydrate are in the form of sugars, so this may be something to bear in mind if you are trying to keep your intake of sugar to a minimum. The manufacturers actually make a 'Weight Watchers' version of this, which contains much less sugar (0.7g).

There are only 0.3g of fat, and only one third of this (0.1g) is saturated.

There is also a significant amount of sodium (the 'Weight Watchers' brand has 0.3g), but a large amount of dietary fibre at 7.3g. The bulk of the remainder of the 100g is made up of water (not shown in the column).

Baked beans are a highly nutritious food item, containing only a trace of saturated fat, a large amount of dietary fibre and a moderate amount of

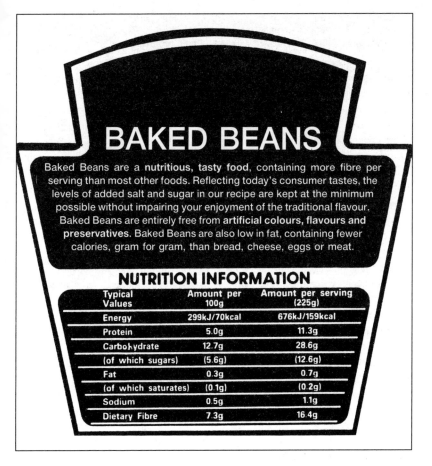

BAKED BEANS

Baked Beans are a **nutritious, tasty food**, containing more fibre per serving than most other foods. Reflecting today's consumer tastes, the levels of added salt and sugar in our recipe are kept at the minimum possible without impairing your enjoyment of the traditional flavour. Baked Beans are entirely free from **artificial colours, flavours and preservatives**. Baked Beans are also low in fat, containing fewer calories, gram for gram, than bread, cheese, eggs or meat.

NUTRITION INFORMATION

Typical Values	Amount per 100g	Amount per serving (225g)
Energy	299kJ/70kcal	676kJ/159kcal
Protein	5.0g	11.3g
Carbohydrate	12.7g	28.6g
(of which sugars)	(5.6g)	(12.6g)
Fat	0.3g	0.7g
(of which saturates)	(0.1g)	(0.2g)
Sodium	0.5g	1.1g
Dietary Fibre	7.3g	16.4g

Label 1 Baked beans — typical nutritional information

carbohydrate for energy. The reduced sugar and sodium options will be of interest to those who are losing weight, or reducing their sodium intake.

Label 2 (overleaf) — Comment

The first thing to note is that for each 100g portion, there are 342 kcals. In other words this is a relatively calorie rich food (compare with 70 kcals for a 100g portion of baked beans). An average serving of this cereal is listed as 37.5g (2 biscuits), which is about 128 kcals.

There is quite a lot of protein (11.2g) and a large amount of carbohydrate (65.8g). However, sugars only form 5.2g of this, so you can see that the overwhelming amount of carbohydrate must be in the form of complex carbohydrate or starches.

Of the 2.7g of fat, only 0.5g is of the saturated type, so again this is excellent. Fibre also is extremely well represented, ie 12.9g of each 100g.

NUTRITION INFORMATION

	per 100g	per 37.5g serving	Vitamins	per 100g	% RDA per 37.5g serving
Energy	1453kj	545kj	Niacin	8.2mg	17%
	342 kcal	128 kcal	Riboflavin (B₂)	0.7mg	17%
Protein	11.2g	4.2g	Thiamin (B₁)	0.5mg	17%
Carbohydrate	65.8g	24.7g		5.4mg	17%
of which sugars	5.2g	2.0g			
Fat	2.7g	1.0g			
of which saturates	0.5g	0.2g			
Fibre	12.9g	4.8g			
of which soluble	4.0g	1.5g			
insoluble	8.9g	3.3g			
Sodium	0.3g	0.1g			

An average serving of two biscuits (37.5g) will provide at least 17% of the recommended daily amount (RDA) for the average adult of the vitamins and iron listed. This pack contains six 2-biscuit servings.

Label 2　Typical nutritional breakdown of a wheat-biscuit type breakfast cereal

Moreover, about one third of this fibre is soluble and the remainder insoluble. It contains 0.3g of sodium, but this is not excessive.

Further information gives the amount of a number of vitamins in each 100g serving. Iron, in particular, is present in significant quantities.

Once again, this is a low fat, very high fibre product, which also has a large amount of complex carbohydrates — the best energy source. It also contains a significant amount of iron and a number of other important vitamins. In short, this is a first rate food which is an excellent source of protein, energy, fibre and iron.

Label 3 — Comment

The amount of information given in this case is very much less than in the two products discussed previously. The first thing to note is that this is a high calorie food; no less than 73 calories per biscuit. There is a reasonable amount of protein (6.5g) but a large amount of carbohydrate and fat.

You will observe that there is no information given as to the exact *form* of carbohydrate, ie whether it occurs as simple sugars or complex carbohydrates. However, if you look at the ingredients box at the top, you will see that sugar is mentioned fairly early on. Since the ingredients tend to be listed in the order of the amounts used, you can be fairly certain that simple sugars make a big contribution to the carbohydrate loading. Further down you will see something called 'partially inverted sugar syrup', which is another form of simple sugar.

When it comes to fat, you can see that for each 100g, almost one quarter is made up of fats. No information is given as to whether or not these fats

INGREDIENTS
FLOUR, VEGETABLE OIL AND HYDROGENATED VEGETABLE FAT AND ANIMAL FAT, SUGAR, WHOLEMEAL FLOUR, CULTURED SKIMMED MILK, PARTIALLY INVERTED SUGAR SYRUP, RAISING AGENTS (SODIUM BICARBONATE, TARTARIC ACID), SALT

NUTRITIONAL INFORMATION

	TYPICAL COMPOSITION	
	per biscuit	per 100g
ENERGY	309kj 73kcal	2099kj 499kcal
PROTEIN	1.0g	6.5g
CARBOHYDRATE	9.8g	67.0g
FAT	3.3g	22.1g

Label 3   Typical sweet biscuit — nutritional information

are unsaturated, but again if you look at the ingredients box there are some clues. The fats are vegetable oil, hydrogenated vegetable fat and animal fat. In other words almost all the fats are saturated. No other nutritional information is provided, except it does mention raising agents (sodium bicarbonate etc) and salt. Thus sodium is represented in two forms: sodium bicarbonate and sodium chloride.

In summary, this is a product which is high in sugars, and high in animal fats. It also contains a significant amount of sodium in the form of salt and sodium bicarbonate.

While an occasional sweet biscuit does no harm, it is not the sort of thing you would want to eat too regularly.

Label 4 (overleaf) — Comment

The calorie content of this pickle is not especially high — roughly the same (per 100g) as that of the cereal biscuit, and very much less than sweet biscuits.

There is very little protein but a large amount of carbohydrates, the vast majority of which (95 per cent) is in the form of simple sugars.

The other nutrient of note is sodium at 1.6g (1600mg), which is three times more than in baked beans, and more than five times that found in the cereal. A low-salt food, by contrast, would contain less than 0.14g of sodium.

NUTRITIONAL INFORMATION

Typical Values	Per 100 g
Energy	630jk/150kcal
Protein	0.7 g
Carbohydrate	34.5 g
– of which sugars	32.8 g
Fat	0.2 g
– of which saturates	NIL
Dietary Fibre	1.8 g
Sodium	1.6 g

Label 4   Nutritional information on the back of a jar of pickle

On the plus side, it does have some dietary fibre, and is virtually fat free.

In summary, this is a product which is rich in salt and sugar, with a moderate amount of fibre.

Not much use if you are trying to lose weight, or control your blood pressure.

CONCLUSION

A simple but fundamentally important proposition underpins everything that I have said in this book, namely that what determines our present and future health has much more to do with the way we live, how much exercise we take and what we eat, than with doctors, hospitals, drugs or our genetic inheritance.

You may think that this is so self-evident as to be hardly worth stating, but my own experience suggests that many people still regard health as being the responsibility of doctors or 'health professionals'. The fact remains, however, that the medical system in this country, indeed in all Western countries, continues to be much more concerned with disease than health. Trying to cure diseases which are already causing symptoms and distress may be what doctors are trained for, but it is surely much less satisfactory than preventing the disease in the first place.

Another commonly held view is that our genetic inheritance is the most important determinant of health and disease. This is perhaps understandable given the tremendous discoveries in genetic science during the last few years, and the advent of the 'Human Genome Project', in which scientists aim to map out the entire genetic structure (genome) of a human being by the end of this century. Once the genes which determine susceptibility or resistance to various diseases have been 'mapped', it should be possible to offer more effective diagnosis and treatment.

But wonderful though this may be, it will not provide all the answers. Early on in this book I made the point that most common illnesses are the result of an interaction between genetic, environmental and lifestyle factors. Relatively few diseases have a purely genetic origin. If it were only a question of 'bad' genes then heart disease, for example, would occur mainly in those individuals with a family history. This is manifestly not the case; many people with heart problems have no family history of the disease at all. Genetics will do much to illuminate the origins of disease and to identify those at increased risk, but it will not remove the need for all of us to pay attention to modifiable factors such as smoking, physical inactivity and poor diet.

So what will happen in the few remaining years of this century? We will see a remarkable growth in our understanding of the interactions between genetic, environmental and lifestyle-related risk factors; there will be an explosion of information about diet and how certain factors such as vitamins, antioxidants and individual fats can contribute to, or can help to prevent, various diseases; research will confirm that poor nutrition during pregnancy and other factors influencing the unborn child, may increase the risk of high blood pressure and heart disease in adult life, and scientists will begin to unravel the complex biological mechanisms by which our psychological state can influence our physical well-being.

This will provide us and our children with even better information on which to make decisions about how we live. *But*, it is the translation of information into *practice* by each one of us which will result in the improved health and well-being of us all.

INDEX